IN GOD WE TRUST

IN GOD WE TRUST

THE ORIGINS OF CHRISTIAN NATIONALISM

By Jimmie R. Hawkins

In God We Trust

The Origins of Christian Nationalism

Copyright © 2026 Friendship Press

All rights reserved. No part of this book may be reproduced in any manner whatsoever without written permission of the publisher, except brief quotations embodied in critical articles or reviews. For permission requests, write to the publisher at info@friendshippress.org.

Print ISBN: 978-1-961088-50-4
Ebook ISBN: 978-1-961088-51-1

Unless otherwise indicated, scripture quotations are taken from the New Revised Standard Version Updated Edition. Copyright © 2021 National Council of the Churches of Christ in the United States of America. Used by permission. All rights reserved worldwide.

Scripture quotations marked ESV are from the ESV® Bible (The Holy Bible, English Standard Version®), copyright © 2001 by Crossway, a publishing ministry of Good News Publishers. Used by permission. All rights reserved.

Scripture quotations marked KJV are from The Authorized (King James) Version. Rights in the Authorized Version in the United Kingdom are vested in the Crown. Reproduced by permission of the Crown's patentee, Cambridge University Press.

Scripture quotations marked (NIV) are taken from the Holy Bible, New International Version®, NIV®. Copyright © 1973, 1978, 1984, 2011 by Biblica, Inc.™ Used by permission of Zondervan. All rights reserved worldwide. www.zondervan.com The "NIV" and "New International Version" are trademarks registered in the United States Patent and Trademark Office by Biblica, Inc.™

Scripture quotations marked RSV are from the Revised Standard Version of the Bible, copyright © 1946, 1952, and 1971 National Council of the Churches of Christ in the United States of America. Used by permission. All rights reserved worldwide. http:// nrsvbibles.org/

Contents

Introduction

> Now I appeal to you, brothers and sisters, by the name of our Lord Jesus Christ, that all of you be in agreement and that there be no divisions among you but that you be knit together in the same mind and the same purpose.
>
> 1 Corinthians 1:10

The premise of this book is that Christian Nationalism has been constant throughout American society. There has been much discussion in academic and ecclesiastical communities on the sudden appearance of the ideology with debates as to how to resist its infiltration into religious circles. Yet Christian Nationalism is not new but has always been present in American culture. The issue is that is has not been identified as a threat to Christian purity and orthodoxy. Rather it has been incorporated in the life and culture of the church and promoted as a component of true religion. It has become so ingrained that few Christians recognize it for what it is: a heresy poisoning the teachings, ministry, and mission of the church.

This book offers a correction to the position that current history is a resurgence of Christian Nationalism. It is not coming back into prominence, for Christian Nationalism, or religious Nationalism more broadly, has always been a plague upon global society. Christian Nationalism is merely the newest manifestation of distortions that have been widely adopted but are suspect in their authenticity. Frances FitzGerald states that "[The] claim that America had been a Christian nation [is] hardly original. Whether it meant that the American population was largely Christian, or whether it meant that the nation itself was Christian, the phrase 'Christian nation' had inhabited evangelical and civil religion from the nineteenth century through the 1950s."[1]

American scholars readily acknowledge the positive impact of religion upon American life and culture. There is ready agreement that the founders did not desire to exorcise religion from society but to protect religious freedom and promote pluralism. Many were of the mind that the religion's influence was positive and did not desire it to be suppressed. At the same time, it was desired that it did not possess political authority to control the policy and regulations of government. The result was a country, on all levels, acknowledging the importance of religion in all areas without granting it power to dictate the lives of citizens. This is known as civil religion.

However, scholars have often mislabeled civil religion as Christian patriotism and ignored the consistent presence of Christian Nationalism. Civil religion and Christian Nationalism have had a corresponding, codependent coexistence. What differentiates the two involves the particular audience and the circumstances under review. The niceties of civil religion had been the common experience of whites, while marginalized communities were treated to the discrimination of Christian Nationalism. Race has been a major determinant in which ideology was applied. Other factors include sexual identity, economic and social class.

Human beings have always valued and sought after a relationship with the divine. This book explores humanity's search for life's purpose and for personal meaning and how religious nationalism interjected itself into the journey. The exploration for meaning, for truth, has been an essential component of the human experience since mortals first scanned the constellations for answers, attempting to comprehend if there is something beyond everyday reality. An earnest desire to identify one's place in life and proof that one's existence has meaning.

It is a search for an individual's worth as she wonders if it matters that she ever breathed the breath of life. Everyone wants to know, "Who am I? Where do I fit in the world? Where do I go to find truth?

Christian Nationalism is one pathway some assert to have discovered revealed truth. Christian Nationalists claim to act out of a desire to serve God as faithful Christians. The merger of political ideology and Christian theology becomes the measurement of one's commitment to Christ Jesus and, for Christian Nationalists, fulfills Christian discipleship. To be a faithful Christian involves being a loyal citizen of the United States of America. Christian nationalism states that it is God's directive for the United States of America, as the instrument of God, to lead the world into a relationship with Jesus. The goal of Christian Nationalism is to establish a theocracy that ensures that America fulfills its purpose as a Christian nation.[2] Hardliners insist that the U.S. government has the responsibility to actively assert that America is and must remain a Christian nation. Frances FitzGerald, quoted earlier, noted the central role of the claim that America is a Christian nation. "Christian Nationalists believe that the American nation was, is, and should remain a 'Christian nation.' It is not merely a historical fact but a moral imperative, an ideological goal, a policy program for the future, a part of the government's responsibility." Many express a frustration that the United States, despite its special calling, has lost its way due to liberalism and special interests. Paul Miller warned of the fallacy of Christian Nationalist rhetoric and the dangers in its doctrine. He wrote that Christian Nationalism appropriated "the message of Jesus as a tool of political propaganda and the church as the handmaiden and cheerleader of the state. The threat to the church is that it becomes a political arm identifying the goals of the country as the same as the goals of the church."[3] Scholars often label this demonstration of patriotic sentiments by Christians as civil religion, but there must be greater specificity as seen later in this book.

This book is divided into three parts with a conclusion, each beginning with Scripture. Christian Nationalists base their beliefs on a desire to be faithful to God's Word. Yet much application is focused upon selective passages and verses, isolated and taken out of context, and interpreted with little depth. Glaringly, there is an absence in the exploration of the teachings of the Gospels and the commandments of Jesus. Rarely do you hear Christian Nationalist sermons that discuss unconditional love and acceptance of the Great Commandment to love God, neighbor, and self (Matthew 22:34-40; Mark 12:28-31; Luke 10:27-28). Evangelicals, Christian conservatives, moderates, and progressives make much of the Great Commission (Matthew 28:19-20) to make disciples of all nations, correctly understanding the primacy of spreading to gospel globally—although often with a limited definition of what that means, usually expressed by verbal testimonies of believers, sermons, pamphlets, and media. But when one explores the fullness of Scripture, one sees that confronting injustice is equally important. James 2 states that faith without works is dead. Jesus accused the religious leaders of neglecting to do the most important work of God, to do justice, love kindness, and faithfulness (Matthew 23:23). Bringing others to a relationship with Jesus involves living out our faith in active engagement with the world to transform it into a place of faithful obedience to God, a God who is described in the Bible as a *"gracious and merciful, slow to anger, abounding in steadfast love, and relenting from punishment"* (Jonah 4:2b; Joel 2:13; see also Exodus 34:6, Nehemiah 9:17, and Psalm 85:15).

The first part, "What Is Christian Nationalism?" explores the diverse manifestations of religious (Christian) nationalism over the centuries within various global contexts. It is an exploration into the ways religion has been distorted by false teachings and exploited by those willing to mislead for their own benefit. People desperate for hope have been susceptible to misinformed leaders claiming to represent Jesus and speak for God. Acrimonious strands of the faith produced division, as adherents have not only distanced themselves from nonbelievers but from one another. Theological distortions abound as age-old misinterpretations regain popularity while others are newly created. False teachings masquerade as sound Christian doctrine and have led people into a misguided certainty that what they have received is biblically and Christologically grounded. Now, for the first time, a significant portion of American citizens find themselves the targets. Throughout the nation's history American whites have either been supportive or silent during its manifestations. African Americans, Native Americans, Hispanics, Asian Americans, women, and members of the gay and lesbian community have been vocal in their resistance to Christian Nationalism.

The second part, "Who Are Christian Nationalists?" explores the identities of different categories of Christians amidst the influence of Christian Nationalism. From conservative to liberal, almost every Christian worldview is affected by this ideology. Ironically, many of the groups previously discriminated against by Christian Nationalist rhetoric have joined its ranks. Blacks, Asians, Hispanics, and women are amongst the primary apologists for a return to biblical standards of patriarchy and suppression of the human rights of non-Christians.

The third part is "What Are Christian Nationalist Issues?" It explores heresies, both ancient and contemporary, that hold Christian Nationalism or religious nationalism at the center. It includes an investigation into the rejection of Christian Nationalism and other religious ideologies by orthodox Christianity. Heresies have been used as a justification to commit a variety of sins in the name of God. Prosperity gospel, millennialism, militarism, and abuse of religious freedom are problematic, heretical teachings posing as Christian truths. Christian Nationalists refuse to critique a capitalist system that produces wealth inequality. Prosperity gospel promotes a doctrine that God's primary promise is to deliver to believers "health and wealth." Prosperity ministers take advantage of the hope of those impoverished yet only offer false promises. Religious freedom has become a rationalization for discrimination in the denial of services publicly available, particularly in the expanded understanding of religious freedom as articulated by the U.S. Supreme Court. For much of the country's history, religious violence has enforced effective caste systems in the form of slavery and Jim Crow laws. All of this despite Christians serving a savior revered as a humble "Prince of Peace."

This book concludes with "The Christian Response to Christian Nationalism." It explores movements where the Christian church has issued a prophetic voice for the global transformation of society. More and more Christian voices are publicly rejecting Christian Nationalism as a danger to the nation, and more importantly, to Christianity itself. The discovery, and for some, the rediscovery of justice advocacy as a Christian discipline has been pronounced in the 21st century. Evangelism complimented by transformative actions calling for societal change has a following within Christian ranks as new generations redefine Christian discipleship.

The author concludes that Christian Nationalism has been a consistent presence in American society. Whether labeled as civil religion or Christian patriotism, sections of the American population have been unduly harmed by prejudicial beliefs based on flawed theological premises. The tragedy is that it has come out of the shadows and no longer lives under the pretense of being Christian doctrine but is now affirmed publicly by the highest religious and pollical leaders in the nation. But it can be resisted and disavowed as unchristian and counter to the teachings of Christ Jesus. It will take the concerted efforts of people of faith to lead the church with a clear message of love reflecting the teachings of a crucified and risen savior.

PART 1

What Is Christian Nationalism?

1

Christian Nationalism

So they watched him and sent spies who pretended to be honest, in order to trap him by what he said and then to hand him over to the jurisdiction and authority of the governor. [21] So they asked him, "Teacher, we know that you are right in what you say and teach, and you show deference to no one but teach the way of God in accordance with truth. [22] Is it lawful for us to pay tribute to Caesar or not?" [23] But he perceived their craftiness and said to them, [24] "Show me a denarius. Whose head and whose title does it bear?" They said, "Caesar's." [25] He said to them, "Then give to Caesar the things that are Caesar's and to God the things that are God's." [26] And they were not able in the presence of the people to trap him by what he said, and being amazed by his answer they became silent.

Luke 20:20-26 (Mark 12:13-17;
Matthew 22:15-22)

For God and Country

Christian Nationalism (CN) is an ideology that upholds national identity as coequal with one's Christian faith. In the United States, Christian Nationalist ideology is so deeply embedded within our consciousness that patriotic passion is intertwined with what it means to be a Christian. This worldview asserts that America is defined by its Christian identity and to be an American goes hand-in-hand with being a Christian. Christian nationalism, in other words, is a merger of Christian and American identities resulting in a distortion of both, misleading adherents into believing that they are equal in meaning. For Christian nationalists, a good American and a good Christian are interrelated, and to be one, it helps to be the other. Adherents profess that Christians are a chosen group and should receive special privileges. Rather than being a stabilizing force in society, Christian nationalist ideology supports and enforces white supremacy and leads to racial subjugation.[1]

A vital ingredient in Christian Nationalism is the belief that America was founded with the intent of being a Christian nation, a belief that persists today. A sizable percentage of American Christians (45%) state that the founding fathers intended to establish a Christian nation. One-third (33%) affirm that presently the country maintains a Christian identity. A 2023 survey disclosed that 80% of Christian Nationalists overwhelmingly support the establishment of a Christian nation utilizing biblical teachings as a foundation for penning legislation. A National Public Radio survey revealed that over half of the Republican Party supports the actions and rhetoric of Christian Nationalism. According to the survey, "Most Republicans qualify as either Christian nationalism sympathizers (33%) or adherents (21%), while at least three-quarters of both independents (46% skeptics and 29% rejecters) and Democrats (36% skeptics and 47% rejecters) lean toward rejecting Christian nationalism. Republicans (21%) are about four times as likely as Democrats (5%) or independents (6%) to be adherents of Christian nationalism."[2]

According to Pew Research Center, 28% of Christian Nationalists want the U.S. government to declare itself a Christian nation. A third (31%) advocate for the elimination of all policies putting barriers between the engagement of church and state; 39% want even greater allowances. Older adults (63%) affirm America as a Christian nation while younger adults (23%) do not. Almost a third want public school teachers to be given the authority to lead students in prayer. Over a third of Christians believe that patriotism and faith are "essential" to being a Christian. For 27% it is "important but not essential."[3] A 2025 Public Religion Research Institute (PRRI) poll updated the percentages. Christian Nationalism is deeply ingrained within the Republican Party. A majority of Republicans register either as Christian Nationalist adherents (20%) or sympathizers (33%), who affirm statements like the following: "being Christian is an important part of being truly American. God has called Christians to exercise dominion over all areas of American society. If the US moves away from our Christian foundations, we will not have a country anymore."[4]

Numerous clergy and scholars have defined Christian Nationalism as modern Christian heresy and a danger to American democracy. Leading clerical figures have denounced the ideology as dangerous and unhelpful for understanding the basics of Christianity. Episcopal Presiding Bishop Michael Curry placed a distinct separation between patriotism and faith: "Christian Nationalism is 'a heresy.' I love my country, but not more than I love my God. [This merger of faith and nationalism] is putting our loyalty to our country on par with our loyalty to our Lord. The early Christians said Jesus is Lord, Caesar is not. And that's true whether it's in the first century or the 21st century."[5]

Christian Nationalism is about power. Pew Research Center reports that Christian Nationalism serves as a pretext for the Christian faith, but in reality, it is a power play for dominance under the Christian banner. It is grounded in racism, authoritarianism, bigotry, and exclusion, while it falsely presents itself as standing for faith and morality. It refuses religious freedom to non-Christians and only offers discrimination and polarization.[6] Cathy Young wrote in the paper, *The Montanan*, "Christian Nationalism is a political movement couched in religious language. Their ultimate goal is earthly power—control over people and issues they don't like—which is the exact opposite of what the gospels teach us. Jesus came as a suffering servant who gave his life for all of us, whether we're rich, poor, gay, straight, Black, white, brown, of any culture, of any creed and of any language."[7]

Christian Nationalists are not monolithic. There are those who are strict adherents to Christian Nationalism, while others adhere to principles who when asked, reject the tenets of the ideology. Conversations about Christian Nationalism should take into account the different levels of support.

Render to God

In Mark 12, Jesus is confronted by his religious adversaries (pharisees, scribes, and Herodians) for the second time out of a total of four in Mark's Gospel. They confront him with an unanswered question: should conquered Jews pay taxes to a hated Roman government? It is a test that he quickly sees through. If he says "Yes!" he is considered a traitor to his own people, and many would disavow him. If he says, "No!" he risks arrest by the pagan government for treason. It is, however, a legitimate question, as both the Jewish leadership and populace are split in their answer. The Herodians and those who benefit from payment answer affirmatively; the Zealots and many of Jesus's countrymen reject payment. Jesus gives the perfect, if inconclusive, answer, as questioners are free to decide what belongs to whom. But a deeper search reveals that each person is to give to Caesar his coinage, which bears his image, and to give to God yourself for you bear the image of God.[8]

Christians seek guidance from the teachings of Jesus on the particulars that govern the relationship between faith and one's political identity. One saying that is most associated with the topic is the passage in Mark 12:13-17, often referred to as the "Render to Caesar" saying. It is one of the more difficult sayings of Jesus that has minute agreement in its interpretation. In it, he addresses whether Jews should pay taxes demanded by the Roman Empire as ransom for being a defeated people. To compound this fact, the hated taxes are collected by their own, Jewish tax collectors, who are treated as traitors. While this passage has served as a cornerstone for debating the relationship between Christians and the nation in which he or she resides, Jesus does not definitively define the boundaries. He does not list the areas of our life that belong to God (service) or what should be allotted to Caesar, or the empire, such as taxes. He does not identify loyalty, taxes, or subservience as belonging to the nation. But, a fuller reading of his teachings reveals that no humans, nor her institutions, are to stand on equal ground in our allegiance and there should be no equal alliance between God and the state.

Biblical scholar Lamar Williamson, in his commentary on Mark, wrote that the "render" phrase called for a priority of devotion. A Christian's primary loyalty is to God, who made humans in the image and likeness of God, while sharing a commitment to the state of one's labor in the service of society. Regardless, Jesus's answer is ambiguous and points to the sense that each must have obligations rendered to it. Williamson explains that "[W]hatever bears the image of God—humankind, that I, which alone in all creation is made in God's likeness—belongs exclusively to God. God is therefore due the highest loyalty and ultimate obedience of persons, who are God's own."[9]

For centuries scholars have interpreted the "render" saying and its implications for Christians. Tertullian determined that earthly money belonged to the world while the soul belonged to God."[10] John Howard Yoder, in *The Politics of Jesus*, wrote most succinctly in reference to the "render" saying of Jesus.

Scripture states that the state and the church have different purposes but also contain limited allegiances. A Christian should fulfill her dual responsibilities of citizenship but only follow limited obedience to the state.[11] Kaitlyn Schiess, in her book, *The Ballot and the Bible*, commented that while the two renderings are distinctly unique, they unite to serve related purposes, the doing of God's will. She offers agreement with Calvin and others that they are not equal in significance nor in requirements of loyalty. "While Caesar has legitimate authority, when his authority conflicts with God's, there's no question about whose authority wins. The coming kingdom of God demotes all earthly power. As many have said of New Testament political theology, 'If Christ is Lord, then Caesar is not.'"[12]

The Two Kingdoms

For some, the saying translated into a dialogue of the existence of two kingdoms, earthly and heavenly, each with its own place and resources. Ambrose of Milan wrote, "Palaces belong to the emperor, churches to the bishop."[13] St. Augustine first proposed the doctrine of "two kingdoms" in his book, *City of God*. God is calling Christians to dual callings to labor in the eternal city of God and the perishable earthly city.[14] Martin Luther modified the "two kingdoms" concept to say that politics and faith were two separate realms: an earthly one and a heavenly one. There was a rigid separation of the secular work of the government apart from the spiritual mission of the church.[15] There must be a refusal to bow too low to human authorities out of reverence for the Lordship of God.[16] Following Martin Luther's example, Ulrich Zwingli wrote his own 67 Theses in 1523 calling for separate realms of leadership. Secular governments legitimately rule under the dictates of the word of God and should be obeyed. Those that govern aligned with God's command to justice are to be obeyed but wicked administrations can be disposed.[17] John Calvin, in his *Institutes of the Christian Religion,* reiterated that Christians are citizens of "two kingdoms" (spiritual and civil) and should give obedience to both. Governments are both appointed by God for the benefit of God's kingdom and purpose. Civil governments are appointed by "divine providence," "holy ordinance," and have been given "God's gifts" to rule. He even urged that Christians not resist "bad kings." He drew the line when it came to a disagreement between the law of God and the law of the land. A Christian's ultimate loyalty is to God above any human government and its representatives. If a ruler tries to prop himself up in the place of God or seeks to lead a Christian away from the one true faith, he is to be resisted. Obedience to government must never become disobedience to God (Acts 5:29).[18] Literary great Dante, in *Divine Comedy,* was adamant about a pure separation of church and state. Throughout the book he argued for complete church-state separation with neither exercising authority over the over.[19]

Christian Patriotism and Christian Nationalism

There are several elements necessary for an ideology to fall under the label of Christian Nationalism. There must be an intersection of Christology (Christian theology), nationalism, and for white Christian Nationalists, nihilistic victimization. Christian Nationalism develops when this merger informs a person's religious and ideological beliefs. Christian Nationalism promotes the establishment of an American theocracy. A theocracy is when a government is installed due to God's perceived intervention, its officials are said to be divinely installed, and their decisions are viewed as God's decisions. The word is based upon the Greek *Koine, θεοκρατία,* "rule of God." A related category is *ecclesiocracy,* where the church has political authority.[20]

Nationalism and patriotism, although related, are distinct from one another. Patriotism is loyalty, devotion, or love of one's country. Patriotism is from the Greek word *patriṓtēs*, translated as patriot, fellow-countryman, lineage member, or fatherland. The first U.S. popular usage dates to the American Revolution, denoting a participant in a resistance movement, a freedom fighter. It generally denotes positive sentiments, attitudes, and actions of loving one's country and serving beneficially for one's compatriots. It is where love and loyalty of country can evoke both praise and criticism. Nationalism has Latin roots, indicating birth or tribe. It relates to the preferential endorsement of the policy and actions of one's nation in international affairs. Nationalism is excessive, aggressive patriotism with negative connotations. It is what happens when patriotism gets out of hand and transforms into something more exclusionary and isolationist.[21]

Patriotism and faith each have distinct purposes and roles in people's lives. The question must be asked, "Can a Christian maintain a degree of patriotism as an identity?" Do Christians assume a Christian identity as their sole one, or can being a patriot exist along with the others (parent, child, profession)? One thing is clear: rather than exist in cohabitation, the two identities of Christian and patriot often fight for dominance. In the early 20th century, there were conflicting views on the relationship between patriotism and faith. Current positions were reversed, as conservatives were anti-militaristic and progressive Protestants accused them of being weak and confused with an "un-American faith." They were confronted with charges of being adversaries to a strong America and a denial of the country being a Christian nation. Evangelicals opposed recruitment for World War I and called Christians to give allegiance to the kingdom of God. A phrase uttered was, "For this reason, patriotism was no virtue; a Christian's loyalty belonged to God's kingdom, not to the nation."[22]

Shirley C. Guthrie wrote one of the most widely accepted books utilized to teach seminarians the doctrines of the Christian faith. In *Christian Doctrine,* he sought to provide a rationale for loving one's country but placing limits on how far to go. He warned against elevating the state to the level of one's god where the demand for loyalty goes unquestioned. To do otherwise is to be subject to tyranny, which must be resisted. "This faith, by its protest against national arrogance abroad and injustice at home, helps to restore a nation to its proper role as servant rather than God of the people."[23]

Patrick Schreiner, professor at Midwestern Baptist Theological Seminary in Kansas City, Missouri, analyzed the differences between the goals of Christianity and those of the nation-state. The former is unselfish service to the other which the latter demands conformity to the whims of the state. Christianity teaches acceptance of those outside of the "nation-state," an appreciation for diversity and welcome to the stranger. The state has its own agenda that must be rigorously followed without exception, even when it excludes others. Christianity follows the agenda of the Prince of Peace."[24]

The adoption of Christian Nationalist beliefs will diminish one's faith, providing little meaning. The empire will not compromise in its quest for power and supremacy. Its appetite for more is unquenchable. It is one's faith and one's exclusive commitment to God that will be called to compromise and accept the rules of the empire. Its tools are violent defeat of its perceived enemies, uncompromising acceptance of the status quo, and an absence of critique. These are the enemies of faith as instituted in the mission of the church. Anything that takes attention away from God as the supreme authority and the words of Scripture as the unchallenged guide is ungodly and will ultimately fail.

Civil Religion and Christian Nationalism

Any study of the relationship between politics and religion in America must begin with an examination of civil religion. They are similar in description, but greater specificity is needed in discussions of faith and politics, as well as analyzing the religiosity that existed within different periods of American history. Civil Religion is the term most often used to describe the American experience and the interplay between politics and religion. In 1967, Robert Bellah marketed the term, "civil religion." It was a descriptor of America's political landscape that was profoundly influenced and inundated by religious meaning and symbols.[25]

Daniel K. Williams wrote that the primary difference between civil religion and Christian Nationalism was the intent of the period and the beliefs of human actors. The civil religion of the founders was not to establish a Christian nation, make Christian converts, or protect only Christians. Williams believed that "perhaps the main difference between Christian Nationalism consists not so much in the words that were said but in the intent. Civil religion was designed to unite the country around broadly shared principles, but Christian Nationalism is designed to wrest control of the country from one group of people (secularists or non-Christians) whom Christian Nationalists distrust and link the identity of the nation with the one group they do trust—namely, conservative Christians."[26]

A chart illustrates the differences between the two:

Aspect	Civil Religion	Christian Nationalism
Definition	A set of shared beliefs, symbols, and rituals that give sacred meaning to a nation and its institutions	A political ideology asserting that a nation should be explicitly defined by and governed according to Christianity.
Core Idea	The nation has a sacred mission or moral purpose, but not tied to one specific church doctrine.	Christianity (often a specific interpretation of it) should shape laws, culture, and national identity.

Aspect	Civil Religion	Christian Nationalism
Religious Scope	Broad and inclusive; may reference God in general terms without endorsing a specific denomination.	Exclusive; prioritizes Christianity and may marginalize other religions or secular views.
Relation to the State	Symbolic religious language supports national unity (e.g., oaths, holidays, monuments).	Seeks direct influence of Christian beliefs on public policy and governance.
Examples (U.S.)	References to God in the Pledge of Allegiance, presidential inaugurations, national memorials.	Movements advocating that the U.S. was founded as a Christian nation and should return to explicitly Christian governance.
View of Pluralism	Compatible with religious diversity.	Often skeptical of or opposed to religious pluralism.
Political Goal	Promote social cohesion and national identity.	Reshape political structures and laws to reflect Christian doctrine.
Criticism	Can blur church–state separation symbolically.	Can threaten democracy, minority rights, and church–state separation.

There are other factors at play that differentiate CR from CN including social factors such as race, gender, sexual identity, and foreign policy.

Throughout American history, CR provided power and status for a select group, whites, as CN controlled and exploitation of the lives of racial-ethnic minorities. For Blacks, Hispanics, and Native Americans life was a series of denigrating oppressions enforced through legal guardrails. CR pacified relations between whites who were treated to a less harsh world where politics and religion transmitted a more affirming society.

Whites in America were greeted with a civil life where religion and politics were affirmed as good for society complete with promises of prosperity. While women, gays, white migrants, and initially Jews and Catholics, were denied their full rights as American citizens, in some cases, this proved to be less severe and temporary. European migrants initially endured first-generation prejudice but were eventually assimilated into white society with a rejuvenated status. Those originally considered "other" could become white and therein find acceptance and offered paths of assimilation. While white Americans looked askew at poor and migrant whites and initially refused their assimilation, the suppression was short-term and less aggressive. Class and economic standings denied fair treatment, but never was there a banner of racial inferiority permanently hoisted. Eventually, their children could become Protestants, change the family names, and become capitalists. People of color could not. Lawrence McCaffrey notes regarding the Irish: "The Irish came about the same time as the Chinese, but they had a distinct advantage: the Naturalization Law of 1790 had reserved citizenship for 'whites' only. Their compatible complexion allowed them to assimilate by blending into American Society. In successfully entering the mainstream, however, these immigrants from Erin pursued an Irish 'ethnic' strategy: they promoted 'Irish' solidarity to gain political power and to dominate skilled blue-collar occupations, often at the expense of the Chinese and Black people."[27]

Race was a major determinant in whether leaders spoke in a CR voice or a CN one. The same individuals who voiced positive affirmations of American life utilized CN foundations to oppress people of color and foreign nations. Amanda Tyler, in *How to End Christian Nationalism*, wrote of the hypocrisy of the Founding Fathers when they discussed the dependency of religious freedom upon the audience. Tyler notes that "Washington and the other founders violated this ideal (of religious freedom) from the very beginning. Citizenship was granted only to white persons from the very beginning, including in the Naturalization Act of 1790. . . . The ideal of equality regardless of religion is discarded in favor of an effective caste system, with only white Christians as full citizens and everyone else having effective second-class citizenship."[28]

Gender complicated relations when politics and policy were based upon religious standards. When the two came together race and gender made life unbearable for women of color. For white women were lessened the discrimination they endured in that while they were denied the basic rights of citizenship, they were not violently raped, murdered, and exploited. Du Mez recalled that southern social policy claimed a need for the protection of white women from Black men while it was the divine right of white men to assume sexual privileges with the bodies of Native American, Black, and Hispanic women. Du Mez surmised that "this blending of racism and the perceived sexual vulnerability of white women had a long history in the South, even if historical evidence irrefutably demonstrates that it was Black women who had reason to fear white men's sexual aggression, not the other way around."[29] Ronald Takaki remarked upon the attitude of white American troops during the Mexican American War. It was the height of manifest destiny and white Americans "seemed to manifest a masculine destiny." He regurgitated the ugly history of the rape of Mexican men of their land and women of their dignity, justified by a sense of racial superiority and divine sanction. White Texans were superior to Mexican men and greatly desired by Mexican women. Takaki elaborates that "American men bragged how they were displaying their prowess in the southwest not only on the battlefield but also in bed. They claimed that their sexual attractiveness to Mexican women was God-given. In an essay on the conquest of California, the editor of the *Southern Quarterly Review* proudly explained the reason why the 'senoritas of California'. . . invariably preferred the men of the Anglo-Saxon race."[30]

21st Century Christian Nationalist Ideologies and Movements

There are voices that defend Christian Nationalism. Presbyterian apologist Stephen Wolfe, in *The Case for Christian Nationalism*, contends that CN is misinterpreted and misunderstood. He utilizes Calvinist rhetoric in support of a "measured theocratic Caesarism" In order to achieve unity through a common religious faith. "If the rise of Christian nationalism in America reflects the decline of Christianity, that is bittersweet news for secular liberals, because it means that they might expect to see more and more of it as the country grows less pious."[31]

American Exceptionalism is one of the most long-standing ideologies undergirding Christian Nationalism. It affirms that the founding of the United States is an act of God and is due to divine favor. America is unique in that it is the current manifestation of the "New Israel" and is in covenant relationship with the divine creator. Legislation should be founded upon Christian values and ardent advocates demand a Constitutional amendment adhering to the principles of Christianity. It is at the heart of Christian Nationalist beliefs in that it provides justification for the acquisition of political power as a means for fulfilling the will of the Almighty. It produced the Manifest Destiny ideology that justified the establishment of an American empire and colonialism. Entangling the work of the government with the divine has always been a popular strategy by both political parties as both Republicans and Democrats have presented America as God's instrument. To entice voters and increase party membership, religious speechifying has endorsed platforms and rallies. Zealous rhetoric materialized in stump speeches and campaign promises to convince listeners of divine sanction. Pious protocols presented themselves through the use of Scripture, symbols, and language promote the image of a party directed by God. Prayers and hymns at government events have become normalized at levels far beyond those expected under civil religion.

Christian Reconstructionism is an ideology that the establishment of a theocratic form of government to establish a biblical worldview is the only solution for the world's problems. Issues of importance include biblical inerrancy, patriarchal hierarchy, and a theocracy controlled by the faithful few. It was originally designed by Rousas John Rushdoony who promoted it during the 1960s and '70s. He was an anti-intellectual who criticized the Enlightenment as misleading in its teachings on equality. He maintained that the self-governing principles of democracy were in opposition to God's desire institutional design for governments. He was an arrogant extremist who taught that slavery was voluntary, and the Civil War was a religious war fought to preserve Christian civilization. His views on race were grounded in white supremacy as he spoke against interracial marriage and education for Blacks. His misogyny was apparent in his denial for the right of women to vote as he criticized women who dared to speak in public. He wrote disparagingly on the rights of the Jewish community. Christian Reconstructionism was founded upon the teachings of biblical law and the CN position that America was founded as a Christian nation. Katherine Stewart wrote in *The Power Worshippers*, "Rushdoony advocated a return to 'biblical' law in America. The Bible . . . commands Christians to exercise absolute dominion over the earth and all of its inhabitants. Women are destined by God to be subordinate to men; men are destined to be ruled by a spiritual aristocracy of right-thinking, orthodox Christian clerics; and the federal government is an agent of evil. Public education . . . is a threat to civilization, for it 'basically trains women to be men,' and represents 'primitivism,' 'chaos,' and 'a vast integration into the void.'"[32] The problems of American society could only be alleviated by the adoption of a patriarchal system as exemplified in Old Testament law. Every institution would function properly only under the strong leadership of a single, strong authority figure who made decisions for the benefit of all. Churches, the family, and government were flawed institutions when decisions were democratically determined, as chaos ensued.[33] Reconstructionists are found amongst the membership of Southern Baptist Convention, the Assemblies of God, Promise Keepers, the Christian Broadcasting Network, the Christian Coalition, the conservative Council for National Policy, and others. True believers are found amongst Presbyterian-oriented educators (Presbyterian Church in America and Orthodox Presbyterian Church), Baptist school headmasters and pastors, and telecommunications.[34]

Dominionists stress that Christians should have "dominion" over all positions of power in government and society. So-called "Apostles" are to assume dominion in every sphere of life that God has identified to destroy Satan's dominion.[35] Lance Wallnau, the originator of the Seven Mountain Mandate, identified the seven mountains as the most important and influential elements of society.[36] True Christians must control these "seven molders" or "mountains" of culture and societal life: government, business, education, media, arts and entertainment, family, and religion. Only through conquest by evangelization by conservative Christians will God's kingdom be established on earth. Christians will be anointed to rule the world to decree righteous behavior. Secular goals such as democracy, pluralism, dialogue, and social acceptance are rejected as pagan ideologies. Former CN adherent Bradley Onishi explained that "the New Apostolic Reformation and the Seven Mountains Mandate have their goal as conquest and power. And so, if your goal is to colonize the earth for God and to dominate American politics and governance, then you want somebody who's willing to go along that road and down that road with you." The goal is not to proclaim a Lord who is one of love, justice, and compassion, but a conquering warrior who will rule by absolute power. Believers scoff at Islamic believers who sacrifice themselves for the promise of paradise, where they are served by a slew of virgins, and organize around a similar promise of a life rewarded by power and privilege.

New Apostolic Reformation (NAR) endorsers stress that Donald Trump has been anointed by God to bring about the establishment of a Christian nation. Mike Johnson associates with Timothy Carscadden, a New Apostolic Reformation pastor, and Dutch Sheets. Sheets mobilized efforts to overturn the 2020 election and called for attendance at the January 6 insurrection."[37] Christian Nationalists, William Wolfe and Russ Vought, were members of Trump's cabinet.[38] Vought was the director of the Office of Management and Budget and was president of The Center for Renewing America think tank. During a meeting with members of the New Apostolic there was a viewing of the video, *God Made Trump*. God anointed him for the presidency as shepherd and caretaker. He is a "cosmic savior" for a "Christian nation."[39] He became Trump's chief of staff during his second term.

A series of events, Jericho March rallies, were implemented from the moment the election was lost and culminated in the January 6 violence. Stewart Rhodes (Oath Keepers) was recruited to fuel the flames of political rebellion and recruit insurrectionists to support Trump.

Former United States National Security Advisor Michael Flynn is touring the nation to promote Christian Nationalism under the ReAwaken tour. Months after the failed insurrection on January 6, Flynn and entrepreneur Clay Clark toured, by 2022, numerous cities and states preaching God, country, and politics. General Flynn uses military language to portray a war between good and evil, where the forces of God are under attack. He defiantly declared that there is a spiritual war and there is a political war," as he endorsed QAnon conspiracies and Christian Nationalist beliefs. NAR endorsers believe that the greatest enemy against God is the government. He stated, "If we are going to have one nation under God, which we must, we have to have one religion. One nation under God, and one religion under God."[40] At the tour, attendees pay for entry tickets and various forms of paraphernalia. Many accept the offer to be baptized and prayed for. At a rally in Batavia, New York, one woman wore a t-shirt that read: "Jesus is my savior, Trump is my president." She was baptized at the political revival on three different occasions, believing it would eventually grant her the gift of speaking in tongues.[41]

The Christian Order of Love is an ideology that teaches a white nationalist term, *kinism*. It is promoted by the TheoBros, a millennial, ultra-conservative group of men unabashedly calling themselves Christian Nationalists. The term is defined as loving those nearest to you as a matter of vital importance. As a matter of fact, it is un-Christian to love foreigners as much as you love those who are citizens of your own country. It lies at the heart of what it means to be patriotic. Nations maintain their ethnic and racial purity, and the United States was founded as the province of white Christians.

This is interesting coming from the mouth of a Christian as it runs contrary to the teaching of Jesus who advocates for loving being the essence of discipleship. Especially caring for those not of one's lineage such as the stranger. Luke 6:32-33, 36 reads: *"If you love those who love you, what credit is that to you? For even sinners love those who love them. If you do good to those who do good to you, what credit is that to you? For even sinners do the same. . . . Be merciful, just as your Father is merciful."*

Conservative organizations exercised an amazing ability to organize and implement their Christian Nationalist strategy with long-term implications. The Congressional Prayer Caucus produced *Project Blitz* to design bills to be pushed in state legislative bodies with the intent of destroying the separation between church and state."[42] What started out as a visionary playbook was put to paper as a 40-page manual that by 2019 it was 148 pages. It was the first installment of *Project 2025*.[43] The Heritage Foundation created *Project 2025* as a handbook for Christian Nationalists to use in their attempts to promote their agenda.[44]

In this program, Congress would lose some of its oversight authority as the president's power is consolidated.[45] Británnica.com notes that "While not explicitly endorsing Christian nationalism, *Project 2025* shares the Christian nationalist views that 'families comprised [sic] of a married mother, father, and their children are the foundation of a well-ordered nation and healthy society.' The Project calls upon the government to 'maintain a biblically based, social science–reinforced definition of marriage and family' and contends that laws protecting the rights and freedoms of LGBTQ persons have effectively violated or at least disrespected the religious freedom of Christians."[46]

A long list of Project 2025's recommendations were implemented by the Trump administration during his second term. It had a devastating impact upon the competency of the federal government when thousands of employees lost jobs, DEI was attached, and prayer services were held at the Pentagon.

The Bible and the Constitution

For Christian Nationalists, there is a standing controversy concerning who should have what rendered unto whom. The question of what is the ultimate authority in the life of a Christian is unresolved. Outside of World Overcomers Church in Memphis, Tennessee, stands a replica of the Statue of Liberty holding a cross instead of a torch, printed with the words, "America Return to Christ." While all would affirm that the authority of the Bible is the ultimate guide, for many, the authority of the Constitution sits alongside it, even if they don't acknowledge it. Christian Nationalists express no conflict between expressing complete and unabashed loyalty to both the Bible and the Constitution. One can be a Christian and an American with equal allegiance to both. Christian Nationalists often defend their rights as Americans by exploiting the Second Amendment and the Bible. Both are quoted as a legitimate basis for owning guns, as well as the freedom to discriminate against persons whose sexual identity is considered controversial. In a counter opinion, a majority of Americans, almost seven-in-ten (67%), see the Constitution as a completely human invention without divine guidance or inspiration. As few as 18% see divine intervention in the drafting of the U.S. Constitution.[47]

CN supporters maintain that America's founding documents (the Constitution and the Declaration of Independence) were inspired by God. They affirm the inerrancy of the Bible and hold almost as high an opinion of the Constitution. America is a Christian nation with a God-inspired Constitution to prove it. Some Christian nationalists go so far as to proclaim that there is no conflict between expressing complete and unabashed loyalty to both the Bible and the Constitution. For some, one is a Christian and an American on an equal basis, with allegiance to both. Some justify their position by holding firm to the belief that the Constitution was inspired by Scripture and has divine sanction. The editors at the *Chicago Tribune* published an opinion piece on the relationship between the Bible and the Constitution. "As the U.S. Constitution is the highest law of the land (in America), so the Bible is the highest law of God. The American Constitution itself was founded upon Biblical standards. It is the Bible that sets forth spiritual laws and records God's enduring promises. The most wonderful message of this document is that it reveals God's plan of redemption for the human race."[48] Paul D. Miller wrote, "If you believe that the Constitution is divinely inspired, that puts you high up on the scale of Christian nationalism. You don't get much more Christian nationalist than that. Sometimes social scientists talk about the ideal type of a thing. In other words, its logical conclusion, its purest form."[49] At an Ohio rally in 2024, followers/supporters of Donald Trump said the nation and its founders, as well as founding documents such as the Bill of Rights, had Christian origins. Historians dispute these assertions.[50]

Kristin Kobes Du Mez offers the opinion that it is not the Bible that determines the issues that white evangelicals, especially Christian Nationalists, endorse. Rather, it is the issues that shape identity. She explains a conflict between what Evangelicals say they believe about the significance of the Bible and just how much impact it has in their lives. "Despite evangelicals' frequent claims that the Bible is the source of their social and political commitments, evangelicalism must be seen as a cultural and political movement rather than as a community defined chiefly by its theology. Evangelical views on any given issue are facets of this larger cultural identity, and no number of Bible verses will dislodge the greater truths at the heart of it."[51]

The Constitution is a tool of democracy to establish democratic governance. The Bible is a book of revelation that opens the reader to the will of God individually and to the world. The allegiance they demand is not equal and to do so places a Christian in a dangerous position of heretical misalignment. Gun rights advocates quote the Second Amendment more often than they do scriptural passages. For Christians, both can have value but require a different set of allegiance and hierarchy. To equate them on equal planes presents an ideologically dangerous position of comprehending the significance of both. The Bible constantly warns of the danger of placing anything above our loyalty to God or even on an equal plane. To hold the Constitution as a document of equal worth to the Word of God elevates the Constitution to sacred status and demotes God's word to just another document.

Meanwhile, Christian Nationalists promote nonconstitutional goals with religious zeal and a sense of righteousness. They stand against the right of a woman to decide whether to undergo an abortion or not. LGBTQIA rights are a nonstarter, and schools should be places where prayer is allowed by everyone.[52] Sociologists Andrew L. Whitehead and Samuel L. Perry examined published surveys and compiled CN dictates, to include: The federal government should declare the United States a Christian nation and adhere to Christian values; a reinstatement of prayer in public schools; and the display of Christian symbols on public property.[53] In these and other situations, Christian Nationalists argue for rights that many Christians have no desire to enforce. American Christians are generally politically moderate and do not want infringement from the state on their religious beliefs, nor the church to be dictating government policy.

But for Christians, there is to be a higher authority, the Bible. And when there are conflicts with our political beliefs, the Word of God should have the last word. There is perhaps no constitutional question, with exception being the controversy over the intent of the Second Amendment, as unresolved as the role of religion in American society in the First Amendment.

In 2024, Donald Trump endorsed a Bible edition that includes U.S. founding documents and the lyrics to Lee Greenwood's "God Bless the USA"—the *God Bless the USA Bible.* It was produced by Hugh Kirkpatrick who stated that he wanted to unite the nation behind God and country as America's founding was greatly influenced by Scripture. The book included a copy of the Constitution as a commemoration of the 20th anniversary of the 911 attacks, as well as lyrics to the song, "God Bless the USA." According to the *Washington Post*, academics in the faith community criticized the American Bible as idolatrous, as an instrument of Christian Nationalism.[54]

Religious Symbols

CN appropriates the symbols of faith into service for the nation. It conflates the language and doctrines of faith with those of national identity. It empties religion of its global significance as one country is more favorable to God than any other. Katherine Stewart, author of *Power Worshippers*, wrote: "Sectarian innovations before public meetings, like crosses placed on public lands, may appear to play a merely symbolic role in our governance and are therefore easy to dismiss. But they point to the broader privileging of conservative Christianity in America, including its superior access to sources of public money and the perversion of our most deeply held constitutional principles."[55] Britannica.com notes that "Among the government policies a Christian nationalist might desire are the display of Christian symbols on public property, the dedication of time for prayer in public schools, government funding for religious institutions, a Christian interpretation of history in public-school curricula, the outlawing of abortion, restrictions on non-Christian immigration, and the policing of what some Christians consider to be immoral behavior, which almost always includes the suppression of LGBTQ+ people. Regardless of the policy, the goal is to privilege Christianity in the public square."[56] CN proponents attempted to build religious monuments on public property. Amanda Tyler, executive director of Baptist Joint Committee criticized any merger of "American and Christian identities." She called for a response from the Christian community: "As Christians, we must speak in one voice condemning Christian nationalism as a distortion of the gospel of Jesus and a threat to American democracy."[57] Supporters argue superficially that the failure of the American school system began when prayer was taken out of the system. Yet, it was never removed as students can lead and assemble in prayer. Teachers and administrators, as agents of the state, cannot endorse a religious preference to the students by offering school prayers. Many individuals who are hostile to Critical Race Theory being taught in public schools support the insertion of a curriculum teaching Christian Nationalist ideology. Fear of the insertion of Islamic Sharia Law into the American criminal code is considered a part of a terrorist invasion.

Religious symbols play an important role in representing America's national identity. Father Eugene Hemrick, author of "One Nation Under God," gave an interview with Catholic News Service and commented, "This country was established with a very strong religious background." He wrote in his book, "We are truly blessed to live in a country that not only respects God, but has chiseled that respect in stone, inscribed it on walls, pierced it together in mosaics, and painted it on canvases so that American generations that will never forget their religious heritage."[58]

As stated earlier, America's religious and political history are joined at the hip. So much so that religious imaginary is found on federal and state buildings around the country. It gives a false impression that America is a Christian nation while injustice has occurred in these same buildings based on prejudice and societal partiality. The U.S. capitol building in Washington, D.C., is an aesthetic display of Christian Nationalist ideology as well as Greek and Roman mythology (i.e. Venus, Minerva, Ceres, Vulcan, and Mercury). It has been referred to as a "sacred center" and a "temple of democracy." The building was dedicated in 1935 and incorporates religious symbols throughout its design in Greek and Roman architecture in the Corinthian style. Each court session begins with the Court Marshall saying before all in attendance, "God save the United States and this honorable court." The Capitol's cast-iron dome is modeled after cathedral domes, particularly those of St. Peter's in Rome and St. Paul's in London. The rotunda is modeled after the Roman Pantheon's replicating the worship place of pagan deities. Inside the dome there is an oculus that opens to a fresco inspired by the Pantheon's Apotheosis of Genevieve. An apotheosis means "the raising of a person to the rank of a god" or "the glorification of a person as an idea." Constantino Brumidi painted within the fresco George Washington rising to heaven. He is surrounded by the mythological Roman gods, Mercury and Venus, and figures representing

Liberty and Victory/Fame. Around the interior of the dome are life-sized paintings containing a mixture of American history and Christian symbols, such as crucifixes. European discoverers, such as Christopher Columbus, were accompanied by Catholic priests, as a symbol of divine blessings. The "Discovery of Mississippi" is depicted by a painting of Hernando de Soto, with priests praying as they stake a crucifix in the ground. On the front doors, Christopher Columbus, is carved into the wooden doors alongside Franciscans with rosaries.[59]

Across the street at the Supreme Court, Moses holds the Ten Commandments on the east side of the building. It is noteworthy that there is a historical debate as to the duality of the artwork. Moses represents the biblical character but also represents the "great lawgivers of history" as he is flanked by Confucius and Solon. In the interior of the building the justices sit beneath a replica of the Ten Commandments as they are also pressed into the doors facing First Street. Again, some historians argue that Adolph Weinman, who designed the frieze, wrote that the Roman numbers I through X represent the first ten Constitutional amendments, the Bill of Rights. A counter argument is that the numbers are written on tablets as recorded in the Bible and could represent nothing else.[60]

Throughout the court building are references to God and faith. In the Cox Corridor, a verse from "America the Beautiful" is carved in the wall. At the east entrance to the Senate chamber are the words *Annuit Coeptis* (Latin for "God has favored our undertakings"). The words, "In God We Trust," are inscribed in two locations: the House chamber, the Senate entrance in the Capitol Chapel. In the Capitol's Chapel is a stained-glass window depicting George Washington in prayer under "In God We Trust." A prayer in the window reads, "Preserve me, God, for in Thee do I put my trust." Above the House gallery door there is a marble relief of Moses.[61]

In 1789, despite strong opposition by James Madison, two chaplains were hired to offer prayers and spiritual counsel to members of Congress and staff. They were paid from public funds. Madison objected,

> The Constitution of the U.S. forbids everything like an establishment of a national religion. The law appointing Chaplains establishes a religious worship for the national representatives, to be performed by Ministers of religion, elected by a majority of them; and these are to be paid out of the national taxes. Does not this involve the principle of a national establishment, applicable to a provision for a religious worship for the Constituent as well as of the representative Body, approved by the majority, and conducted by Ministers of religion paid by the entire nation? . . . [If] it be proper that public functionaries, as well as their Constituents should discharge their religious duties, let them[,] like their Constituents, do so at their own expense."[62]

In a December 6, 1884, ceremony an aluminum capstone was placed atop the Washington Monument containing the Latin phrase *Laus Deo*, "Praise be to God." The cornerstone includes a Bible, a copy of the Declaration of Independence and the U.S. Constitution. Inside is a memorial plaque from the Free Press Methodist-Episcopal Church. On different landings there is a prayer, a memorial by Chinese Christians, carved blocks inscribed with attributes to God and the Scriptures."[63]

Abraham Lincoln was another president for whom faith was important. He made constant references to God and would often quote Scripture. The Lincoln Memorial was designed similar to a Greek Pantheon inscribed with the Gettysburg Address. "We here highly resolve that these dead shall not have died in vain—that this nation, under God, shall have a new birth of freedom." Also is his second inaugural address that referred to God 14 times and twice quoted the Bible. On the walls of the memorial, the words of Isaiah 40 were later added in reference to Martin Luther King Jr.'s "I Have a Dream" speech."[64]

Combating Christian Nationalism

The existence of CN does not mean that all Christians have universally agreed on Christian Nationalism. Percentages hold that while religion is an important element in the land, its influence should remain neutral, if not negated to the realms of the church. Few are familiar with the concept of Christian Nationalism and many doubt that it has meaningful impact.[65]

Francis Schaeffer, an American evangelical, coined the term "existential methodology." Society had been greatly influenced by humanist ideology rather than the ultimate truth of Christianity. He wanted a return to a government based upon God's law as exposed in Scripture. He even advocated for civil disobedience against any government that was authoritarian and repressed freedom. He, however, was clear in that he was not calling for the establishment of a theocracy and rejected outright the principles of Christian Nationalism as supported by Falwell and others of the Christian Right of his day. He argued, "There is no New Testament basis for a linking of church and state until Christ, the King returns. The whole 'Constantine mentality' from the fourth century up to our day was a mistake. . . . [T]hrough the centuries it has caused great confusion between loyalty to the state and loyalty to Christ, between patriotism and being a Christian. We must not confuse the Kingdom of God with our country. To say it another way: 'We should not wrap our Christianity in our national flag.'"[66]

Even among those who label themselves as Christian Nationalists, opinions vary concerning what it means for America to be a Christian nation. Most feel that the adage of separation of church and state should remain status quo. Only a handful want the federal government to declare the nation a Christian state. Only 5% view CN positively and 25% do not view it as something that should be promoted. No religious demographic has a majority with a favorable opinion of the ideology. It is of interest that while most Americans are not endorsers of CN, many do affirm the contributions that the Christian faith makes to society and stress that the federal government *should* be in the business of promoting Christian values. Over half value the qualities that the Bible promotes and want it to influence the country's laws. And if a majority of Americans disagree with the position of Scripture, it should be implemented regardless.[67]

Andrew Torba, founder of *Gab*, wrote a 78-page booklet defending Christian Nationalism. He called for an end to speech restrictions that limited the rhetoric of far-right extremists. Only by being more aggressive can Christians win over secular culture that is less receptive to the Word of God. Real Christian men need to step up and lead in the battle for Christ's dominion. He commented, "We need Christian men who will embrace their God-given masculine energy to conquer and lead. We are done being footstools. We are done being pushovers. Now we want to win. Win souls for Christ. Win elections. Win in the culture. Win in the education system. Win with our own technology. Our own media. Our own entertainment. Win for the glory of God."[68]

2

Global Origins of Christian Nationalism

King Nebuchadnez'zar made an image of gold, whose height was sixty cubits and its breadth six cubits. He set it up on the plain of Dura, in the province of Babylon. . . . And the herald proclaimed aloud, "You are commanded, O peoples, nations, and languages, that when you hear the sound of the horn, pipe, lyre, trigon, harp, bagpipe, and every kind of music, you are to fall down and worship the golden image that King Nebuchadnez'zar has set up. And whoever does not fall down and worship shall immediately be cast into a burning fiery furnace". . . Chaldeans came forward and maliciously accused the Jews. . . "Shadrach, Meshach, and Abed'nego. These men, O king, pay no heed to you; they do not serve your gods or worship the golden image which you have set up."

Then Nebuchadnez'zar in furious rage commanded that Shadrach, Meshach, and Abed'nego be brought . . . before the king. Nebuchadnezzar said to them, "Is it true, O Shadrach, Meshach, and Abed'nego, that you do not serve my gods or worship the golden image which I have set up? . . . (I)f you do not worship, you shall immediately be cast into a burning fiery furnace; and who is the god that will deliver you out of my hands?"

Shadrach, Meshach, and Abed'nego answered the king, "O Nebuchadnez'zar, we have no need to answer you in

> this matter. If it be so, our God whom we serve is able to deliver us from the burning fiery furnace; and he will deliver us out of your hand, O king. But if not, be it known to you, O king, that we will not serve your gods or worship the golden image which you have set up."
>
> Daniel 3:1-18, RSV

Daniel chapter 3 indicates that one of the dangers of Christian Nationalism is the confusion of whom one is to bow down to, God or the king. Getting too close to political power means to conflate allegiance. Christian Nationalists desire political power, even to hold it and make decisions based on their truths. They operate as prophets only when those holding office differ in party and policy. They rarely see themselves as the critics to abuses committed but look to curry favor with politicians who can advance their agenda.

In this story from Daniel, his three friends Shadrach, Meshach, and Abed'nego demonstrated not only tremendous courage, but outstanding faith. They had incurred the wrath of the king whose decision could endanger their lives. Rather than fear the king, they maintained their loyalty to God and refused to commit idolatry. The book of Exodus contains the Ten Commandments that command, "Thou shalt have no other gods before me" and to refuse to bow down to graven images (Exodus 20: 3-5 KJV). There is no compromise in our steadfastness to an omnipotent God in opposition to worship finite human beings. Rarely do we find such a consistency to being able to separate the loyalty due to God and our understanding of the finiteness of human authority. Almost every religion has compromised their worship of God by incorporating instances of human adoration of each other. Far too often we comprise places set aside for a sacred purpose by allowing the worship of humans to merge with the divine.

History of Religious Nationalism

Christian Nationalism is being widely discussed in the media and critiqued by religious leaders. The willingness of Christian Nationalists to combine faith and politics has caused consternation that the country is headed down a path from which democracy won't recover. Much of the conversation focuses upon its current manifestation in the United States, but it is a global phenomenon with historic and international manifestations. Long before Christianity came upon the scene, the merger of religious and sociopolitical components existed under the guise of what could be referred to as religious nationalism, and rather than being the exception, it was the norm.

American Christian Nationalists consider their beliefs to be God's unique revelation of God's will. Christian Nationalists affirm that their American identity is closely associated with their Christian identity and that the state of the nation is dependent upon their fidelity to God. Christian Nationalism adheres to a belief that the welfare of the nation is intertwined with how well faith is maintained. America is a Christian nation founded by Christians whose sole desire was to assert the United States as the dominant world power for the glory of God. If today's Christian Nationalists fail, the nation will fail, as its fortunes are dependent upon the favor of God. One of the reoccurring features of religious belief has been a people or tribe maintaining that the fate of the nation was determined by the faithfulness of its people. The well-being of one's nation is maintained by a mandated subservience to a god who will punish the innocent for perceived disloyalty. Christians, both progressive and conservative, instinctively worship a God who is in control of all of life and distributes blessings for those who are faithful. Even when not using the language of CN, many believe that the divisiveness and problems of the country are due to disobedience and the failure to "give God the glory." African Americans have a long history of equating the suffering of the nation with God's displeasure and that there will be a reckoning. John Brown prophesied that the sin of an unrepentant nation could only be purged with blood.

The antecedents of CN did not originate with the founding of the nation, but in the Fertile Crescent passing from the Sumerians to the Babylonians to the Assyrians to the Egyptians as a spiritual inheritance for diverse religions. Key to understanding today's controversy is the knowledge that this is part of the human search for revelation for contentment and inner peace. And that itself is problematic, for as much as we seek clarity on the meaning of life, we want it to be uniquely ours and that we are the ones called by a mysterious God to open the eyes of non-believers. We want to be special. And that is a problem for those who embrace CN and those who reject it: we want to be right and have God on our side. Dr. William Newton Clark wrote in his 1898 book, *An Outline of Christian Theology,* that Christians should have an appreciation for the contributions of all religions. Humans have sought knowledge of an unknown God who has bequeathed knowledge upon all races without leaving them spiritually destitute. Truth, mostly partial, is God's gift to those who have sought the divine over the eons. "Though Christian theology thus possesses the best light in the world, it should not be contemptuous toward other religions, or rule them out as containing nothing valuable. Christians should view such religions, not with contempt, but with generous and compassionate consideration."[1]

Ancient revelations have had an enormous influence upon the world's monotheistic religions. Religious concepts that are popular today have foundations in ancient religions. Throughout centuries of theological wrangling, the concept of a single deity won out. However, many ancient beliefs remain unchanged. The hardest to overcome has been religious nationalism as humans desperately need to feel that their relationship with God is unlike that of others. We desire for God to give our lives a special purpose by appropriating God's ability to choose who is good and what is evil. Who we are, in our everyday lives, is never enough. When in reality, what makes life worth living is the ability to accept our finiteness and maintain faith and trust in God. To be able to live a complete life filled with joy and purpose.

Beliefs were refined and reformed as primitive notions were dropped for more contemporary sensibilities. The reverse happened as well as ancient myths and rituals allowed quick adaptation of newer religious beliefs similar in ideology and custom.[2]

A large percentage of religious doctrines and revelations have connections to ancient mythology. Many of the modern beliefs about God, creation, nature, and human beings are not limited to our religious traditions as we oftentimes assume, as many have their source in ancient religions. There is a connection between the religious dogmas of antiquity and modern theologies such as religious nationalism, creation, incarnation, resurrection, and sin. The power of myths is that they have lasting power and influence over the religious beliefs that followed, even Christianity. Karl Barth, writing in *Dogmatics in Outline,* refuted the thought that pagan myths infiltrated Christian theology. But he admitted that in Genesis 1 and 2, "certain mythical elements are to be found there."[3] Paul Tillich and Reinhold Niebuhr concluded that every religion was composed of myths and religious legends. For them it was absurd to regard the narratives of Adam and Eve, the Flood, and others as literally true and dispel with their mythic composition. "Myths, they proposed, were the essential mode of encounter with the sacred: the means of expressing the dimension of depth in life that transcends history and points to 'the ultimate ground of existence.'"[4] Bernhard W. Anderson, in his book *Understanding the Old Testament*, studied the link between the stories, myths, and narratives of the Old Testament and their predecessor religions. He had no issue with crediting their origins as being beyond Israel. Myths that were part of

Canaanite culture include many of the sagas in Genesis, Abraham's sacrifice of Isaac (Gen. 22) and Jacob's dream at Bethel (Gen. 28). They were not just borrowed but appropriated."[5]

In the ancient Near East, religion and spirituality met at the center of everyday existence. For the ancients, there were no individual spheres as all of life was intertwined; religion was immersed into politics, society, and family. Ancient civilizations believed that religion influenced every moment of living. People worshipped a variety of gods whose behavior and actions influenced their daily lives as well as impacted future events. Divine favor was assumed in every region and a nation's fate was determined by their gods. Religious expectations and those of the state were interlinked and mutually important for well-being. To be a citizen of the state meant being identified under the banner of a national deity.[6] The *Time Magazine* series, "Great Ages of Man: Ancient Egypt," revealed, "Because all Egyptian life was permeated with religion, there was no distinct church-state separation as is known in the modern West; where the ruler is god, civil and religious affairs run together. . . ."[7]

Divine Origins of Nations

The history of the United States is one of a nation obsessed with, and possessed by, religion. The combination of nationalism and religious faith has produced a constant stream of belief in "American Exceptionalism." Christian nationalists insist that America is a Christian nation, and the future of the country is guided by that vision. Internally, the U.S. has been enthralled with the belief in its divine nationhood. Throughout her history, there has been an unwavering belief in the divine sanction of God controlling America's destiny. It has a unique relationship with God, unlike that of any other, with a divine destiny. Around 1783, pastor George Duffield, Third Presbyterian Church (Philadelphia), preached a sermon that compared the colonies to Israel in the Bible. America was a "banner of civil and religious liberty," and was an "asylum for the poor and oppressed from every part of the earth and was "God's American Zion."[8] Author Kelly J. Baker stated, "Arguably we can talk about how the combination of Christianity and white supremacy goes to the American founding, with early folks like Puritans showing up and claiming they're the nation upon a hill and that this is now their land, and they have dominion over it. . . . [A] variety of different movements in different time periods pick up the same ideas and rhetoric and practices."[9] Throughout the seventeenth, eighteenth, and nineteenth centuries, the United States was self-described as a "new Israel" and later in the twentieth century as a "Christian nation." Consistently it has been part of a nihilistic mindset that promoted the belief that "to be a faithful Christian in America, one must be loyal to the American nation [and] that the American nation is defined in part by Christian values and Christian culture." For Christian Nationalists America "was, is, *and should remain* a 'Christian nation'—that America's identity as a Christian nation is not merely a historical fact but a moral imperative, and ideological goal, and a policy program for the future, which also means that defining the nation's religious and cultural identity is rightfully part of the government's responsibility."[10]

Ancient mythologies connected earthly kingdoms with supernatural ones. States and towns had a protector god who was responsible for their well-being and who demanded fidelity to their commands. For Sumerians and later Mesopotamians, a divinely appointed king was responsible for the stewardship of all property that was under divine ownership. Survival was in the hands of regional and national deities who determined one's success or failure. Nothing was undertaken without first appeasing the gods who were intimately involved in human affairs either as benefactors or adversaries. Rituals, rites, and ceremonies were performed to ensure the safety and protection of the community and the individual. In ancient Sumer each city was owned by a local deity. Mesopotamia, designated as the "Cradle of Civilization" and one of the first to deify the kingship.[11,12] For 3,000 years, Egypt was a land not of one god, but of many regional deities. Egypt's various cities, town, and villages each had their own deity who was responsible for the prosperity of the region. The list grew as decades grew into centuries. As the nation unified, local gods were not abandoned but were integrated into the wider belief system.

Rulers found that their administrations were more readily accepted if they had divine sanction. Dissatisfaction on the part of the populace was quieted when authorities and priests wrapped the right to rule in heavenly dictations. The apprehension of being out of line with the will of God was a dominant force in keeping the populace subjugated. Supreme deification was cast upon the monarch as he himself evolved into a deity at the moment of his death. Lionel Casson wrote, "Religious nationalism provides a unique source of authority by giving a leader or government unwavering moral support for its policies. Since it ultimately pursues power, religious nationalism does not have room for prophets who seek to hold the government to a higher standard, only yes-men interested in blessing government action."[13]

As a part of ancient belief systems, not only were nations divinely favored, but a secondary connection was the insistence that kings were of cosmic descent and godly origin."[14] "At first, the rulers of Sumer were outstanding commoners elected to lead their people during crises, but soon these democratically chosen chieftains were transformed into hereditary monarchs who ruled with divine sanction, setting the pattern for centuries to come. Some of their successors, like Greece's Alexander the Great and Persia's Shapur II, actually considered themselves to be gods; others, like the legendary King Arthur, thought merely to be vicars of the Lord: France's absolutist Louis XIV saw kings 'occupying, so to speak, the place of God.'"

Divine Origins of Kings, Pharaohs, and Presidents

One would think that ancient beliefs that a ruler was sent by God and whose reign was the handiwork of a divine being would no longer resonate. But much of this belief system remains inherent as a part of contemporary political beliefs, especially as it relates to presidents. According to PRRI (Public Religion Research Institute), in 2025, up to two thirds (67%) of Christian Nationalists "either completely or mostly agreed that God ordained Trump to be the winner of the 2024 election."[15]

Attributing divine intervention as the cause for a leader is as old as time itself. Numerous African cultures (Fipa, Tutsi, and Yoruba) taught that human beings were created by divine or semi-divine beings who descended to the earth from heaven. Numerous cultures believed that their kings were descended from divinity and were equipped with mythical powers).[16] Egyptian pharaohs were amongst the first to claim divinity as a part of their lineage. They claimed direct descent from the gods and defined themselves as both human and divine. Pharaoh was "god and king," embodied the gods, and was the soul of the state. Pharaohs initially claimed that they were the children of Isis and Osiris. After the Fifth Dynasty each pharaoh held the title, "Son of Re." As such, they were responsible for management of the affairs of state, the beneficial tides of the Nile River, successful harvests, business prosperity, the military, and establishing a peaceful reign. He was considered omnipresent and represented all spheres of life in his personhood: political, social, and religious. He served as the orchestrator of civil society, the military, and religion.[17]

The Greeks worshipped and honored human heroes with divine origins as the children of gods.[18] Alexander the

Great was told by his mother, Olympias, that he was the son of Zeus, the supreme deity of the Romans. His father, King Philip claimed that the son of Zeus, Heracles (Hercules) was his father. Alexander was extremely religious and was tolerant of other religions, even of those he conquered by military battles. He stressed that any victory won was the will of the gods and before battles he made sacrifices and prayed for victory. In 332 BCE he arrived in Egypt and received confirmation that he was the son of Zeus. He was told that "he was the son of Zeus and had been given the rule of the world. Alexander now honestly knew whose blood ran through his veins; he was truly the son of Zeus. Upon his return to Memphis, he made a sacrifice to Zeus. While there he received two delegations—one from Miletus and another from Erythrae—and both told him that their city's oracle confirmed him to be the son of Zeus. Although he believed they may only have been saying that to win favor, he hoped they would still spread the word. The always unruly Greek cities of Athens, Sparta and Thebes might think twice before causing the son of a god trouble."[19]

Roman gods could start life as human beings and reach immortal status. Emperors demanded to be worshipped as gods, with temples and sacrifices made to them. This practice started in the recognition of emperors once they died but evolved into the deification of those living. Founders Romulus and Remus were children of the god Mars and a human mother, Rhea Silvia. Emperor Diocletian put into legal code the divinity of the emperor and ordered all who came before him to bow down in worship and adoration.[20]

South American cultures included the Mayan and Incan peoples. Polynesians, including the Hawaiians, the Japanese, and Chinese, often associated their rulers as children of the sun. Polynesians told stories of human beings being the children of the Earth and Sky. Every area of life for the Mayan people had a divine presence and figures had anthropomorphic features. South American civilizations had semi-divine rulers. The Incas had a divine ancestor, Inti, and the emperor was known as the "son of the sun." Her sister, Mama Kilya, the goddess of the moon, was revered as the mother of the Inca people.[21]

European monarchs, and countries as a whole, claimed a "divine right of kings" to rule without any supervision or collaboration with any human authority. King James I (Great Britain, 1603-1625) said that, "The State of MONARCHIE is the supremest thing upon earth: For Kings are not only God's Lieutenants upon earth, and sit upon GOD'S throne, but even by GOD himself they are called GODS."[22]

Throughout the 1700s, France was controlled by a restrictive monarchy, the Ancien Régime, that claimed a divine right to rule as God's representative on earth. Even today Great Britain maintains a royal family, faithfully referred to as The Royals. The British coronation of the king contains both civic and religious symbolism and represents dual duties as monarch and "Defender of the Faith."[23]

Glimpses of past divinity claims of pharaohs and kings were seen in the messianic hopes draped around the shoulders of American presidents. One of the most intriguing positions of CNs who support Donald Trump is the pronouncement that he has been sent by God. Christian supporters confirmed their belief that Donald Trump's election was a godsend. *The Washington Post* explained, "(T)oday's Christian nationalist power brokers are dedicated to the monarchical strand within biblical texts. Trump is not just any president. He is the anointed one, 'God's candidate.'"[24]

This ideology has had much more impact on global religions with the exception of the Jewish people who completely reject any sort of divinity for human rulers. Throughout their history, they have maintained this stance and held the Creator in a position above the creation. The first six commandments of the Ten Commandments (Exodus 20) have been followed with a rigid determination. They lay the framework for the Jewish understanding of what it means to revere God, the image and name of God. A person of the Jewish faith does not even mention the word for God, acknowledging that it is too other, too holy, to be uttered.

Myths and the Bible

The Bible is of supreme importance to Christian Nationalists. CNs and conservative Christians charge progressive Christians with not fully revering the Bible as the Word of God and for not stressing its inerrancy. There is rigidity when it comes to other global religions and the connections between beliefs and historical traditions. Many proclaim "Jesus Only" motifs and would consider it to be blasphemous to even engage in a conversation alluding that the Bible appropriated other traditions. This erases opportunities for connecting around shared beliefs and for engagement in community mission.

Christian Nationalists are insistent that only Christianity contains the original word of God and refuse to consider that there are myths, narrative creations, and allegory present in the Bible. However, the Hebrew people utilized numerous concepts from neighboring religions.[25]

A major influence was the Persian (Iranian) religion of Zoroastrianism. It stressed faith in one God, good and evil personified in deity, and free will. It moved followers away from rituals and sacrifices to a focus on the inward thoughts, words, and deeds of the individual. Charity toward others was mandated through the living of an ethical life.[26]

The Old Testament story of Paradise (Genesis 2:4b-3:24) tells of the Tree of Life and the serpent, elements found in various myths and cult narratives. The Hebrew faith invoked a god who made covenants with people and nations through a personal relationship. Not all that Abraham brought with him from Mesopotamia and nearby belief systems was rejected. The Hebrew God was one of a wandering Aramean; Baal was a god of agriculture and harvest in a land flowing with milk and honey. It was easy for the people to embrace elements of Baal worship that promised successful crops and food for their children. Even though they were forbidden to worship other gods, the pagan name of Baal was given to children, including by kings Saul and David. Gideon, the judge, was named Jerub-baal, "Let Baal contend," or "may Baal multiply." The prophet Hosea accused the people of referring to Yahweh as Baal and worshipped him falsely (Hosea 2). The Israelite people incorporated figurines, small statuettes of the goddess of fertility, Ashtart, in their homes and worship. There are biblical references to the city of Ur of the Chaldeans (Southern Mesopotamia) as the birthplace of Abraham, the Father of the monolithic religions. Sumerian cities and rulers are mentioned (Genesis 10:10-12): Babel, Erech, and Akkad, in the land of Shinar; Assyrian capital city of Nineveh, Rehoboth-ir, Calah, and Resen between Nineveh and Calah. The biblical story of the Tower of Babel in Genesis 11 and ethical references to widows and orphans reflect Sumerian influence. Sumarian ziggurats, such as the White Temple of Uruk, rose to great heights centuries long before the pyramids of Egypt.

The book of Exodus is tightly wrapped in Egyptian history and religious culture, including the stories of Moses and Joshua. Moses was a popular Egyptian verb, *mose,* meaning "is born." In the Hebrew, Mosheh, means "to draw out." Tuthmose (the god Toth is born); Ptah-mose (born of the god Ptah), and Ra-meses (born of the god Ra.)[27] The story of the liberation of the Hebrews takes place in Egypt and dominates the latter half of the book of Exodus. The Egyptian story, *The Tale of Two Brothers,* has been linked to the story in the book of Genesis of Joseph and Potiphar. According to Bernhard W. Anderson, "(T)he biblical story about Jacob and Joseph contains elements of folklore, such as the motif of the false accusation of adultery with Potiphar's wife after Joseph had in reality rejected her sexual advances—a motif found also in the Egyptian 'Story of Two Brothers.'"[28] Both have a seduction that they refused.

The younger brother is approached by his brother's wife who attempts to seduce him.

The Origins of Monotheism

Central to Christianity is the belief in one God (monotheism), a creator God from whom Christian Nationalists discern being called to their specific mission. It is this call from God that gives them a sense of righteousness that they are working to bring about his kingdom. They reject that God has acted within other religions, even Judaism, and act as if only Christians can serve God to save the world from sin. Ironically, it was not Christianity that first declared that there was only one God. In the 5th century, in Iran, a religious ideology was given the name of its founder Zoroaster (628 BCE). His followers consider him the first prophet with divine relation from the one true god, Ahura Mazda, who was omniscient, omnipresent, and omnipotent. Zoroastrianism influence can be seen in all three monotheistic religions: Judaism, Christianity, and Islam. All share its most prominent elements of monotheism, dualism, eschatology, duality, and messianism. Its prophetic references are echoed by Ezekiel, Nimrod, Seth, Balaam, Baruch, with similarities attributed to Jesus. God has an evil opposite, Agra Mainyu, the lord of hell. A person spends eternity, based on the quality of the life lived, either in heaven or in hell.[29]

Despite early attempts at polytheism, civilizations evolved to the belief in a single godhead. Basil Davidson early attributed to Africans the worship of one God. In *African Kingdoms*, he wrote, "Nearly all Africans believed in a single High God from whom all things flowed. He was seldom regarded as human in form, but rather as the Energy that differentiated life from matter, a sort of Life-Force."[30]

The Egyptians were polytheistic for the vast majority of each dynasty, with the exception of the 18th Dynasty. It inaugurated one of the first monotheistic religions two centuries before Moses was born, by the pharaoh known as Amenhotep, the "heretic king." His effort failed but had long-lasting impact in the region. It ushered in an encounter with a god who was not cold and impersonal as the Egyptian pantheon, but one approachable by everyday people.[31]

Creation

Almost every ancient tradition has a creation story. Creation myths contain a great deal of similarity to the Hebrew version of creation with chaos being the norm before the act. Several, including the Hebrews, Egyptians, and Greeks tell of creation being brought forth out of chaos. Greek mythology introduced five gods who created the cosmos out of chaos. Gaia (mother earth), Tartarus or Hades (underworld), Erebus (darkness), Night (darkness over the earth), and Eros (love).[32] The Mesopotamians revered water as "primeval and eternal," the "source of all things from which came the universe, the heavenly arch and the disk of earth." The act of creation "separated 'Father Heaven' from 'Mother Earth,' and produced the shining stars, the sun, and the moon, thus setting the stage for the creation of man and the establishment of civilization."[33]

Several creation stories have human beings created in the image and likeness of God from the earth. African mythology displayed a rich tapestry of creation stories. The creation of human beings was at the center of the created order called into being into a cosmos that existed beforehand. The Babylonian god Marduk created the sky and the earth and humans from clay mixed with the blood of the god, Kingu.[34] For the Greeks, the Titan Prometheus (forethought) created human beings out of mud in the image of the gods.[35]

A prominent element in the creation stories is the consideration that the world was created by the utterance of a spoken word, a command of God. The Hebrews utilized this supernatural ability wherein each act of creation occurs after God speaks. This was a rare and unique feature that existed before the Genesis telling of creation as an intentional act of God. This concept was passed down from one world religion to another and figured prominently in God creating the heavens and the earth out of nothing by merely speaking, and it was so. Samuel Noah Kramer wrote, "Creation was not too difficult or laborious, for once the gods had decided what they wanted to do, they had merely to voice their plan of action and the thing was done. This idea developed into a credo that was shared as an accepted article of faith throughout the Near East: The Word of God—or of various gods—has the power, of itself, to create something out of nothingness."[36]

Global Flood Narratives

Civilizations around the world (Mayans, Assyrians, Babylonians, Israelites, Greeks, Romans, etc.) spoke of a worldwide flood that destroyed all of life. The narratives of the biblical story of Noah have similarity to Mesopotamia's Enlil's flood narrative. The earlier version, Atra-Hasis and the "Flood Story from Nineveh" predate the narrative in Genesis. An immortal, Utnapishtim, told of Mesopotamia's Enlil's flood that killed all humans except him when he was warned by the god Ea. It lasted seven days. He built a boat and survived the deluge with every kind of seed.[37] The god Ea warns Utnapishtim of Shurrupak that the gods are about to destroy the world through a worldwide deluge. He is given the exact measurements for a boat, loaded with his family, silver and gold, and each animal species. After seven days of rain, he sends out first a dove, a swallow, and a raven, which do not return to the boat. He prepares a sacrifice, and the mother goddess vows never to forget what has happened.[38] Greek mythology taught that Zeus punished humanity with a destructive flood in punishment for Prometheus stealing fire and bequeathing it to humanity. Prometheus saved his son, Deucalion, and his wife, Pyrrha, by warning them to build an ark. Humans were created from the soil of the earth and redeemed themselves by throwing dirt and rocks over their shoulder in recognition of the earth mother, Gaia. Women sprouted from those cast by Pyrrha and men from those thrown by Deucalion.[39] Norse mythology had a strange story of a deadly flood. A giant frost giant, Ymir, emerged when Ginningagap, cosmic emptiness, began to melt. His three sons killed him, and a flood of blood drowned all the frost giants.[40]

The same is true of Native American religions, among which English naturalist John Josselyn, writing in the 17th century, found what he described as stories of God and the devil, immortality, and a flood.[41]

Religion and Sacrifice

For ancient religions, the obtaining of a sacrifice was mandatory for interaction with the gods. All of this was done so that the nation might retain the favor of the gods. Most, including ancient Judaism, offered animal sacrifices as payment for sin. According to Jareb Krebsbach, in *The Collector*, the Bible makes mention of human sacrifice and prohibits it as a practice by the Hebrew people. Various Near Eastern rituals, including the Phoenicians and Carthaginians, were used it to secure divine blessing.[42]

The first-century BCE Greek historian Diodorus (*Library of History*, 20.14) referred to the pagan deity Baal by the Greek name "Cronus." He examined the practice by the Phoenicians who, rather than slaying the children of the poor or prisoners, they uniquely sacrificed the children of the nobility.[43]

Mesoamerica immersed successful living with a dangerous, sacrificial interplay with the gods. The Aztecs sacrificed prisoners of war to appease the sun god, Huitzilopochtli.[44] In Peru the Chimú people sacrificed 76 children and 2 adults to secure a blessing for a newly constructed irrigation system at Pampa la

Cruz.[45] The Incans sacrificed their own children to their gods as messengers and gifts. They become a part of the family of deities upon death. Historians are not in agreement that the Phoenicians sacrificed their children, but large burial sites filled with the bones of sacrificed animals and children have been found by archaeologists. Southeast Asians practiced human sacrifice. On Sumba Island, watchful heads were planted in trees as a sign of divine protection.[46] The Pawnee people believed in a god of creation who was represented by the North Star. To maintain a peaceful relationship with the Morning Star, warriors would murder women from other tribes.[47]

While not widely associated with the rite of human sacrifice, Europeans have instances where humans were sacrificed to appease the gods or to ensure comfort in the next world. Wealthy Vikings were buried with murdered servants whose labor was extended even after death.[48] Women were labeled as witches and murdered by public execution, often burning, for communal safety. In Massachusetts, priests hunted down women during the Salem Witch trials in June of 1692. Cotton Mather, a minister, was a witness of and participant in the persecution of the women tried and executed as witches in New England. He recorded firsthand observations in *Wonders of the Invisible World*. Mather believed that the "New-Englanders" were "People of God" planted in that part of the world by the Hand of God personally. They were intentionally targeted by the devil who wanted them for their own.[49] He described the atmosphere in the colony and went into great details concerning the trials. In the course of 16 months, February 1692 until May 1693, almost 200 arrestees, mostly women, were accused of witchcraft. Thirty were found guilty resulting in 19 public executions.[50]

The Reality of Resurrection

The concept of resurrection is prominent in Islam, Judaism, and Christianity but has a legacy that far precedes monotheistic religion. Egyptian folklore focused upon the resurrection from the dead. There was a bodily resurrection as the soul was reunited with its mummified remains. Originally resurrection was reserved for the pharaoh and royal families, but eventually it spread to nobles, and then to ordinary families by the end of the New Kingdom. They were the first to ascribe to a resurrection wherein each individual soul was to be judged.[51] The god-king Osiris was credited with planting the seeds of civilization in Egyptian society. Each pharaoh ruled as his son Horus and when he died, assumed the position of Osiris and lord of the underworld. The cult of Isis was adopted by the Greeks who passed it on to the Romans. Women participated in a ten-day ritual that symbolized a rebirth that was extended to them as they were granted immortality.[52] The Canaanite god, Baal, was resurrected to symbolize the transition from winter to the new life of spring.[53] Norse Vikings had a complex afterlife. National consciousness was influenced by a religious belief that your present reality determined your future reality. Similar to Roman Catholicism, there was a purgatory realm for the unworthy.[54] Both Christianity and Islam make use of two death stages. In the book of Revelation and the Koran there is a first and second death. Both mention being in the grave and the sounding of a trumpet to usher in a rebirth.[55]

Even in death, Americans have sought to attribute the death of leaders with divinity. President Abraham Lincoln, after being assassinated, was close to being deified. He was shot on Easter's Good Friday and Easter sermons resonated with sermons about his divine nature. Christian ministers equated him with Christ Jesus and Jewish rabbis referred to him as Moses. Rev. A. D. Mayo proclaimed Lincoln's death as an extension of that of Jesus. Lincoln was glorified as "one of the country's greatest secular saints and evermore as the nation's 'savior' and a 'Christ-figure' who died for the sins of his nation, and who would now rise into the hearts of his flowers."[56]

Ancestor Worship

Christian Nationalists absolutely revere the founding fathers and make sacred the founding of the nation. In every culture and resulting religions, ancestors are to be honored, revered, and worshipped. Recognition started within families but spread throughout communities. Ancestors were approached with the same dignity accorded to the living. Ceremonies were performed on their birthdays and to commemorate the dates of their death. The spirits of parents and grandparents who recently died as well as those who died long ago were remembered by acts of reverence as food was offered as an act of esteem. Respect and veneration for one's elders remain a part of Chinese life and culture. Despite the vast variation found on the African continent, ancestors held a prominent place as they were protectors, guides, and even adversaries if not treated with the proper amount of reverence and care. For Africans there is an unwritten contract between the living and the dead wherein both sides have duties and actions to maintain. The living was to perform rites and rituals of ancestors who were descended from the founders through ceremonies, rituals, public festivals, secret rites, and sacred objects. These "appointed ancestors" were to provide protection from dangers and help in times of need. The ancestors were a direct link to the gods who enabled them in establishing their tribal community and who directed their actions in the present. To disrespect the ancestors was to disrespect the deities who watched over them."[57] The Romans started slowly with spirits and artifacts that contained little spiritual value to the people rather was more ritualistic in form. *Numena* (divinity) were nebulous spirits that were not imaged anthropomorphically, unnamed, and without gender. The *Lares* (spirits) were responsible for one's home and family. They existed for individual families and were often ancestors who were revered and worshipped in household shrines. Romans would retain the memories of dead family members and retell them year after year.[58] Southeastern Asians recited stories of a first ancestor who arrived by canoe. Those who followed were of a semi-divine nature and were often deified. Those recently deceased watched over younger generations and guided them throughout the rest of their lives.[59]

The Christian church participates in various forms of ancestor veneration. Catholics have special reverence for the saints canonized by the faith.[60] Protestant theologians argued for centuries that there existed in Roman Catholicism a remnant of a divine-human being that existed in the exaltation of the saints and the pope. Unlike other Christian denominations, Catholic saints have a semi-divine status. Greek Orthodox followers utilize icons, paintings of saints, as a reminder to pray. Protestants erect churches for deity worship but name them after humans, usually men. Families honor one another by paying to place the names of the deceased in windows.

The Damaging Legacy of the Doctrine of Discovery

One of the most reprehensible extensions of Christian Nationalism was the Doctrine of Discovery (DOD). At its heart, it intertwined religion and politics during the period of European Exploitation, commonly known as European Exploration. It originated with the Catholic Church as it provided divine justification for European governments to invade other lands. It was the first unabashed merger between church and state with global implications. Papal declarations issued divine authority to European countries to seize by violence the territory of foreign populations. Papal Bulls sanctioned the brutal conquest and global colonization of non-Christians who could be conquered for Christ by violent and racist actions. International invasion had a divine mandate.

The most despicable aspect of DOD was the marriage between theology and racism. DOD victims were mostly Black and brown as it ushered in the reign of white supremacy. Racist ideology endorsed human dehumanization and dispossession through murder and violent assimilation. It provided the foundation for white supremacy designating European colonizers as instruments of divine design authorized to offer salvation to nonbelievers. European invaders *discovered* lands inhabited for centuries and exploited, displaced, and murdered those who resisted, and those who did not. In its wake, genocide was committed against indigenous peoples as cultural traditions and customs were appropriated and destroyed. Pope Nicholas V issued a papal bull, *Dum Diversas* (June 18, 1452) that provided theological justification for the military conquest of the "enemies of Christ." Addressed to King Alfonso V of Portugal, it justified the seizure of sovereign territory and the brutal conquest and colonization of non-Christians. It listed Saracens (Muslims) and pagans as susceptible to European conquest under a Christian banner. In 1455 another bull, Romanus Pontifex, was issued again to Portugal who used it to initiate the African Slave Trade."[61]

Church and State

One of the significant goals of CN is the absolution of the separation of church and state doctrine. It is, essentially, "the political belief that the United States is and should be a Christian nation."[62] The reasons are theological with many believing that God called Christians to dominate all areas of government. For others there are economic incentives in the dismantling of the controls of government over education and other sectors. Privatization is very profitable.

During the 13th and 15th centuries, a complete merger between the affairs of the state and the doctrine of the church strengthened in the Western Hemisphere. In light of the writings of the Apostle Paul in the New Testament, Christians were to "obey governing authorities." His writings had innumerable impacts and to disobey the state's authority was to disobey a God who put both church and state in place. According to National Catholic Review, "Christian nationalism is not new. One can trace its roots to the Roman emperor Constantine's conversion in 312 that forged a seemingly unbreakable link between Christianity and power. Not long before, Christianity had been a powerless, sometimes persecuted religion. With state backing, it began its evolution into a powerful political and social force that often persecuted others. This revolution laid the foundation for the Christian nationalism we have seen throughout Western history."[63] It birthed "whiteness" as a deadly consequence embedded within the country's institutions and societal life privileging whites the availability of status and power. As more and more foreign lands were encountered, there arose a need to justify conquest. This imperialistic instinct is quite common for empires seeking world domination. Before citizens will support acts of exploitation directed toward other nations, there must be a divine mission worth killing over. The British were saddled with the "white man's burden" to civilize the world. The French embarked on a civilizing mission through *la mission civilisatrice*, and the Portuguese, *missão civilizadora*.[64]

The American South

The American South has been described as a "nation within a nation," while the conditions of the entire country cannot be ignored, as slavery and Jim Crow were present throughout every region. Southern policies have disproportionately impacted discrimination in the U.S., referred to as the religious, political, and cultural Southernization of the nation. W. J. Cash wrote a highly controversial book, *The Mind of the South*, that explored the unique cultural and psychological nature of the American South. He insisted upon its unique mindset and listed a set of hates: "anti-Negro, anti-Alien, anti-Red, anti-Catholic, anti-Jew, anti-Darwin, anti-Modern, anti-Liberal, Fundamentalist, vastly Moral, militantly Protestant." Its isolated landscape, flawed theology, and history inclusive of slavery, the Civil War, and Reconstruction combined to generate a sense of separateness from the rest of the country. These and other factors resulted in a religiously endorsed racial caste system that embraced white supremacy as a means of pretending to be something it was not, an honorable and religious society. It developed a damaged psyche where racism, romantic idealism, anti-intellectualism, and violence were displayed throughout every section of the region. Cash romantically described life in the South as a paradoxical interaction where the dispossessed were dominated by the delusion of religious obedience. He wrote, "Here is ghostly rides through the moonlit, aromatic evening to whip a Negro or a prostitute or some poor white given to violating the Seventh Commandment or drinking up his scant earnings instead of clothing his children, or merely given to staying away from church; to tar and feather a labor organizer or a schoolmaster who had talked his new ideas too much—in slow, swaying noonday parades through the burning silence of towns where every Negro was gone from the streets, and the Jews and the Catholics and the aliens had their houses and shops shuttered—here was surcease for the personal frustrations and itches of the Klansman, of course. But also the old coveted, splendid sense of being a heroic blade, a crusader sweeping up mystical slopes for White supremacy, religion, morality, and all that had made up the faith of the Fathers: of being the direct heir in continuous line of the Confederate soldiers at Gettysburg and of those old Klansmen who had once driven out the carpetbagger and tamed the scalawag; of participating in ritualistic assertion of the South's continuing identity, its will to remain unchanged and defy the ways of the Yankee and the world in favor of that one which had so long been its own."[65]

Nazi Germany

Religious nationalism influenced the domestic and foreign policy of nation-states. Countries utilized a collaboration with the church to justify racist and religious oppression. Germany's Third Reich sought to establish a Christian Nationalist state. The Third Reich successfully convinced German churches to endorse the horrors of the Nazi regime. The Nazi regime sought to justify its actions through the endorsement of the German church. Its programs received the blessing of the church by creating partnerships that benefited the institution. It did not take force or intimidation, as promises of relative independence produced the desired acquiescence. German youth organizations were directed to attend worship services and to recruit their families to accompany them to increase membership. The end result was a unification of the German government with the church as Protestant Christians endorsed the ideology of an Aryan Church. Even as the state rounded up millions of Jewish citizens, the church was eerily silent and did little. Christian Nationalist propaganda promoted divine protection for the actions of the state. Ministers publicly sanctioned the regime as an instrument of God. They expelled Jewish Christians from ordained ministry and adopted the Nazi "Führer Principle" as the defining principle of church government. The pro-Nazi "German Christian" movement glorified Adolf Hitler as a "German prophet" and preached that racial consciousness was a source of revelation with biblical foundations.[66]

There was resistance to this horrific Christian Nationalist movement that occurred within Germany. The Confessing Church Movement condemned the church's idolatry that falsely stated that the government was an agent of God. Convicted clergy produced the Barmen Declaration in 1934 to challenge both the Nazis and fellow churches. It was drafted by Reformed theologian Karl Barth and Lutheran theologian Hans Asmussen as a call to resistance against the theological claims of the Nazi state. It expressly repudiated the claim that any source apart from Christ could be a source of God's revelation. Barmen declared, "We reject the false doctrine, as though there were areas of our life in which we would not belong to Jesus Christ, but to other lords—areas in which we would not need justification and sanctification through him. . . . We reject the false doctrine that beyond its special commission the State should and could become the sole and total order of human life and so fulfill the vocation of the Church as well."[67]

South African Apartheid State

In South Africa the apartheid era represents the most obvious existence of a Christian Nationalist government as the South African Christian Church partnered with the government to endorse its apartheid policies.

The South African Dutch Reformed Church was insistent in its validation of the government policy of racial segregation. Allan Boesak, in his book *Black and Reformed*, rebelled against the role of the DRC and repudiated it as anti-Christian. He insisted that the role of the church in South African apartheid was unique in world history wherein the policy of apartheid was essentially the "missionary policy of the white Dutch Reformed Church." The church was responsible for providing a theological classification but, more so, it supplied the strategic vision for the policy. Boesak concluded, "There's no wonder that the Kirk boat, official mouthpiece of the white Dutch Reformed Church, wrote with pride in 1958: as the church, we have always worked purposefully for the separation of the races. In this regard apartheid can rightly be called a church policy."[68]

The DRC did not reverse course until the late 1980s when it offered an apology for past legitimization of racial discrimination. In 1986, church moderator Nelus van Rensburg acknowledged the church's role in maintaining the system and pledged to help to restructure the nation. "We were very much complicit in propping up Apartheid. We provided the theological base for Apartheid. And that's how ideology works."[69]

South Korea, South Vietnam

When the Korean peninsula repelled Japanese domination, it established a merger of Korean identity coupled with a Christian identity that continues today. Between the 1950s and the early years of the 1960s, the Roman Catholic Church was prominent in South Vietnamese life and culture. President Ngo Ding, a proponent of Christianity, was overthrown as the religion threatened to overtake Buddhism as the nation's spiritual belief system.

Islamic States

Several states are governed by Islamic laws, including the Islamic Republics of Iran, Afghanistan, Pakistan, and Mauritania. Pakistan was the first and founded itself as an Islamic state in 1956. It was followed by Mauritania in 1958 and by Iran in 1979. Sharia law provides the foundation for the laws of the nation. Afghanistan had two terms between 1996 and 2001 and later in 2021. Saudi Arabia is self-described as a sovereign Arab Islamic State while others describe it as an Islamic theocracy. Either way, Islam is the official state religion and other religions are prohibited. Sunni Islam has a head of state, a Caliph, selected by a Muslims or their representatives. Their counter religion, Shia Islam, the Caliph is an Imam who is chosen by God. Once in office, the Caliph governs with both religious and secular authority.[70]

Hungary

In Hungary, a new constitution was passed in 2011 that praised "the role of Christianity in preserving nationhood" and called for a "spiritual and intellectual renewal." Prime Minister Viktor Orbán was instrumental and used his influence to deny entry into much of Europe Islamic refugees fleeing their homeland of Syria. He openly stated the reason that they were of the Islamic faith, and not Christians."[71]

Brazil

Conservative Christians in Brazil embrace an exclusionary language and mirror their U.S. Christian Nationalists. Since the 19th century Brazilian evangelicals have been grounded in the ideology of southern U.S. evangelicals. Northern evangelicals and politicians (Mike Pence, Mike Pompeo, and Ralph Drollinger) have trained clergy in CN ideology. Following the American CN model, their avowed enemies are "moral relativism, social liberalism, alleged neo-Marxism, and LBGTQ rights."[72]

Global Patriotic Religious Symbolism: Flags and Monuments

Countries continue to seek divine protection and favored status by incorporating religious symbols and colors on their national banners, the flag. There are 196 countries with flags containing symbols of faith with Islamic and Christian symbols being found on over 75%. Sixty-four flags (48%) have Christian symbols. Thirty-three percent of the total are from Islamic nations. Pictorial images of the Christian faith are found on those of 31 European nations, Asia, the Pacific, and the Americas. Some design of a cross is present on most. Denmark, Norway, Sweden, Finland, and Iceland use the Nordic cross.

Georgia has five "St. George's Crosses" representing the "five holy wounds of Christ." Both the Republic of the Marshall Islands and Slovakia have crosses placed in prominent positions. British Commonwealths have adopted Great Britain's Union Jack: Fiji, Tuvalu, Australia, and New Zealand. Some countries incorporate three different Christian crosses designs: St. George, St. Patrick, and St. Andrew. Four countries (Spain, Greece, Norway, and the Dominican Republic) have their various Christian symbols.[73]

Islam has 21 countries displaying Islamic symbols including sub-Saharan Africa, the Asia-Pacific region, the Middle East, and North Africa. Islam is represented by the crescent and star; the colors red and green are often accompanied by white and black. The Five Pillars of Islam are represented by five stars on the flag of Bahrain. The Islamic Republics of Iran, Iraq, and Saudi Arabia have references to Allah and the Prophet Muhammad. The state of Israel is the only country with the symbols of Judaism, a Star of David and the white and blue colors worn on a Jewish shawl. Religious symbols for Buddhism and Hinduism are configured on five flags including Cambodia, Nepal, and India. The official flag of Japan carries a *hinomsru*, or "rising sun" of Shintoism. The Axtec sun god, Huitzilopochtli, rests upon the flag of Mexico in the form of an eagle with a snake in its beak. Uruguay and Argentina honor the Incan god Inti by shining golden suns.[74] Several American state flags have religious symbols including Alabama and Florida using the St. Andrew's cross. Hawaii, once colonized by Britain, is the only U.S. state to insert the flag of a foreign nation, Great Britain's Union Jack, into its state emblem. The Virginia state flag has the pagan goddess Virtus standing over a defeated tyrant.[75]

3

American Origins of Christian Nationalism

Be subject for the Lord's sake to every human institution, whether it be to the emperor as supreme, or to governors as sent by him to punish those who do evil and to praise those who do good. For this is the will of God, that by doing good you should put to silence the ignorance of foolish people. Live as people who are free, not using your freedom as a cover-up for evil, but living as servants of God. Honor everyone. Love the brotherhood. Fear God. Honor the emperor.

1 Peter 2:13-17 ESV

Let every person be subject to the governing authorities. For there is no authority except from God, and those that exist have been instituted by God. Therefore whoever resists the authorities resists what God has appointed, and those who resist will incur judgment. . . . Therefore one must be in subjection, not only to avoid God's wrath but also for the sake of conscience. For because of this you also pay taxes, for the authorities are ministers of God, attending to this very thing. Pay to all what is owed to them: taxes to whom taxes are owed, revenue to whom revenue is owed, respect to whom respect is owed, honor to whom honor is owed.

Romans 13:1-7 ESV (Titus 3:1; 1 Timothy 2:2)

The Bible and Governing Authorities

Both of the above passages (1 Peter 2 and Romans 13) could be considered the basis for a Christian Nationalist ideology. Both center around the relationship between a Christian and her obedience to the government. Both state unequivocally that the state must be obeyed and not only that, but that the government has been instituted by God. Therefore, to disobey governing authorities is to disobey God. These passages could provide strong evidence that Christian Nationalism is a correct theological position, as least in the minds of adherents. But a deeper dive into the totality of these passages, and the whole of the Bible itself, reveals that there are conditions upon obedience to the government. The state has been established for the well-being of those who are residents, not to demand their obedience and sacrifices for the state. The state must provide for the poor in the same manner in which God charges individuals to be generous stewards of God's harvest. The state becomes an opponent of God who revokes its authority when its policies and laws are oppressive toward the vulnerable.

Theology of Church and State: Romans 13

Academics and clergy debated a Christian's dual citizenship as belonging to the nation and to the kingdom of God. Both the "render" saying of Jesus and Paul's "subject to the governing authority" were at the forefront of arguments. Early Jewish and Christian theologians listed separate spheres where God ruled and another belonging to the earthly kingdom. The Roman Empire adopted an early stance that there was equal deference to God and to Caesar, largely influenced by the writings of the Apostle Paul to show godly obedience to the government (Romans 13).

Moses Hadas wrote that since the writing of Romans 13, Christian theologians debated the relationship between the empire and the faith. Many conceded that it was possible to be both a faithful Christian and a good Roman citizen. By the fourth century a compromise compressed the history of Christianity to the history of the Roman state. Therefore, obedience to the state equaled loyalty to Christ.[1]

Theologian John Howard Yoder, in *The Politics of Jesus*, wrote that on the surface the Romans 13 adage was to be obedient to governing authorities. Yoder insists that the responsibility of the Christian in relation to the government is not to be obedient, but submissive. Jesus did not follow the dictates of Roman law, but God's law of love. He modeled the highest form of obedience to the powers of the world whom he acknowledged would have no power over him if it had not been granted from above. H. Richard Niebuhr, in *The Social Sources of Denominationalism,* contended that the church has been in contention with nationalism but with the Constantinian adoption of the faith it lost its spiritual identity. The church succumbed to the state as the ultimate authority of faith and life. The church was unable to convert political systems and was inundated by their ideologies. In Rome, the empire won out and the church surrendered any impact the teachings of Jesus and Paul would have had.[2] As church and state moved closer together, rather than transform the state, the church was immersed into the mentality of the empire. Leaders could regard "Caesar as a divine representative, the political head of a new theocracy."[3] By the fifth century, Christianity became an office of the Roman Empire. Rather than transforming Graeco-Roman culture, it was transformed into a series of state-churches. The Reformation splintered Christendom into divided national churches based upon the model of nation-states, not only in hierarchical structure but in ideology. Wherever it was established, Protestant Christianity adopted nationalist and cultural principles that impacted the structuring and principles of creed and confessions. The churches became miniature replicas of the nation-state."[4]

The American Colonies and Christian Nationalism

As the monolithic religions gained global dominance, the intermixing of religion and politics continued to be the paradigm. Once Christianity became a world religion, countries transformed religious nationalism into Christian Nationalism. It infiltrated European countries and was transported across the oceans to the United States. Unmistakably, Christianity has exerted tremendous influence on all aspects of American life. British scholar Berndt Ostendorf observed that American democracy was deeply rooted in religious belief and had a reciprocal relationship.

> As early as 1830 the French aristocrat Alexis de Tocqueville noted with surprise that in the U.S.A. religion and democracy were not in opposition. Unlike in Europe there was a marked compatibility, if not reciprocity, between religious and democratic passions. After all, had not the American clergy supported the revolutionary struggle? James Bryce, British ambassador to the U.S. from 1907 to 1913, noticed that Christianity in America, although based on doctrinally weak voluntary associations, had become the "common law of the United States." And the English novelist G. K. Chesterton concluded in 1920 that the U.S. was "a nation with the soul of a church." Chesterton captured the synergy between religion and nationalism and called it "civil religion" which he, like Max Weber, attributed to the influence of Puritans and Calvinists on the American body politic.[5]

Study of the relationship between politics and religion in America begins with an examination of civil religion. Christian Nationalism bears a striking resemblance to civil religion. Any discussion on Christian Nationalism starts with examining each concept and then analyzing the religiosity that existed within different periods of American history.

It cannot be argued that the United States was founded as a Christian nation. But neither can it be argued that religion, specifically Christianity, did not play a major role in the country's development and exalts a lasting impact today. Christian Nationalists mistakenly argue that they are returning the country to its Christian origins. This is true only to a point, for while many of the founders, and American society, were grounded in the Christian faith, even the founders who wanted the country to express a Christian identity did not want a government controlled by religious loyalty. America was founded by designers who did not desire to duplicate the European model of secular/religious monarchs. They valued the imprint of religion as a blueprint for living a moral life, but it could not be a requirement for government participation. They resisted tremendous pressure to insert God and the Christian religion pointedly into the framing of the government. This pressure makes the achievements of the Declaration of Independence and the Constitution even more remarkable: men who were nurtured within a culture of Christian religiosity did not interject God into their founding documents. So, no, America was not founded as a Christian nation, but one founded by Christians who created a secular system that granted religious freedom for all.

In 1620, the Pilgrim Puritans arrived upon the shores of Turtle Island, the name given to the land that was to become America by indigenous peoples. John Winthrop, the future governor of the Massachusetts Bay Colony, spoke to the families headed for the colony. Each family was represented by a male member who signed the Mayflower Compact on November 11, 1620. It credited both God and king for the establishment of the colony for the glory and honor of God.[6]

In 1631 the Massachusetts Bay Colony's General Court ruled that the Congregational Church was the established state church and only its members would be acknowledged as citizens. Church attendance was mandatory, and annual taxes were received for its support. One could be fined for behavior that was contrary to church doctrine. Ministers did not control the government, but their influence was monumental. They could not hold public office, and civil authorities controlled the churches, including who could be a church member. Only members could vote, and members consulted officeholders on matters of importance. Tolerance for different beliefs was not accepted. Between 1644 and 1661, Baptists and Quakers were banished, beaten, and publicly executed by hanging. Ann Hutchinson was banned from the colony in 1643 and later murdered by a local Indian tribe.[7] In 1639, the colony of New Haven (Connecticut) was formed with the Bible being the basis for the government and only church members could vote. It was decreed that "Scripturs doe holde forth a perfect rule for the direction and government of all men in all dut(ies)."[8]

Religious Freedom and Christian Nationalism

In 1636 Roger Williams founded Providence (Rhode Island), the first colony with almost complete religious freedom. He welcomed banned Baptists, antinomians, and Quakers but not Jews. He upheld the authority of the state to uphold morality and its discipline. Northampton's Congregational minister, Solomon Stoddard, was both clergy and "political boss." He relied upon religious tolerance to increase settlement of the frontier by allowing any Christians to sit at the Lord's Table for the sacrament of Holy Communion. The grandfather of Jonathan Edwards controlled the colony with a dictatorial hand to promote the advance of God's kingdom. In 1609, the Netherlands found New Netherland; in 1664 the English assumed control and renamed it New York. The Netherlands was the only western European nation to welcome the Jewish people as refugees and extended the welcome to its new colony. In 1693 the British *Act of Toleration* permitted religious freedom in the colony for all Protestants and political service was determined by property ownership and no longer church membership.

William Penn founded Pennsylvania in 1682 and railed against religious intolerance and a state church. His brand of religious tolerance was deemed a "Holy Experiment" and a model for what God was doing for the rest of the world through America, and especially Pennsylvania. He was not completely removed from Christian Nationalism, as the theists approved state punishment for religious crimes. Adulterers, blasphemers, and Sabbath breakers were given hard labor and fines. The 1776 state constitution prevented non-Christians from holding membership. Maryland (1630) continued the hybrid of political governance with policies promoting religious freedom. It first used the "free exercise thereof" later inserted into the U.S. Constitution. Virginia (1607) inserted in its charter that its mission was economic and commercial, with a focus on planting Christianity in the New World. Anglicanism was the state-church administered by the colonial governor who allocated land for clergy and church buildings, mandated worship attendance, and raised funds through a church tax.

Gorski and Perry, in *The Flag and the Cross*, surmised that around 1690 the country made a decisive move toward establishing a strong, unapologetic Christian Nationalist position. It adopted racial authoritarianism under two sets of rules: one for whites and another for non-whites. This period in American history was one where profit and class won out over equality and human liberty. "[I]t was around 1690 that racism, apocalypticism, and nationalism first fused into a deep story. . . . The death of that vision went hand-in-hand with the birth of a new vision: a social order dominated by white Protestant men and defined in opposition to 'red savagery,' Black bondage, and Roman popery. Within that order, race, religion, and nationalism were to be aligned—by force, if necessary. That is the spirit of 1690: the spirit of white Christian nationalism."[9]

America Awakens

Two Great Awakenings (1740s-1790s) created an interruption in the public acceptance of any marriage between church and state. The first Great Awakening was a revolution of religious freedom for everyday Christians. A new teaching proclaimed that God was not a distant deity of anger and wrath but one who was up close and personal, available to each believer. God cared for ordinary people and desired a personal relationship and was intimately involved in their daily affairs. Races mingled freely with one another without adherence to caste boundaries as racially diverse crowds called one another brother and sister. God was a God of grace and love. It created a challenge to Christian Nationalist instincts as the influence of emerging revivalists created questions in the hearts and minds of the laity about the authority of ecclesiastical structures and the dissolution of a formal relationship between church and state. New Side Presbyterians, Baptist Separatists, and Methodists rejected the rigors of Calvinist teachings and rebelled against a status quo that desired a strong church-state connection.[10]

The Second Awakening continued the movement of the masses of Americans from support for state-controlled churches as being divinely sanctioned. It also ushered in an awareness that the individual was free from state dominated religion, but the individual was free as well from dominating ecclesiastical restriction that restricted religious freedom to choose. For the first time the church began to oppose the actions of the state as a part of the mission of the faith. Stands for the abolition of slavery, public education, women's equality, prison reform, mental health asylums, temperance, pacifism, and protection of Native Americans were promoted by leaders such as Charles Finley.[11] By the end of the period of spiritual-political awakening, the seeds for revolution were planted by seeds of the right of the individual against government oppression.[12]

For Blacks, the Great Awakenings offered a different theological perspective and played a role in establishing the roots of Black theology born in slave fields and cabins. After first rejecting the submissive messages inflicted upon the enslaved, the gatherings were racially mixed, and Black preachers began to emerge in Virginia and the upper South. The faith of the enslaved presented a growing challenge to the institution of slavery in full rejection of any sermonizing in support of bondage. Slaves could not only fully receive the message of salvation but deliver it in a priesthood of all believers. The God of Exodus cared about their enslavement as a God of deliverance. Revivalists prohibited adultery and urged slaveholders to honor slave marriages. This was the beginnings of a Christian theology birthed in slave cabins based upon their own faith experience. It rejected Christian Nationalism and utilized its rhetoric against white supremacy utilizing the Constitution and Declaration of Independence. Anthea Butler wrote of the Black church: "[T]he style of the Black church that developed following the Great Awakening and in the antebellum period was one of prophetic witness to the moral outrage of racism in America. It was the rhetoric of dissent . . . excoriating white Christians for their role in the slave trade."[13]

The Revolutionary War and Christian Militarism

America's two major wars, The Revolutionary War and the Civil War, could be considered religious conflicts complicated by social and economic factors. The Revolutionary War was a call for rebellion complete with Christian Nationalist ramifications. Religious faith as a motivator for fighting for independence should not be minimized. Many defined the war as a religious crusade. Kevin Phillips affirmed the religious and political intertwining of the wars. . . .

> [R]eligion's powerful role in U.S. politics and warfare goes back to the seventeenth century. . . . From colonial days to the present, war and politics in the United States have borne a heavy imprint of church leadership and denominationalism, the latter frequently overlapping with racial, regional, and ethnic self-identifications. . . . [Any examination] of the American Revolution, and the 1861-1865 War Between the States—will show religion as a major factor, often the decisive one, in how individuals and communities chose sides. Moreover, in these cases the clergy were commonly among the most prominent drumbeaters. . . . America's founding event, the Revolution, was in many ways a religious war. . . .[14]

The two largest denominations were the Presbyterians and the Congregationalists, who not only overwhelmingly supported the Revolutionary War effort but exegeted their support religiously. Presbyterians called for rebellion from the stranglehold of an earthly king by repeating, "No King but King Jesus." Loyalist clergy Thomas Hutchinson and Jonathan Boucher bitterly acknowledged that a multitude of sermons preached war and that "God favored independence." Hutchison, "Our pulpits are filled with such dark covered expressions, and the people are led to think they may lawfully resist the King's troops as any foreign enemy."[15] The latter complained, "In America, as in the Grand Rebellion in England, much execution was done by sermons. Those persons who have read any out of the great number of puritan sermons that were then printed as well as preached, will cease to wonder that so many people were worked up into such a state of frenzy."[16] Presbyterian clergy were amongst the main proponents to justify Christian Nationalism. After the war concluded, around 1783, pastor George Duffield, Third Presbyterian Church (Philadelphia) preached a sermon that compared the colonies to Israel in the Bible. America was a "banner of civil and religious liberty," and was an "asylum for the poor and oppressed from every part of the earth and was 'God's American Zion.'"[17]

Political leaders sought to undergird their war efforts by utilizing religious fundamentals. The colonies that metamorphosed into the United States were populated by highly religious persons who beliefs were more aligned with ancient traditions and anachronistic theological beliefs. Global societies perceived that God, or gods, controlled life's daily occurrences, as did the American colonists. They were ideologically closer to Egyptians and Mesopotamians than contemporary secularized society. The cause of life's blessings and curses were attributable to the favor or disfavor of God. The wrath of God displayed in one's life daily depended upon the strength of one's faith and obedience. The colonists were supernaturally religious, and the divine dominated their interpretation for all of life's major events. As in antiquity, if political and religious leadership convinced people that their authority came from God, public support would follow.

Throughout the fighting, both patriots and loyalists insisted that God was on their side, and they were fighting as a fulfillment of God's will. Both sides had favorite Scriptures, biblical stories, and upheld liberty as their motto. The patriots depended on readings from the Old Testament: Micah 6:8, Proverbs 29:2, and Galatians 5:1. The insertion of corrupt kings and the story of Esther provided further inspiration, illustrating corrupt administrations. Loyalists made special use of New Testament passages: Romans 13:1-7, 1 Timothy 2:1-3, and 1 Peter 2:17, commanding submission to governing authorities.[18] General Washington recruited troops by calling for "Christian soldiers" to defend the country's liberty. He stated that during battle he was divinely protected: "By the all powerful dispensations of Providence, I have been protected beyond all human probability or expectation."[19] When he was sworn in as president in 1789, he inserted the concluding statement that has become standard: "So help me God." He advocated for military chaplains and mandated that soldiers attend worship services each Sunday. In his Farewell Address, he stated,

> "Of all the dispositions and habits which lead to political prosperity, religion and morality are indispensable supports. . . . And let us with caution indulge the supposition that morality can be maintained without religion. Whatever may be conceded to the influence of refined education on minds of peculiar structure, reason and experience both forbid us to expect that national morality can prevail in exclusion of religious principle."[20]

The Continental Congress distributed 20,000 Bibles and later printed an American edition. Historian Edward Humphrey analyzed Congressional papers and concluded that they were filled with many biblical phrases and resembled "Old Testament ecclesiastical documents." Proposals for the official seal focused upon the use of biblical images from the book of Exodus portraying the people of Israel. Thomas Jefferson suggested images of the Israelites following the pillar of smoke while they wandered in the wilderness. Benjamin Franklin wanted an image of the drowning of the Egyptian army in the Red Sea as the people watched. Battles won were attributed to God being on the side of the patriots. At the Battle of Bandywine, a minister cried, "Remember, soldiers, that God is with you! The eternal God fights for you! God, the awful, the infinite, fights for you, and will triumph!" One reflected that impressed Long Island troops were saved by God sending a fog at two in the morning to cover their escape. Perhaps, as great a contribution received from the pulpit was the gift of unity and a call for cohesiveness. Testimonies spoke that there might have been domestic terrorism and violence had not the church created a spirit of calm.[21]

The Constitution and The First Amendment Set a Different Course

After the war ended, the Constitution was adopted on September 17, 1787. A major debate concerned the role religion would have in governance. Americans were divided by two differing opinions: those who wanted the influx of religion and those who feared the consequences of such an entanglement. Thomas Jefferson maintained a lifelong distrust of clergy and wanted them barred from holding office. He adamantly advocated for distinct separation between the roles of religion and government and proposed a bill for the disestablishment of a state church. It was only after the revolution ended that states included in their constitutions an end to the sponsoring of the Anglican church as a state church.[22] In 1776, the Virginia Constitution was approved weeks before the Constitutional Convention and granted unequivocal religious freedom: "All men are equally entitled to the full and free exercise of religious freedom." A law freed non-Anglicans from the church tax and later Anglicans as well. Even so, the founding fathers desired for religion to have a presence in the nation's consciousness as it provided morality and decency.

The decision to limit religion's role won the day. The First Amendment was adopted in September 1789 and ratified by the states in December 1791.[23] The Religion Clause prohibited the establishment of a national religion and forbade the state governments to establish state churches. The Free Exercise clause granted each citizen the right to believe and worship freely as she chooses. Chronicler Alexis De Tocqueville, in *Democracy in America*, toured the country after the war. His observations about the "great democratic revolution" were presented in such a scholarly fashion that his reflections are still popular with American historians. He listed true religion as being a vital element in the establishment of a democracy.

He compared the role of religion in the newly liberated colonies and the traditional merger of church and state in Europe. He greatly approved of the constitutional separation of church and state as defined in the First Amendment and predicted seductive entanglements endangering religion if barriers are crossed. He was somewhat optimistic in his observations of American clergy having no religious desires for involvement in politics.[24]

Yet there remained a conviction that religion must play a role in the shaping of society. Author A. James Reichley captures this outlook among America's people following the Revolution:

> As the leaders of the generation of the Revolution passed gradually from the scene, they left a nation that saw no contradiction between the concept of separation of church and state and the concept that the legitimacy of republican government must ultimately be rooted in religion. . . . The founders, guided by the constellation of values . . . sought to construct a charter of fundamental law that would maintain a balance between the dual, and they believed ultimately complementary, goals of a largely secular state and a society shaped by religion.[25]

Patriotism and religion were constant companions as the nation subconsciously promoted them equally. Patriotism was often defined along religious lines. The judiciary, from the Supreme Court to state courts, refused to enforce a strict adherence to the separation of church and state up until the mid-19th century,

A Reckoning: The American Civil War

Despite the sentiment that America was chosen by God to promote democratic liberty, the American Civil War was brought about by an inability to unite the country around a solution concerning issues of slavery and racial equality.

White mainline Protestant denominations in the South fully supported the war, with few exceptions, and provided religious foundations.[26] The Southern Baptist Convention (1854) impressed upon Confederate soldiers Bibles, hymnals, pamphlets, and written resources providing religious justifications for their sacrifices. By the war's end, over 100 different tracts totaling over 50 million pages were placed in the hands of Southern troops.[27] The Civil War resulted in splits within denominations (Presbyterian, Methodists, and Baptists) as southerners isolated themselves from their northern counterparts.

The Ultimate Manifestation: Manifest Destiny

In 1823, the country initiated a foreign policy inaugurated by President James Monroe commonly known as the Monroe Doctrine. It stipulated that America would not interfere in European affairs under the prerequisite that Europe remain out of American affairs in the hemisphere. Europe could maintain any colonies it held but could not establish new ones. Monroe's foreign policy established the theological underpinnings of American territorial expansion overseas. Johan Galtung identified elements of the Doctrine of Discovery in the development of an American ideology that God constructed the world with America as a mediator between good and evil. Anyone who speaks otherwise is roundly ridiculed and accused of political heresy. U.S. foreign policy must be grounded by its covenant with God, and the U.S. had the right to use force to bring misguided countries into compliance.[28]

America's belief about her special role was founded upon a false religiosity that the hand of God uniquely predestined her to play a special role in human history. It was the foremost rationale for Christian Nationalism as it proclaimed a divine mandate to spread civilization and Christianity across the continent under a celestial mandate. America was destined by God for greatness, prosperity, and the preeminent model for democracy. Historic public statements, political policy, and sermons preached reveal a belief that the hand of God was at work in the nation's domestic and foreign affairs. Americans readily embraced a religious justification that the nation had a divine mandate to save the world.[29]

Christian Nationalism has always lain dormant in the United States, rising, settling back down, only to later reappear in the public space. It is always present, as religion and politics have always been a part of the national fabric. But it has been uttered time and time again during the onset of war, providing a justification for conflict. It caused the emergence of divinely justifiable conflict often articulated by politicians with clergy serving as accomplices. Behind words of providence and destiny, lay greed, genocide, disease, war, and empire-building undergirded by religious justification. In 1899, newly elected U.S. senator, Albert J. Beveridge, promoted the conquest of the Philippines utilizing specifically missionary terms, stating, "It is ours to bear the torch of Christianity where midnight has reigned a thousand years."[30] President William McKinley recalled God's act of creation in the founding of the country as a Christian nation in his first presidential address: "Our faith teaches that there is no safer reliance than upon the God of our fathers, who has so singularly favored the American people in every national trial, and who will not forsake us so long as we obey His commandments and walk humbly in his footsteps."[31] He defended his decision to invade the Philippines as a directive from God "to educate the Filipinos, and uplift and civilize and Christianize them, and by God's grace to do the very best we could by them, as our fellow-men for whom Christ also died."[32]

Southern Reconstruction, Resurrection, and Redemption

For the next 100 years, Southerners would regain their dignity by exploiting and oppressing every racial minority within their reach and upholding white supremacy as public policy. This age was one where under the double sword of nationalism and Christianity and CN beliefs were rampant. For white America white supremacy, nationalism, and Christianity were a regular aspect of the American landscape. To link the three was not considered controversial nor out of the mainstream. Southern Jim Crow culture had repressive impact in the North as it adopted many of the racist attitudes and behaviors toward Blacks. Without putting up signs it relegated Blacks to slums and low-paying jobs. Southern redemption was built upon the backs of Black Americas utilizing political power justified by a religious mandate. This period of violent, racial suppression was to last for over a century.

Kevin Phillips dissected the South's form of American exceptionalism. Throughout its history it was convinced of the righteousness of Manifest Destiny and that it was in a covenant relationship with the Almighty. Southern clerics defined the relationship between religion and politics as key to their identity. After the war white Southerners amplified their Christian nationalist rhetoric filled with bad theology, myths, rituals, urban legends, and saints. The Civil War was redefined into a religious conflict, not between regions of the country, but between orthodoxy and those who fell into infidelity. Only those who remained faithful to the commandments and covenants of God would receive the commandment of God for their noble cause. The South was redeemed when Reconstruction ended. Its story mirrored on one hand the story of the Israelites of the Old Testament, Job, and even Jesus. Like Job the region had been tested by God and like Jesus it, too, had risen from the dead, redeemed from its oppressive past.[33]

CN Resistance: The Social Gospel Movement

The Social Gospel Movement was powered by a determination to address the issues that plagued the world, as well as the American nation, by Christianizing both. Washington Gladden and Walter Rauschenbusch were its major architects. Gladden was the "Father" of the movement and stressed that America had a divine mission to Christianize the world. Rauschenbusch went even further and wrote about the revolutionary nature of Christianity. Both Jesus and the prophets were revolutionaries calling for social change. "[T]he Messianic hope was a revolutionary hope."[34]

Christian Nationalism in the 20th Century

Christian Nationalism during the early part of the 20th century had a dislike of unions and were adamantly opposed to any support for the rights of workers. Impoverished farmers and other workers rejected both political parties and challenged the failures of America's economic system. The Scopes trial, Darwin's theory of evolution, and Prohibition were all events where religion and politics merged to influence American life and culture. The 1898 Wilmington *coup d'etat* was a violent overthrow of the Wilmington city government governed by a Black-white coalition of political leaders, clergy, and social progressives. Lawyers, politicians, and former Confederate officers went throughout the state calling for white rule as the natural order dictated by God.[35]

American foreign policy reflected a Christian Nationalist favor despite the political party of the president. The administrations of Theodore Roosevelt and Woodrow Wilson carried America's sense of divine destiny overseas as foreign policy became the new mission with a theological foundation. Roosevelt equated patriotism and religion into a vision of an overseas American empire for the glory of God. Woodrow Wilson said in 1915 before the ecumenical Federation of Churches that the United States was created as "a mighty Christian nation to Christianize the world."[36] The institution of Christianity joined on the side of the judiciary and offered theological justifications for the oppression of people of color.

In the 1930s Gerald Lyman Kenneth Smith served as a political organizer in Louisiana for Senator Huey Long. He held strong views against Communists and the Jewish people and used his hatred of others to promote Christian Nationalist ideas of a white-only America. His efforts led to the Christian Nationalist Crusade, the Christian Nationalist Party, the America First Party, and published monthly *The Cross and the Flag*. Professor Seth Cotlar offered an explanation of the attitude of the day amongst many Americans: "The idea that America belongs to Christian people, to white Christian people, and that others are maybe to be tolerated as kind of guests, as visitors, as second class Americans—but not quite real Americans like us—builds upon a history that is surrounded by patriotism around the Founding Fathers and how Christian they were."[37]

Christian Nationalism's prevalence fluctuated between highs and lows until the 1930s. Denominations stepped headfirst into political lobbying full-time during the 1940s. This was a new approach as even in the mainline denominations, many members were uneasy with direct activism on the part of their churches. In 1923 Methodist women ushered in the age with the construction of the Methodist Building on Capitol Hill. In 1943 the Friends Committee on National Legislation was instituted by the Quakers. These were followed by Presbyterians (1946), Baptist Joint Conference Committee, Lutheran Council (1948), Methodist Women's Division of Christian Service (1948), National Council of Churches (1950), and the Union of American Hebrew Congregations. By 1951 there were 16 denominational offices serving advocacy services in D.C. This service revealed that the progressive efforts were in conflict with members who wanted the church to focus on ecclesiastical matters and evangelism. Most members were not even aware that offices had been established, and the level of political advocacy being done in their name.[38]

Most historians focus on the conservative movements involving the white church that opposed communism and largely ignore that there were rivaling movements within the Christian church family. They are normally examined separately but are reactions to the mainstream adoption of Christian Nationalism by the American public that supported white supremacy and militarism. Black Christians mobilized to combat Christian Nationalism's support of segregation as God's will and beneficial for the nation. Desegregation was an enemy to be defeated as it worked against the word of God. Progressive Christians spoke out against the proliferation of nuclear weapons and for global disarmament.

Throughout the 1940s until the '70s there was a widely held opinion that it was the duty of the churches to support efforts by the federal government to establish racial segregation in housing as public policy. Richard Rothstein, *The Color of Law*, wrote,

> Racial segregation in housing was not merely a project of southerners in the former slaveholding Confederacy. It was a nation-wide project of the federal government in the twentieth century, designed and implemented by its most liberal leaders. Half a century ago, the truth of *de jure* segregation was well known, but since then, we have suppressed our historical memory and soothed ourselves into believing that it all happened by accident or by misguided private prejudice. Popularized by Supreme Court majorities from the 1970s to the present, the *de facto* segregation myth has now been adopted by conventional opinion, liberal and conservative alike."[39]

Churches and synagogues, led by ministers and rabbis, utilized the courts to prevent Blacks from moving into white neighborhoods under government-enforced restrictive covenants. The Reverend Constantine Dzink, pastor of the King Catholic Church testified before the United States Housing Authority, wrote, [C]hurch involvement and leadership were commonplace in property owners associations that were organized to maintain neighborhood segregation. . ."[40]

Rothstein wrote,

> The construction of a low-cost housing project in the vicinity . . . for the colored people . . . would mean utter ruin for many people who have mortgaged their homes to the FHA, and not only that, but it would jeopardize the safety of many of our white girls. . . . It is the sentiment of all people residing within the vicinity to object against this project in order to stop race riots in the future.[41]

Christian Nationalism has always been wrapped in the American flag. Two world wars heightened awareness that patriotism was a virtue and the responsibility of all citizens, and of all Christians. In 1949 and 1954, the National Association of Evangelicals proposed a constitutional amendment inserting mentioning of both God and Jesus in the United States Constitution. Mainline denominations joined forty-eight Jewish organizations in opposing this effort to declare the USA as an official Christian nation. American children were taught to not question their country and to trust leaders who were protecting them from the evils that threatened them on a daily basis. Fascism, communism, nuclear bombs, Black people, Jews, Catholics, immigrants, and homosexuals were everywhere and would disrupt and destroy the American way of life. Baby Boomers grew up learning to fear the bomb and hate the Communists. An internal danger was in the presence of Blacks who were only kept at bay by white supremacy and Jim Crow laws.

By the 1950s, the aftermath of World War II created an environment of fear that galvanized the American public into an adoption of the religious ideology of CN. The perceived threat of Communism produced an intense fear of atheism and nuclear destruction produced the most concentrated support of CN in contemporary America. Up until then, conservative Protestants were obsessed with the kingdom of God in the heavenly realm, not maneuvering for political prominence in the present world. In the 19th and 20th centuries there was a determination to separate from worldly affairs with a mind toward the separation of church and state. Evangelicals were not engaged in merging with any political party, but they were also detached from the societal plagues of racism, misogyny, and homophobia.[42]

The popularity of Billy Graham created a class of evangelicals whose revival ministry created a gentler, more persuasive form of Christian Nationalism. Christian Nationalist rhetoric infiltrated his messages. He often preached, "If you would be a loyal American, then become a loyal Christian." While they disagreed on issues of theology and foreign policy, their messages converged on the deep importance of religion during national periods of crisis. The global growth of communism threatened American stability centered around faith in God. Frances FitzGerald, in *The Evangelicals*, concluded that American churches and political leaders marched to the same drumbeat when it came to justifying CN. "They agreed that patriotism and religious belief were synonymous, and that America had a moral and spiritual mission to redeem the world. . . . Graham's position was closer to Eisenhower's than to that of liberal Protestant leaders, all of whom objected to the conflation of Christianity with Americanism."[43]

The American Cold War was propagandized as a religious war, with the U.S. portrayed as a God-fearing nation opposed by godless Communists. Every institution in the country promoted it as such with religious, political, and entrepreneurial talking points. Communism became the common enemy of all Americans, especially Christians. Christian Nationalism reemerged as the unchallenged ideology as global tension was justified by religious faith. As a result, new generations of Americans were enamored by a Christian Nationalist worldview as intense as any moment in the nation's history. The faith community was moving toward being more open to utilizing religious rhetoric for the advancement of a political agenda, slowly leading to the development of the religious right. Rather than the faith community being an objective voice for the nation advocating for diplomacy, it took sides and adopted adversaries as evil and godless threats to Christianity. Rather than helping to promote world peace, it added righteous fuel to the fire.[44]

For the moment, Americans were solidly in favor of a distinct separation between government and religion. A 1968 Gallup poll found that 53% of Americans felt distinctively that churches should play no role in the functioning of politics. This sentiment alongside anti-Catholic distrust were exposed when John F. Kennedy announced his candidacy for president. It produced trepidation in the heart of Protestant America who feared a Vatican puppet.[45]

A similar suspicion was addressed by former Massachusetts governor and 2004 presidential candidate Mitt Romney, a member of the Church of Jesus Christ of Latter-Day Saints (Mormon). He felt compelled to offer a similar rebuttal that, if elected president, he would not be dictated to by the Mormon Church. He promised to be an independent thinker as president and that his decisions would be what was best for the country without influence of religious leaders.

Between the mid-1970s through the mid-1980s, another unabashed merger of religion and politics occurred with the appearance of the Christian Right. This movement has played a major role in American politics into the 21st century.[46] Those who followed in Graham's wake, Jerry Falwell and Pat Robertson, wanted to guarantee Christians, specifically white Christian leaders, a seat at political tables to reshape the country into a functioning theocracy. They possessed radically different personalities from that of Graham, displaying assertiveness and extreme self-confidence. What they shared with Graham was the desire to reconfigure America into a Christian Nationalist nation.

The beginning of the 21st century saw the emergence of political parties that were more aligned with religious agendas than policy issues. The Tea Party was the perfect marriage between religion and politics, with religion being the dominant factor. In the past, persons of faith joined forces with a political party, the Republicans. In this instance, the party itself was a religio-political organization posing as a political one. It could be considered the first authentic Christian Nationalist political party.[47]

It experienced qualified success as candidates Rand Paul and Ted Cruz won local and congressional elections. Candidates for state office won over 500 seats, and the 112th Congress had more religious conservatives in its history as youth ministers and a Mennonite went to Washington. Its political platform opposed oppressive taxation, government regulations, anything considered to be an intervention in a citizen's freedom, and immigration. Tea Party members had two related characteristics; they attend church on a weekly basis and tend to lean religiously conservative to a greater degree than Americans overall. A majority of conservative Christians (69%) were in support of the policy issues endorsed by the TEA Party (Taxed Enough Already) such as being pro-life (63%) and against gay rights (82%). Forty-four percent were in favor as opposed to only 8% in disagreement. Surprisingly, 48% were not knowledgeable of the movement. Supporters included white Catholics (33%), white mainline Protestants (30%). Dissenters included Jews (49%), unaffiliated voters (42%), Black Protestants (56%), atheists and agnostics (67%).[48]

Professor Matthew N. Schmalz of the College of the Holy Cross, Worcester, Massachusetts, determined that the Tea

Party was "in part a religious movement" and that its political rhetoric found a home in the hearts of white evangelical Protestants.[49] A 2010 PRRI poll revealed Tea Party members related American identity as that of Christian.[50] Attendees at a 2010 rally sponsored by then Fox News commentator showed illustrated t-shirts printed with "One Nation Under God" and "It is impossible to rightly govern a nation without God and the Bible." Marchers held a sign that read, "In God We Trust Not Congress."[51] NPR concluded that the majority of supporters were members of the Christian Right and religious opinions motivated many. NPR labeled it as "a 'civil religion' that [appealed] to many Tea Partiers: the idea that America was a divine experiment, that the Founding Fathers were Christian men who created a nation on biblical principles."[52]

Many of the January 6, 2021, insurrectionists at the nation's capital were motivated by Christian Nationalism. Prayers, Christian symbols, crosses, and signs reading "Jesus Saves" and Jesus 2029 were littered along the landscape. Huge crosses were used as prayer posts as rioters pressed their forehead against it before barging into the building. A shofar sounded the call to arms accompanied by a female voice singing, "Peace in the name of Jesus. The blood of Jesus covering this place!"[53]

4

White Christian Nationalism

> And they were all filled with the Holy Spirit and began to speak in other tongues as the Spirit gave them utterance. Now there were dwelling in Jerusalem Jews, devout men from every nation under heaven. And at this sound the multitude came together, and they were bewildered, because each one was hearing them speak in his own language. And they were amazed and astonished, saying, "Are not all these who are speaking Galileans? And how is it that we hear, each of us in his own native language? Parthians and Medes and Elamites and residents of Mesopotamia, Judea and Cappadocia, Pontus and Asia, Phrygia and Pamphylia, Egypt and the parts of Libya belonging to Cyrene, and visitors from Rome, both Jews and proselytes, Cretans and Arabians—we hear them telling in our own tongues the mighty works of God."
>
> Acts 2:4-11 ESV

An Impartial God

Christian Nationalists insist that they are the only true Christians and reject any acceptance of those of other faiths as recipients of the love and grace of God. For white Christian Nationalists, God is partial toward those with white skin and they are to separate from those not of their race. The Bible, however, says throughout that God is "no respecter of persons." In other words, God does not have favorites, neither individuals nor countries. The righteous are beloved by God because they understand that God has a heart for all people. It is God's will to embrace all people, and the mission of Christianity is to bring people into a relationship with God to receive protection, love, and forgiveness.

Defining White Christian Nationalism

White Christian Nationalism is an ancient ideology that has threatened the country since the days of Black enslavement and the genocide of indigenous nations. It has a long tenure as a fixture in American folklore. A core tenet is that America was founded by white men as a Christian nation based on the principles of the Christian faith. Its goals have been constant: a hierarchy with white men on top, freedom from government regulation, and the willingness to resort to violence to achieve its goals.

To be a Christian Nationalist does not automatically assign one into the ranks of being a white Supremacist. For not every Christian Nationalist is motivated by white supremacy, as there are people of color who also affirm its merger of faith and patriotism. But a significant percentage of whites do rigidly adhere to the principles of White Christian Nationalism. Therefore, as Christian Nationalism is an ideology held primarily by whites in the United States and Europe, it cannot escape fostering racial and ethnic exclusivity. Basic precepts state that to be an American one must fit into a certain profile of being white, Christian, and culturally pure. A belief in racial superiority drives many who want America to be great again, or to be white again. Christian Nationalists warn that whiteness is being erased by the far left as gains in equity, education, job advances, and healthcare availability become normalized.

The mission is to maintain the status quo in legislating racially partisan policy, economic privatization, and the subjugation of communities of color.[1] Moreover they have no qualms over capital punishment, torture, and not only support the right of nations to engage in war, but that nations could initiate preemptive war. They widely support the right to own a gun and public carry policies that allow a prevalence of open display throughout a community. Over half do not agree that the prospect of America being mostly non-white in the near future is a positive development for the country.

In the background the knowledge that makes white Christian Nationalism a seductive enticement is the nation's transitory racial demographics. Rapid growth from racial-ethnic populations partnered with a decrease in the white population can be a polarizing realization for white Americans. Over the past four decades, the percentage of the American population categorized as white and Christian has decreased by almost one-third. In the 21st century, white Christians constitute 44% of American Christians; 14 % identified as white evangelical Protestants. Examining the transition, by the close of the 20th century, almost two-thirds (65%) self-defined as being white and Christian. Within a decade the percentage dropped to 54% and decreased to 43% by 2017. One year later it was only 42%. In 2020, there was a brief rebound to 44%.[2] As the country becomes less white and Christian, there is a growing desire to maintain the reins of political and economic power.[3]

Christian Nationalism is undergirded by racist violence and intimidation to promote a conservative political agenda. Many publicly deny that white supremacy plays a role in the country's day-to-day interactions. Christian Nationalist proponents defend negative stereotypes of immigrants and people of color. White Christian America needs enemies to overcome, ranging from Native Americans, Catholics, Communists, Black radicals, atheists, Muslims, and socialists. The only viable solution is violence and intimidation with communities of color being the primary targets.[4]

Race, Politics, and Christian Nationalism

Race has always played a varying role in America's spiritual life. Denominations and congregations operated in communities where race determined leadership and limited membership. Whiteness evolved into an instrument of demonstrating power and dominance over non-whites, as it played a dominant role in culture, religion, and politics. The Christian Nationalist movement is embroiled in identity politics. It is often referred to as a white movement that involves recovering a nation defined by being both Christian and white. To be American one must match a profile of being white, Christian, and culturally pure. Christian Nationalist clergy inform their church members on which candidates to vote for. Political engagement is encouraged in the form of volunteerism in campaigns and to run for elected offices. They must do whatever it takes to save the country from humanists and the advancement of LGBTQ rights. The nation must be retaken for God.[5]

Throughout U.S. history, White Christian Nationalist policies have voiced support for anti-democratic and pro-authoritarian goals, especially as it related to the rights of people of color, primarily Blacks.[6]

White Christian Masculinity

At the heart of WCN is a nostalgic search for an ultra-masculine manhood. That desire birthed a search for a "rugged, aggressive, militant white masculinity."[7] The fate of the nation indissolubly connected the control of a father in the home with the valiant rule of the nation. A white patriarchal society needed heroes who represented a faith that was white, masculine, strong, and unbending. Each generation appropriated a worldview that men were the divine operatives in the home but had lost their place of dominance. After WWII the Civil Rights Movement, opposition to the Vietnam War, and women achieving independence in the workplace battered and bruised the egos of white men. There were wars to be fought and ideologies (communism) to be defeated, and only a warrior Jesus could lead the nation from the brink of disaster.[8]

White evangelicals have been as influenced by American culture as much as the teachings of the Bible and the church. Evangelical leaders utilized Christian nationalist rhetoric to instill in the church a rugged, frontier mentality. Megachurch pastors preached and exemplified a hypermasculine image of a warrior Jesus and a church that bullied punks.[9]

This ideology was partnered with a call for Christian women to be submissive to their husbands. They were to be highly sexualized and to cater to their man's needs. Women were born to be feminine and to fulfill the dream of all little girls to grow up to be princesses.[10]

For decades sermons have preached these beliefs on a weekly basis. These messages are circulated by books, curriculum, and speeches all around the evangelistic world. Since the 1970s megachurch and small-church pastors have manipulated parishioners into believing that this was the message of a Prince of Peace who rejected popular definitions of what it meant to be a child of God.

The Challenges to White Christian Nationalism

We must continue to pay close attention to this threat to democracy and support federal and state-level policy efforts aimed at eradicating white nationalism and hate crime. Various nonprofits and faith groups have opposed the precepts of white Christian nationalism. The *National Catholic Reporter*: "We must be clear and unequivocal: White Christian nationalism is a betrayal of what it means to follow the one who was crucified. At stake is the integrity of Christianity itself."[11] Robert Jones, in *The End of White Christian America*, writes of the demise of the dominance of white Christianity. He affirms the good that it achieved over many decades instilling values into American society with global impact. But he concludes that it ultimately failed to be racially and ethnically inclusive, eventually giving its soul to politics.[12]

5

Black Christian Nationalism

> Then an angel of the Lord said to Philip, "Get up and go toward the south to the road that goes down from Jerusalem to Gaza." . . . So, he got up and went. Now there was an Ethiopian eunuch, a court official of the Candace, the queen of the Ethiopians, in charge of her entire treasury. He had come to Jerusalem to worship and was returning home; seated in his chariot, he was reading the prophet Isaiah. . . . Then Philip began to speak, and starting with this scripture, he proclaimed to him the good news about Jesus. . . . He commanded the chariot to stop, and both of them, Philip and the eunuch, went down into the water, and Philip baptized him. When they came up out of the water, the Spirit of the Lord snatched Philip away; the eunuch saw him no more and went on his way rejoicing.
>
> Acts 8:26-39

Black people are Christian Nationalists! Black people have always been Christian Nationalists! This is perhaps shocking to most who do not associate Christian Nationalism with the Black race given their history of oppression and systemic discrimination faced in the United States. On the surface there appears to be little to no appeal for Black

Americans, as Christian Nationalism is most often associated with white evangelicals and linked to white supremacy. Why would Black people seek to merge their Christian identity with an American identity that has been historically denied to them? But just as there are whites who affirm Christian Nationalism, there are also Black Christian Nationalists with the emphasis on Christian.

Contemporary scholarship often refers primarily to White Christian Nationalism, but there must be a more robust examination. Christian Nationalism is neither a new phenomenon nor is it limited to those who espouse white supremacy. It exists in almost every expression of the Christian faith and amongst many of Christ's followers. There is no denomination, no racial group, no class, that does not demonstrate aspects of Christian Nationalism on a regular basis. That includes African Americans. Black Americans play an intimate role in every sphere of American life, and politics is no exception. They are liberal and conservative, Democrat and Republican, and yes, they are Christian Nationalists.[1] In Black congregations, flags populate sanctuaries and patriotic music echoes in worship. It is a rarity to visit a sanctuary in a majority Black congregation wherein a flag is not present. The most prophetic Black Afrocentric minister preaches from a pulpit with a flag displayed nearby. Patriotic hymns are lifted up during worship, especially on the Fourth of July, Memorial and Veteran's Day weekends. Black veterans have pushed for more and more recognition for their service, with worship being infiltrated with nationalist songs and annual services with a military focus. One North Carolina African American parish associate recommended to the senior pastor that American flag lapels be given out to veterans during a service. The request was denied.

A poll on Christian Nationalism by the Public Religion Research Institute (PRRI) *Christian Nationalism Survey* revealed that a surprisingly large percentage of African Americans gave themselves the label of Christian Nationalist. Three in

10 Black Americans registered themselves as Christian Nationalist "sympathizers" (21%) or "adherents" (12%). Similarly, three in 10 multiracial Americans are "sympathizers" (19%) or "adherents" (8%)."[2]

Black Christian Nationalists hold in common with one another at least four characteristics. Most do not have a four-year college degree. They are highly active in the life of their church and attend services as often as once a week. They are attracted to other unorthodox religious beliefs such as prosperity gospel. They share a determined history of social justice advocacy since the founding of the country.[3]

Categories of Blacks and Nationalism

An initial category could be best described as Black Christian Patriotism. Equal loyalty to both country and God is for Christian Nationalists an assumed position; to be one is to be the other. Black Christian Patriots have been nurtured in a community that stresses that to be religious is to be political. While acknowledging the doctrine of separation between religion and politics, their rhetoric and practices have come close to straying across that spectrum, usually for the purpose of bringing about a great manifestation of equality and justice for all.

Black Christian Patriots merge the connection between the eternal and the temporal. For Black Christians there has never been a problem with wrapping oneself in the flag while holding upward the cross. They have affirmed their religious affiliation while at the same time espousing pride in being an American. Blacks have demonstrated a higher-than-normal degree of patriotism for a nation that has constantly denied them their basic rights. They feel no contradiction due to the fact that love for country has been grounded in the demand for access to all the rights of American citizenship: the right to vote, operate businesses, quality schools, and full societal participation, absent the danger of violent retaliation. They rejected the castigations that they were inferior and unworthy of the privileges of being called an American. This was their homeland as much as it was for anyone else. Alongside white Christian Nationalists, they alluded to the hand of God being evident in the American story. Blacks have gone from severe criticism for the nation's shortcomings while uttering words of highest praise to what the nation stands for.

Dr. Nikole Hannah-Jones, in her book *The 1619 Project*, was bemused by her father's patriotic commitment to hoisting a flag at their family home each year. When one became old and worn, he replaced it with another. She questioned why a man who had experienced so much hardship would be so patriotic. Even his being a veteran did not help her understand his commitment to that piece of cloth. She knew that Black men served in the military, fought, killed, and died for America and yet during wartime their bravery was questioned. She wrote,

> My dad always flew an American flag in our front yard. . . . So, when I was young, that flag outside our home never made sense to me. How could this Black man, having seen firsthand the way his country abused Black Americans, the way it refused to treat us as full citizens, proudly fly its banner?. . . I didn't understand his patriotism. It deeply embarrassed me. . . . I wish now that I could go back to the younger me and tell her that her people's ancestry started here, on these lands, and to boldly, proudly, draw the stars and those stripes of the American flag. We were told once, by virtue of our bondage, that we could never be Americans. But it was by virtue of our bondage that we became the most American of all.[4]

An element that separates Christian Black Patriotism from Christian Nationalism is the fact that Blacks have had to overcome opposition to claim their American identity, one that was not granted outright. Their expressed pride and admiration were not mindless applause, but the means to an end, liberation. Black Christian Patriots exploited patriotic sentimentalities as an instrument in the fight against white supremacy and oppressive laws. The Black Christian Patriotic voice has been filled with patriotic commendation yet also contained the most constant strands of criticism that the country has had to contend with throughout its founding, as it addressed issues relevant to the Black struggle. Such rhetoric, more often than not, was used as a tool in the fight against racial discrimination.

Tracing a path from slavery through Reconstruction to Jim Crow, the Black Church was the most powerful religious and political institution in the Black community, with the Black preacher holding the highest social status.[5]

On July 27, 2016, Bishop William Barber II spoke at the Democratic National Convention. *The Washington Post* described him as giving "'evidence of a long tradition of liberal, religious patriotism.'. . . It was . . . an articulation of a liberal and patriotic philosophy with what Barber said was the moral force to shock and resuscitate the heart of the nation. 'We are being called like our forefathers and foremothers to be the moral defibrillators of our time. . . . We need to embrace our deepest moral values . . . for revival at the heart of our democracy. . . . When we love the Jewish child and the Palestinian child, the Muslim and the Christian and the Hindu and the Buddhist and those who have no faith, but they love this nation, we are reviving the heart of our democracy."[6]

Christian Black Nationalism is a political and theological movement that combines Black religious identity with a focus on self-determination and racial justice. It emphasizes the unique experiences of Black Christians and seeks to create a society where Black people have autonomy and control over their own destiny. It enjoined a call for Black independence economically, spiritually, socially, and consciously. A primary goal was the ownership and control of Black businesses, schools, and the institutions that affected Black people. Historically Black Nationalism involved connecting religious belief with the creation of a Black nation, or a nation within a nation. It's important to understand that Black Christian Nationalism isn't a single, unified movement. There are different interpretations and approaches within it, and not everyone who identifies as a Black Christian Nationalist will hold the same beliefs.

There are a few key aspects to Christian Black Nationalism. It calls for a reinterpretation of Christianity. Black Christian Nationalists often reinterpret traditional Christian teachings to center the experiences of Black people and emphasize themes of liberation and social justice. It has a focus on community. Building strong Black communities is central to this movement. This might involve things like economic cooperation, social programs, and a focus on Black-owned businesses. While not always the case, some forms of Black Christian Nationalism advocate for greater Black political and cultural autonomy, or even complete separation from white society.

In the 1960s, Rev. Albert Cleage proudly referred to himself as a Black Christian Nationalist and has been crowned the "Father of Christian Nationalism."[7] Duke University professor C. Eric Lincoln labeled him a "Christian Black Nationalist." Cleage called for self-determination, control over the institutions functioning within the Black community, and complete separation from whites. He founded the Shrine of the Black Madonna Church in Detroit, as well as sites in Michigan, Atlanta, and Houston. His 1972 book, *Black Christian Nationalism,* described Jesus as a Black savior who offered salvation for the whole of the race, not just the individual.[8]

Marcus Garvey was a most influential founder of a Black Nationalism movement in the United States. His movement was part of a broader Black Christian Nationalism. Garvey believed in a strong connection between race and spirituality. He promoted the idea of a Black Christ and a Black Virgin Mary, and he emphasized the importance of African-centered religious traditions. Garvey's message had a strong focus on building up Black economic and political power.

Black Nationalism was a religious call from God to establish a nation foreordained, as Black people were the original people. Its foundation is built on faith in a God of liberation who was not only a God of Black people, but a Black God acting on their behalf. Were not the original Jews and Jesus from Black people? Black Nationalism transcended Christianity, as people of other faiths espoused Black Nationalism, especially Islamic men and women. Throughout American history, Black Nationalism has had appeal in the midst of the struggle for human and civil rights and its most prominent spokesperson, Malcolm X.[9]

Many of today's Black Christian Nationalists have embraced Christian Nationalism, completely rejecting the past priority of their Christian identity. The tide has turned as modern Black Christian Nationalists have rejected positions of social critics and have adopted the rhetoric and tactics of white Christian Nationalists. Many have adopted the beliefs of white Christiain Nationalists in order to assimilate into Christian Nationalist society. They are more Nationalist than Christian. They have given up their unique voice and only echo a 21st-century Christian Nationalist perspective. No longer do they hold the country accountable for her sins but sing American praises while proclaiming that white supremacy and racism are things of the past. They have lost the prophetic voice of the elders who loved their God and their nation and complained when paths parted. They only offer polite platitudes and banalities when it comes to critiquing the social structures in the United States of America and the conditions of the poor and marginalized.

They are Christian Nationalists without reservation and, like their white Christian Nationalist counterparts, reflect the most orthodox Christiain Nationalist principles. Their expressed sentiments about their nation insist that America is a Christian nation and always has been. Like white Christian Nationalists, they merge their religious and political identities and operate in the public sphere simultaneously as a Christian and an

American. They are motivated by a desire to fulfill a God-give vision wherein the greatest country in the world is governed by God's chosen people, Christians. And like other Christian Nationalists, they see the hand of God at work in America and make the claim that the United States is the greatest nation in the world. They affirm the righteousness of their country without critique and reject political and social wokeness. There is an attempt to affiliate with whites and be normalized. It is a desire to say, "See, we are just like you." There is a level of acquiescence in today's Black CN community that differs from the past. There is a reversal in the speeches of Black Christian Nationalists in the past when compared with that of those today.

Black Republicans are more likely to express Christian Nationalist thoughts and perspectives at a higher percentage. But as more Blacks are Democrats, they are present but with different conclusions. Especially prominent are former members of the Trump administration and fellow Republicans. Presidential candidate and Trump's Secretary of Agriculture Ben Carson validated common Christian Nationalist positions connecting American history with a providential call from God:

> [God] is the reason that our nation excelled the way that it does. And those people who like to criticize America—criticize people in America—and always talking about separation of church and state, which is not in the Constitution, by the way—do they realize that our founding document, the Declaration of Independence, talks about certain unalienable rights given to us by our creator, a.k.a. God—do they realize that the Pledge of Allegiance to our flag says we are one nation under God—in many courtrooms, on the wall, it says "In God we Trust"—every coin in our pocket, every bill in our wallet says "In God we Trust."[10]

Presidential candidate and South Carolina Senator Tim Scott, has tried to demonstrate his moderate stances on everything, including Christian Nationalism. During his campaign he strongly verbalized his Christian faith and wanted to revisit George W. Bush's compassionate conservative image. But when pushed, he has asserted his Christian Nationalist credentials.[11]

The former Lt. Governor of North Carolina and gubernatorial candidate in 2024, Mark Robinson, is one of the strongest African American supporters of Christian Nationalism. He constantly spouts Christian Nationalist rhetoric on the campaign trail, especially when speaking in churches. He regularly uses calls to attack those who deny America's greatness and its Christian roots. The country is under attack by anti-Christian forces that present a danger to the nation. "The United States of America is a Christian nation, founded on the principles and wisdom of Jesus Christ," he said, and he called on "patriots to stand up and reclaim who we are as Americans."[12]

Blacks have been grounded in their Christian faith and committed to politics as a tactic of liberation. And, like others, have adopted a variety of ideologies about the engagement of faith and politics. But overall, they have chosen to support the separation of church and state. Mostly. Often, they have had to make a choice, and they chose Jesus. But often with compromise.

There are Blacks who are engaged in political circles, yet who post that their primary identity is that of a Christian. Several defiantly boasted that there was no comparison in their heart between their loyalty to their God and to their nation. Many, even the most Christian Nationalist advocates, identify a divine origin for their sense of identity.[13] Cornel West, in *Democracy Matters*, strongly stressed that his faith compels him to engage in politics for a more just nation. He wrote,

> I speak as a Christian—one who commitment to democracy is very deep but whose Christian convictions are even deeper. Democracy is not my faith. And American democ-

racy is not my idol. . . . To see the Gospel of Jesus Christ bastardized by imperial Christians and pulverized by Constantinian believers and then exploited by nihilistic elites of the American empire makes my blood boil. . . .To be a Christian—a follower of Jesus Christ—is to love wisdom, love justice, and love freedom.[14]

6

Hispanic Christian Nationalism

> You shall not oppress your neighbor or rob him. The wages of a hired worker shall not remain with you all night until the morning. . . . When a stranger sojourns with you in your land, you shall not do him wrong. You shall treat the stranger who sojourns with you as the native among you, and you shall love him as yourself, for you were strangers in the land of Egypt: I am the LORD your God.
>
> Leviticus 19:13; 33-34 ESV

The Attraction of Christian Nationalism

Hispanic persons of faith are the biggest surprise among those who endorse Christian Nationalism. First, Christian Nationalists often are anti-immigrant and espouse the hateful, racist rhetoric of Donald Trump. Nevertheless, their percentages are disproportionately higher than other racial and religious demographics. This is remarkable because much of the rhetoric by supporters of Christian Nationalism includes language that demonizes immigrants and is anti-immigration. Many of the issues important to the Hispanic community do not register with the Christian Nationalist base.

Latinos/as are the most racially and ethnically diverse and the most politically conservative. According to sociologist Jonathan Calvillo, "Latinx Protestants identify more with the U.S. than their prior home countries. Ethnic minorities who are Pentecostals are very likely to vote for a Christian nationalist agenda."[1] Politically, Hispanic Christian Nationalists are evenly divided among Republicans (32%), independents (27%), and Democrats (27%). Almost half (53%) of Hispanics think that the church should speak to issues in the community. Hispanic Christian Nationalists (39%) are the most likely to agree with the idea that violence is a legitimate strategy to shift the country to Christian Nationalist support. Only 1/3 of white Christian Nationalists (33%) agree, followed by only 28% of Black Christian Nationalists.

Between 2022 and 2023, Hispanic Protestants uniquely increased their support of Christian Nationalism by 12%. Hispanic Pentecostals identify as Christian Nationalists at a higher rate than any other religious body (44%). In 2024 polling between Hispanic, Black, and white Protestants, Hispanics were the only religious group where there was an increase in support for Christian Nationalism.[2]

In the United States, 10 million Hispanics wear either the evangelical or Protestant label with 28%, or three in ten, being Republicans and evangelical Protestants. For them, the themes of Christian Nationalism resonate deeply, for it is their hope for America to be a Christian nation, living according to Christian standards and values. For Hispanics who embrace Christian Nationalism, their ideas line up with the belief that God has ordained America as a promised land. They affirm the legend of a land of opportunity where hard work pays off for everyone. Unfortunately, this myth was constructed at a time when white men were considered to be the recipients of the dream, and all others were secondary or left out. It was a time when women and marginalized communities knew their place.

The Latino Christian community has been infiltrated by Christian Nationalism in such subtle ways that many are not even aware of the position they are supporting. Many would not recognize that they are being indoctrinated with beliefs that don't coincide with many of their political positions. Many attend congregations where there is constant reiteration of Christian Nationalist positions. The increasing numbers of Latinos joining Pentecostal or other evangelical churches mean that they increasingly hear messages from prosperity-gospel preachers, including those who believe Trump was ordained by God to be president. Elizabeth Rios, founder of Passion Center in South Florida, said that Latino Americans are drawn to conservative ideas about the value of hard work and family values. They encounter groups online that lead them down a rabbit hole "where the direction and the depth and the acceptability of aggression become more fixed. . . . I think this is happening because most of our Latinos have been discipled in these white megachurches where a lot of nationalism is taking place."[3]

CN concepts can be extremely attractive to Latinos who have forgiven Trump for his slurs of "bad hombres, rapists, thugs, and animals."[4] Axios reported on efforts to recruit Latino voters to Christian Nationalism and the moderate success it has had. California Pastor Samuel Rodríguez is torn between embracing Christian Nationalism and the political embrace of the Republican Party, which seem to go hand-in-hand. He stated that he considers the rhetoric of the Republicans as "nativist and racist" but that the nation needs to be based on the Christian faith.[5]

Extreme white-wing conservative leaders and pastors have been actively recruiting Latinos to the ranks of the Republican Party and Christian Nationalism. A deep motivation was the realization that the voter base was much more racially diverse and becoming even more so. Materials were translated into Spanish with Hispanic speakers being a part of the presentations of a series of recruiting events targeting Hispanic pastors. The enticement was a focus on the economic opportunities offered by capitalism in order to break the relationship between the community and the Democratic Party, labor unions, and other progressive initiatives.[6]

The *Faith & Freedom Coalition* worked for years amongst millions of evangelical and conservative Catholic voters in the 2024 election cycle with a focus upon conservative Latinos. Director Nilsa Alvarez endorsed the call to deport illegal immigrants but focusing on those who were committing crimes. "We're not worried at all, because we know who he's targeting."[7]

Carlos Malavé, the president of the *Latino Christian National Network*, believes that many Latinos who endorse Christian Nationalism do not have a thorough understanding of all its dimensions. Many positions run counter to where many Hispanics report support. Christian Nationalist ambassadors endorse anti-immigration policies and are constantly hostile to the rights and protection of immigrants. He stresses that the ideology promotes racism and patriarchy and contributes to greater marginalization of vulnerable groups or minorities, especially immigrants. He commented, "When you generally ask the public, in churches, what Christian nationalism is, people cannot give an answer. . . . A magnificent job has been done by groups that are extremists to convince even the immigrants themselves that the new immigrants are a threat."[8]

According to *The Guardian*, various citizens were shocked by the Christian Nationalist rhetoric during the campaign season. Joyce Hamilton raised concerns on the violations of the sacredness of churches that she observed during election cycles. She was troubled by the misuse of one's religious views in order to win an election and felt that it was a form of voter manipulation. "It's problematic to me as a person who follows Christianity and has my own spiritual search . . . It feels offensive to me for someone to claim that they represent God, family and country. I wouldn't be pretending that I'm the biblical candidate." She commented, "It makes me feel very uncomfortable . . . mixing politics and church, and possibly pressuring people in the sense of making them feel that 'I must vote that way as a Christian' doesn't fit with my views." Jan Demro, a Lutheran, was a determined endorser of the separation of church and state. "I am totally opposed to the idea that political campaigning belongs in a church. It both angers and it saddens me because I feel like she's taking advantage of the people that she's preaching to. What she is preaching on is more Christian nationalism than Christianity."[9]

7

Asian American Christian Nationalism

You therefore must be perfect, as your heavenly Father is perfect.

Matthew 5:48 ESV

Since the 1960s Asian Americans have been stereotyped as the "model minority." In 1966, *The New York Times Magazine* and *U.S. News and World Report* both portrayed Chinese and Japanese Americans as the model people of color. They were an example to others that the American dream was possible for it did not matter what color you were or where you were from. It was used to demean the demands of African Americans and others that white supremacy was wrong, and that discrimination prevented advancement into the professional fields.

In 1987 *Time* magazine published a similar lead story, "Asian American Whiz Kids." They were portrayed with admirable characteristics of hard work, strong family ties, submissive to authority, intelligent, doing well, with natural ability in math and science, and other attributes that made them enviable.

They were presented as high achieving in contrast with other people of color, Black and brown people. Asians have a different story to tell, as many of the struggles of people of color is their story. They are not monolithic but have varying economic situations and backgrounds. Along with the lifelong struggles many have experienced, they have been emotionally impacted by stereotyping, feeling pressure to excel, and a sense of failure when it does not come. It has placed levels of animosity between African and Asian Americans as their mythical success has been translated into African American failure. Those in power pointed to this myth to justify oppressive policies that blame those who are oppressed for not trying harder to succeed.[1]

Asian Americans participate to a lesser percentage in Christian Nationalism than other ethnic groups; they are more often the victims of Christian Nationalism. This became frighteningly apparent in the episodes of violence that targeted the community during the COVID-19 pandemic. Racist caricatures that linked the Asian community with the outbreak of the virus led to escalating violence targeting them. Politicians have mouthed stereotypical slurs against the Asian community, with Senators Ted Cruz and Josh Hawley painting themselves as Christian warriors in combat against "godless Communist China." FM (*Faithful Magazine*) bloggers asked, "Why are so many Asian American Christians willing to not just tolerate sanctified Sinophobia, but actively propagate the Christian nationalism underpinning it?"[2]

Surprisingly, some Asian Americans embraced the ideology of Christian Nationalism. Why? Those who are first, or second, generation are extremely patriotic and proud to be American citizens. Having migrated to the U.S., many escaped brutal conditions in their homelands and feel blessed to live in America. They do not expect handouts and place high expectations on others. They favor a strong police presence that offers protection from autocratic threats and reckless individuals. The rhetoric of biblical authority appeals to a people who have a high regard for the Word of God. Asian American Christians, in particular, often resonate with the combination of biblical interpretations, anti-Communist propaganda, and "family values" motivating Christian Nationalists.

FM Editors wrote, "Asian American Christian nationalists . . . hold to the Bible as the scriptural authority in our spiritual lives, and we hold to the American empire to protect our material well-being. . . . We cannot ignore the fact that Asian Americans of both older and younger generations have cast their lot with Christian Nationalism."[3]

Asian American support of Christian Nationalism is a growing concern in the community. Endorsers tend to be more conservative than Black Christian Nationalists. Amongst the January 6 insurrectionists there were Vietnamese, Khmer, Korean, and Filipino migrants who invaded the capitol building. South Asian flags were visible as well as *walis tambo* Filipino brooms. They are ardent Trump supporters who assume that he is the best candidate for their issues. They agree with white Christian Nationalists who identify issues such as abortion, support for Israel, secure borders, xenophobia, and national sovereignty as having primary importance. They strongly affirm that America is God's chosen nation and must return to traditional hierarchies and other patriarchal models in order for God to redeem the nation and restore it to its place of prominence.

Despite growing numbers of Christian Nationalist supporters, twice as many Asian Americans voted for candidate Joe Biden as did for Trump and their votes in Georgia helped flipped the U.S. Senate to the Democrats. After African Americans Asian Americans examine Christian Nationalism with the most concern as 71% poll that Christian Nationalism is a danger to the country. Voters (57%) respond that the lives of racial-ethnic groups and immigrants are presented with threatening situations by their presence and influence in the nation.[4]

A letter was produced from the Asian American community entitled, *"Asian American Letter Against Christian Nationalism."* It read in part,

> As Asian American Christians, Asians of diverse nationalities and creeds, and allies from various ethnic and religious backgrounds, we condemn the Sinophobia demonstrated by Christian politicians and enabled by their churches today. . . . While combatting Sinophobia may involve more than opposing the religiosity that presently sanctifies it, it cannot involve less than that. We Asian followers of Christ, whose most sacred beliefs have been weaponized against us, and our non-Christian loved ones, especially affirm this. As such, we cannot wait for politicians and their associated churches to address racism on their own private timetable. The stakes are too high. We demand that the named politicians publicly repent and take steps to remedy the harm they have caused, both to Asian Americans and to the reputation of Christ's church. We also demand that the religious leaders who have chosen to ignore their congregants' bigotry, often while claiming to care about racial justice, make amends for damaging the church's witness. Finally, we call for solidarity from members of these churches in the event that their leaders do not take sufficient action. We demand transformation because we love both those with power and those without it."[5]

PART 2

Who Are Christian Nationalists?

8

The Church and Christian Nationalism

> And they devoted themselves to the apostles' teaching and the fellowship, to the breaking of bread and the prayers. And awe came upon every soul, and many wonders and signs were being done through the apostles. And all who believed were together and had all things in common. And they were selling their possessions and belongings and distributing the proceeds to all, as any had need. And day by day, attending the temple together and breaking bread in their homes, they received their food with glad and generous hearts, praising God and having favor with all the people. And the Lord added to their number day by day those who were being saved. . . . For a whole year they met with the church and taught a great many people. And in Antioch the disciples were first called Christians.
>
> Acts 2:42-47; 11:26b ESV

Christian Unity

The early church was less an institution and more of a group of people gathered as a unit galvanized around the teachings of Jesus. Christians created a community that focused upon the welfare of its members who were often impoverished and in need. They shared freely to the degree that members sold their possessions and property for a community collection where anyone could receive according to their need. The church grew because of the recognition that they were a unique group of people who cared for one another. They were less concerned about doctrinal differences, nationalities, or race. They were united in purpose and mission. The point is reiterated in Acts 4:32-33: *"Now the full number of those who believed were of one heart and soul, and no one said that any of the things that belonged to him was his own, but they had everything in common. And with great power the apostles were giving their testimony to the resurrection of the Lord Jesus, and great grace was upon them all"* (ESV). William Willimon, in his book *Acts*, writes,

> [T]he real miracle of Pentecost is to be found here—that from so diverse assemblage of people 'from every nation under heaven' (2:5) a unified body of believers is formed. . . . The gathering of the fellowship at the table is another tangible, visible expression of the work of the Spirit among the new community. . . . Eating together is a mark of unity, solidarity, and deep friendship, a visible sign that social barriers which once plagued these people have broken down. . . . [W]hen the blessing is said at the table, the table becomes a holy place and eating together a sacred activity. . . . In the midst of all the newness, the community does not neglect the traditions of the ancestors, does not cease being devoutly Jewish. In all these activities of teaching, fellowship and sharing, breaking of bread, and praying we were a well-rounded picture of the church, the marks of authentic embodiment of the Spirit in the community's life, a canon for the measurement of the church's activity today.[1]

The 21st Century Church

Christian Nationalism is one of many false ideologies that is causing a disintegration in the church's mission, reputation, and effectiveness. It is by far not the only false teaching, as prosperity gospel, millennialism, integralism, a sense of piousness on the part of every Christian denomination and sect, are doing extensive damage. The church in the 21st century has lost much of that sense of cohesiveness and unity. It has also lost its popularity with those outside of the church due to distaste with a perceived caustic culture. It is not known by its love of others, but rather by its intolerance and judgmental behavior. It is also judged as an arm of political parties, engaging in efforts to position itself to gain power. Christians have been pulverized by accusations of self-interest and intolerance by previous generations. The church has endured legitimate criticism from young adults and those with no church affiliation that it is an isolationist institution only concerned with its own well-being. Many criticize the church for its silence and ostensible apathy in the face of societal injustice. Christians are only concerned with salvation of the soul while ignoring the pains the body endures. The church faces charges of prejudice against marginalized groups such as LGBTQIA+, Islamic, and racial-ethnic communities. The adoption of Christian Nationalism has damaged the image and reputation of the church as Christians conflate nationalism and Christian doctrine.

Pushback is occurring as denominations and church councils are rejecting the tenets of CN. The National Council of Churches published a statement that CN is heresy. It objects the tenets of Christian Nationalism and its affirmation of American exceptionalism bonded to Christianity. It criticized the belief that the "U.S. was founded as a Christian nation. That America is exceptional. That is, God has given the United States particular blessings and privileges not available to people in other countries, and the nation must remain Christian in order for those blessings to continue." The Presbyterian Church (USA) strongly condemned "the merging of faith and politics into a single ideology is idolatrous and dangerous. [W]e must also at times, in our role as active Christian members of a civil community, take seriously our prophetic role." In its 2026 document, "White Christian Nationalism," "The Presbyterian Church (USA) repudiates the ideology and practices of White Christian Nationalism in all its forms and affirms the PCUSA's historical support for disestablishment of religion as enshrined in the First Amendment to the Constitution." The Episcopal Church's Presiding Bishop and Primate, The Most Rev. Michael B. Curry, wrote, "The violence, intimidation and distortion of scripture associated with 'Christian nationalism' does not reflect the person and teachings of Jesus Christ, and so I stand with fellow leaders in the Christian community and call for a better way." In 2019, the Baptist Joint Committee for Religious Freedom (BJC) released a statement, *Christians Against Christian Nationalism*. The document called on religious Americans to push back against fusions of religion and government as deformations of the Christian faith. "We reject this damaging political ideology and invite our Christian brothers and sisters to join us in opposing this threat to our faith and to our nation. . . . As Christians, we must speak in one voice condemning Christian nationalism as a distortion of the gospel of Jesus and a threat to American democracy."

The early stance of denominations had lasting impact as there was persistent resistance by the church to encourage active engagement in the world for justice. The Christian church's motif was *protest-against-protest*. The church defined itself as a spiritual institution that abstained from worldly conflict. Societal transformation was not in the purview of a church with a purely spiritual mission. Its primary purpose was to redeem the world for Christ Jesus through evangelistic ministries. For centuries denominations, influential congregations, and theologians resisted any outright adoption of any ideology that compelled Christians to participate in advocacy, as worldly matters were of minimum concern. Leaders were reluctant to challenge injustices in society from a scriptural mandate to obey governing authorities—church leadership endorsed as biblical respecting the authority of governments and political leaders. As patriotic Americans, Christians must maintain a separation of church and state and obey all human laws, for they were from God. Rather than confront members, political authorities, family, or friends, they acquiesced and were silent in the face of discrimination. Mainline Protestants endorsed white supremacy and wrote thesis and doctrinal statements in support of slavery, xenophobia, and misogyny. Mainline denominations rejected a call to advocacy and prohibited protest against earthly powers and principalities. Injustice must be expected in an evil, sinful world. The path to a just society was by the destruction of one's sinful nature. Social reform would be achieved by individual regeneration as a result of evangelism and conversion.

Dan Kimball, in his 2007 book, *They Like Jesus but Not the Church*, critiqued the 21st century church as being out of touch with the contemporary standards of youth and young adults. Young people don't want to connect with the church as an institution, rather they desire a spiritual encounter with God. They reject its formality and hierarchal structure and accuse it of neglect. Emerging generations find Jesus to be interesting and provocative, but find that the church betrayed him as a tool for political purposes. "Many people think church leaders not only have political agendas but also use Jesus to promote them. But the reality is that it's generally politicians (not church leaders) who are the ones who use the church and Christians for their agendas and to gain votes. . . . As a result, we in the church have become stereotyped as being blindly obedient to one political party. . . [W]hat I think most people mean is that they like Jesus, but they don't like what people have turned the church into."[2]

The church is currently engaged in a reevaluation of what it means to serve God in secular society. The mission of the church is undergoing rapid reinterpretation and becoming redefined. The church has long announced that Jesus is priest, prophet, and king. But his identity as a prophet has rarely maintained equal status. Historically, service in the form of charity manifested the church's mission to help the poor. But it has rarely translated into a call for justice advocacy to confront the sins of systemic and structural injustice. This became problematic due to the fact that regardless how much help was provided, charity has been inadequate to meet the totality of human need as systems prevented persons from full utilization of communal resources.[3]

Today, a newly acquired part of its mission is the transformation of the world into a likeness of the kingdom of God, to create the "Beloved Community" as defined by Martin Luther King, Jr. It exists when poverty, racism, and militarism are replaced by love, equity, and reconciliation. It is not enough to evangelize for faith in Jesus, but faith-based justice advocacy is fundamental to being a Christian. Christianity is a religion focused on the person and work of Jesus Christ as illustrated by the Christian Bible. In the sense that its adherents appreciated that their faith is to challenge, affect, and transform the world. Christianity is political, therefore people of faith are called to be political. It means to engage political systems on behalf of the vulnerable, the poor, children, the elderly, and the exploited.

Today more and more Christians have turned to advocacy to complete the call of the Great Commission. Christians are motivated by their faith in a God of justice who demands service on behalf of and with those identified by Jesus as the "least of these."[4] Worship is vital, but rather than being the completion of a life of faith, it is the beginning. Scripture reminds us that "faith by itself, if it has no works, is dead" (James 2:17).

9

Evangelicals and Christian Nationalism

I charge you in the presence of God and of Christ Jesus, who is to judge the living and the dead, and by his appearing and his kingdom: preach the word; be ready in season and out of season; reprove, rebuke, and exhort, with complete patience and teaching. For the time is coming when people will not endure sound teaching but having itching ears, they will accumulate for themselves teachers to suit their own passions and will turn away from listening to the truth and wander off into myths. But as for you, always be sober-minded, endure suffering, do the work of an evangelist, fulfill your ministry.

2 Timothy 4:1-5 ESV

The Apostle Paul wrote to his mentee Timothy to encourage him in his ministry as a leader in the church. He told Timothy not to be intimidated because of his age but to be confident and ready to reprove unsound teaching. In this instance Paul is issuing a warning to the church in modern times, for throughout its history various heresies have arisen that mislead those seeking to follow Jesus in sincerity and faith. Christian Nationalism is one of those heresies.

Antiquity was awash with the emergence of one set of teachings after another. Hellenistic culture prided itself on philosophical expositions to explain the meaning of life, and new discoveries created excitement. The Apostle Paul wrote to his young mentee to be confident in his ability to teach sound doctrine and to beware of those who were attracted to the latest theological fad. Ultimate truth was revealed through the gospel message. The word *evangelical* is from the Greek *euangelion*, "good news" and "gospel." Evangelicals are Protestants who assert that the Bible is the ultimate source of divine authority and reveals God's self-revelation. Many evangelicals believe the Bible is inerrant, without error, and often prioritize a literal interpretation to understand it.

Evangelicals are a successor to fundamentalism, a term that came to prominence in the 1970s in conjunction with the rise of the Moral Majority. They inherited from Jerry Falwell (Moral Majority) a distrust of "secular humanism" that denied the authority of God in human affairs. That distrust of anything outside of their religious community, especially outside of the teachings of their churches, was a continuance of the teachings of the conservative Christian right. Most evangelicals self-identify through church membership rather than any denominational connection. They are committed to a mission of spreading the gospel around the world, often through charismatic preaching.

Evangelicals tend to be more conservative on social issues than the American public as a whole. Evangelicals demonstrate differences in everything from separation of church and state implementation to the Bible and social justice advocacy. In Tim Alberta's 2023 book, *The Kingdom, the Power, and the Glory: American Evangelicals in an Age of Extremism*, he details how he spent time analyzing the role of evangelicals in contemporary American society. He discovered that as a group they were devolving into fractures. The reason being due to self-inflicted wounds and becoming more and more alienated from the rest of society. It is the most misunderstood body of believers and most internally contentious. Many are ardent Christian Nationalists who have lifelong commitments to a form of Christian patriotism that identifies their nation as equivalent to the kingdom of God. In this view, America is in a covenant relationship with God and is uniquely blessed with favor. It has sought to usher in the reign of God by acquiring political power and by aligning itself alongside the Republican Party as a means of living in accordance to the teachings of Scripture. It has gained the reputation of supporting the most controversially unpopular policies such as restrictive anti-abolition legislation and political figures such as Donald Trump. He questioned the reason for the existence of the American evangelical movement if it did not glorify God.[1]

White evangelicals ignored the lack of Christian attributes, faith, or behavior in presidential candidate Donald Trump and voted for him in overwhelming numbers (81%). He fit their preference for a strong, confident, white male who browbeat his opponents into submission by mockery and derision. Kristin Kobes Du Mez, in the book *Jesus and John Wayne: How White Evangelicals Corrupted a Faith and Fractured a Nation,* clarified that evangelicals were not abandoning their religious beliefs by voting for and supporting candidate Donald Trump for president, they were fulfilling them. After decades, since the '70s of hearing the need for American greatness through strength, Trump fit the bill. She wrote,

> By the time Trump arrived proclaiming himself their savior, conservative white evangelicals had already traded a faith that privileges humility and elevates "the least of these" for one that derides gentleness as the province of wusses. Rather than turning the other cheek, they'd resolved to defend their faith and their nation, secure in

> the knowledge that the ends justify the means. Having replaced the Jesus of the gospels with their vengeful warrior Christ, it's no wonder many came to think of Trump in the same way. In 2016, many observers were stunned at evangelicals' apparent betrayal of their own values. In reality, evangelicals did not cast their vote despite their beliefs, but because of them.[2]

For many, Trump was the lesser of two evils whom they could vote for. For some, it was, in business terminology, a political transaction. In return for their vote, Trump promised to protect religious liberty and appoint anti-abortion judges to the Supreme Court. Contrary to some beliefs, it was not a betrayal of the values of their faith but the ultimate manifestation of what their theological definition of being a Christian had become. Trump merely capitalized on their emotional shift from following a meek and humble Christ figure to the idolization of a warrior savior. Trump, like Reagan before him, epitomized for them a masculine, outspoken advocate for white America. Over half of evangelicals do not agree that the prospect of America being mostly non-white in the near future is a positive development for the country. For them, Islam is a religion that promotes violence, causes societal division, and is naturally anti-democratic. Christians in the 21st century faced higher levels of discrimination than do Muslims whose rights supersede their own. Blacks have rejected calling themselves evangelicals due to the racial neutrality and hostility of white evangelicals. For many it was no more than a "religious brand," rather than a life of belief.[3]

Karen Swallow Prior, a Christian author and literary scholar, has spoken against fellow evangelicals' embrace of Trump, despite his character flaws and inability to represent anything close to a person of faith. In the past, she said Trump supporters hoped but weren't certain that Trump shared their Christian faith but have resolved the tension by simply discounting any doubts. In 2018, Georgia Public Broadcast reported that a 2014 Pew Research Center survey identified that 14% of African Americans in the state labeled themselves as Evangelical Protestant. Nationally, the overall number was even smaller for a people for whom 80 percent identify as Christian.[4]

Blacks have largely rejected calling themselves evangelicals due to the racial neutrality and hostility of white evangelicals seeking to establish a politically neutral "religious brand." The issues of importance differ across categories of evangelicals by racial identity. There is especially a disconnect when it comes to issues of racial justice and being prophetically vocal. For African Americans, there has been a constant struggle not only for their human rights, but for a simple recognition of their humanity as a child of God.

Kristin Kobes Du Mez,in her book *Jesus and John Wayne*, writes, "Black Christians have long resisted embracing the evangelical label because it is clear to them that there is more to evangelicalism than straightforward statements of belief. Survey data indicate that on nearly every social and political issue, Black Protestants apply their faith in ways that run counter to white evangelicalism. The differences may be rooted not just in experience but in the faith itself. . . . To many Black Christians, evangelicalism had become 'a white religious brand.'"[5] Thus, Du Mez clarifies that Blacks have emotional investment in their faith and political activism. Their experience with evangelical leaders and congregations is filled with rhetorical language of the blessings of a relationship with Jesus, but short on how that relationship will impact their lives in the here and now. Sermons rarely give voice to racial discrimination nor issue a call for justice throughout society, especially for those on the margins.

10

Progressive Christians and Christian Nationalism

"And to the angel of the church in Thyatira write: These are the words of the Son of God, who has eyes like a flame of fire and whose feet are like burnished bronze:

"I know your works: your love, faith, service, and endurance. I know that your latest works are greater than the first. But I have this against you: you tolerate that woman Jezebel, who calls herself a prophet and is teaching and beguiling my servants to engage in sexual immorality and to eat food sacrificed to idols. . . . And all the churches will know that I am the one who searches minds and hearts, and I will give to each of you as your works deserve. [24] But to the rest of you in Thyatira, who do not hold this teaching, who have not learned what some call 'the deep things of Satan,' to you I say, I do not lay on you any other burden; only hold fast to what you have until I come."

Revelation 2:18-25

The book of Revelation begins with a warning to seven churches in Asia Minor. Six of the seven are first affirmed and then elements of their spiritual life criticized. The church at Thyatira was a loving congregation where their love for God and each other was apparent. They were active offering help and service to the poor. But they allowed heretical teachings within their church body to be put forth under the banner of authentic Christianity. The writer condemned this as unacceptable, and the offender should be cast out. They are told that not all have fallen under the sway of this falsity and should remain faithful. All will be judged according to their commitment to true teaching.

The Christian church must undergo constant self-examination as to the correctness of her teachings. Progressives are often accused of elitism standing in judgment of those without the benefit of societal status, wealth, or education. Christian conservatives accuse them of judgmental behavior and arrogance. Another complaint is that the left is unbiblical and out of step with the Word of God. The left charges conservatives with protesting for the rights of the unborn while ignoring the hardships of those already born. Both left and right profess that they are on the side of God, and that God is on their side. Jim Wallis's book's title is on point: *Why the Right Gets It Wrong and the Left Doesn't Get It.*

The inability of Christians in the United States to engage in critical self-critique has been a consistent blind spot. Marginalized communities that have faced political discrimination and violence have rarely found an advocate in neighborhood congregations outside of their own racial-ethnic identity. Churches throughout history have sided with the majority by either open endorsement or silent compliance.

In the U.S., Christian Nationalism is normally associated with white evangelicals and is often referred to as White Christian Nationalism (WCN). While much of the research and scholarly articles written focus on its infiltration into evangelical ranks, Christian Nationalism is not limited to evangelical embrace, for every denomination has been contaminated. The difference is that there is more of an unfiltered adoption by evangelicals from top to bottom, as both clergy and laity associate with its ideology. Progressives are limited in the public endorsements of Christian Nationalism but rarely address Christian Nationalist elements present throughout their worship communities.

Churches of every race and class are filled with the components of Christian Nationalism. Enter any Christian church, and one will find the visible symbols of faith. All Christians, especially regular church attendees, are quite used to seeing these symbols throughout the building. The pulpit for preaching the word of God, a baptismal font, and a communion table for the sacrament of Holy Communion. Bibles and hymnals are placed in the back of pews. They are so obvious that few feel a need to acknowledge their presence. But there are also symbols whose existence should generate questions about their appropriateness—emblems that represent not the Christian faith, but the secular state. Their presence is so subtle that it is even tolerated by those who outwardly reject Christian Nationalism as a belief. The acceptance of Christian Nationalism has been through a steady repetition of pledging allegiance to the nation as a duty to Christian citizenship. Christian churches were breeding grounds for loyalty to both the flag and the cross. Congregations have the cross and the flag in close proximity in sanctuaries across the nation. On Memorial Day, Veterans Day, Presidents' day, Patriot Day, and the Fourth of July, patriotic music dominates worship services. The Boy Scouts of America's use of houses of worship combined, in young minds, a connection between faith and love of country.

There is need for frankness on the part of the progressive community, as elements of Christian Nationalism exist in every aspect of American life. A progressive Christian is one who identifies as a Christian but interprets the faith in a way that emphasizes openness, social justice, and community activism to implement change. Their motivation is their Christian faith as found in the teaching of the Bible and their faith tradition. There are very progressive Christians, generally

Protestants, who publicly oppose Christian Nationalism, its ideology, and its presence in churches among the mainline denominations. Yet even as church leaders question its authenticity, its members embrace Christian Nationalism. And when one examines the intersections between politics and religion, there are remarkable similarities in jargon and tactics from both progressives and conservatives. Both ranks have prominent activists who describe themselves as evangelicals and affirm the importance of a personal relationship with Jesus.

Another striking similarity progressives share with conservatives, who both seek to promote faith through politics, is that it is largely through a domestic agenda. This aligns with the Christian Nationalist perspective that what happens in the United States is of the greatest importance to the world. They speak of America as the greatest nation in the world and must therefore assume leadership while exercising global influence. But the U.S. is not the most important nation nor the instrument of God's desire for the world. Christians must have both a domestic and global mission to fulfill the mission of Christ to positively impact the lives of others suffering immensely. War, hunger, violent misogyny, theft of mineral resources, famine, drought, the devastating effects of climate change, and so many other sins are producing suffering on a massive scale. Often it is church members and leaders who contribute, reinforce, and mirror the oppressive mindset of larger society. This is not to say that there is no mentioning of these problems by progressives, but they are brief and rare. Jesus would never ignore Haiti, Gaza, Ukraine, Sudan, Democratic Republic of the Congo, Cuba, and other places of desolation and neglect. A prophetic voice has to speak to the issues of "the least of these" and build connections between what is happening overseas to life in this nation. The Rev. Dr. Martin Luther King, Jr. demonstrated this when he spoke out against the Vietnam War. He lost the support of a president, his Civil Rights colleagues, ecumenical partners, and his people. Progressives have a domestic agenda as limited as that of conservatives with an eye on America despite the fact that we live in a global community. Primarily because there is a price to be paid by God's prophets who address the sins of a nation both domestically and globally. Often, their lives. If you think a prophet has no honor in his own country, start talking about American global injustice and neglect on a regular basis and you will discover how many allies you truly have.

This is not to say that a measurable percentage of mainline Protestants are rigid Christian Nationalists. Most disavow Christian Nationalism and reject its primary premise that to be a good Christian is synonymous with patriotic citizenship. But some walk perilously close to that line when urging Christians to engage predominantly in the political realm. Mainlines, like evangelicals, see politics as the means for being obedient to God's word—at times, to a degree greater than its potential. Politics is one wrench in the toolbox that must also include societal, individual ethical, means. Both conservatives and liberals have issues they are promoting as being of God and from God. Both indicate, overtly and subliminally, that God is on their side and that America won't be true to its destiny if it does not follow their prescriptions. Politically oriented Christians use similar theological reasoning in their use of politics to fulfill God's work. Both link politics and religion in ways that are not entirely biblical, promoting political activity as the means for a more just world. All uphold democracy, especially American democratic principles, when living true to its meaning, as a divine pathway to achieve equality.

The irony is that both wind up being ultimately disappointed by elected officials. Both conservatives and liberals complain of betrayal by their candidates who once in office fail to be bold in addressing issues they hold to be important. Conservatives only recently felt that their candidate delivered when the Supreme Court, filled with Trump appointees, reversed *Roe v. Wade*. No progressive candidate has ever had a truly progressive platform addressing the issues that liberal theologians list as being important: poverty, white supremacy, human trafficking, domestic violence, etc. The reason being that any candidate with such a platform would never hold office. Pursuing change through politics involves compromise on the part of prophets who learn that to have an audience with power, you must bend the knee to the throne. First a little, then a lot. To get invited to the White House means that you are not perceived as a threat, rather you can help those in power stay in power. Often it is an opportunity to be photographed with the President and members of Congress.

Liberation theology and Black liberation theology both impacted mainline denominations. Their theologies emphasized how faith should lead to action, especially working for justice and helping the oppressed. This pushed mainline churches to focus more on things like poverty, racial inequality, and political engagement. It made some mainline churches more activist-oriented, paying closer attention to how their faith should play out in the real world. Liberation theology influenced Black theology and in many ways the goals are indistinguishable. Liberation theology broadened Black theology's framework to think about oppression and how to fight against it. Its emphasis on questioning traditional church structures and power dynamics resonated with Black theology's critique of white-dominated churches.

Progressives and the Symbols of Christian Nationalism

Scholars might argue that theological conservatives and progressives fall under the category of civil religion, but again, a close look reveals elements of civil religion and Christian Nationalism in both camps. The most visible evidence is the presence of the American flag frequently located in the sanctuary. It is often placed near the pulpit where the Word of God is proclaimed. It takes tremendous effort to find a Christian church that does not have an American flag in a place of prominence. The flag represents the nation of residence without any religious symbolism. Even with a superficial examination, it communicates a distortion of the phase "separation of church and state."

The question must be asked, "What does the presence of the American flag signify to those who observe it, as it has no religious significance?" Many would disagree with it being an issue where they must choose between the two. One Presbyterian minister in Charlotte, North Carolina, agreed with the issue but responded during a panel discussion, "You pick your battles." Congregations are faced with a choice between the cross and the flag as the symbols of faith. You cannot worship with both the flag and the cross. They are not equal in symbolism or significance for the church and should not share the same space. Each has its place of proper location, the cross in the church and the flag in the statehouse. Christians must decide what level of societal accommodation they are willing to accept. This is so commonplace that there is little to no discussion on what it means to follow Jesus who called his disciples to travel light as they shared the good news. No one, from clergy to laity, questions the appropriateness of the church representing both kingdoms within its confines. Donald J. Bruggink and Carl H. Droppers in their book, *Christ and Architecture*, examined the proper design and use of a church building. They inquired about the presence of having flags placed in the sanctuary of a church: "[Does this] tell us that this church is subject to the nation? Are they to tell us that the Word of God may be proclaimed in this church only as long as it does not conflict with the will of the nation? . . . Or do they mean that the nation is also a means of God's grace?"[1] Their answer was an emphatic "No!" They equated its presence as one of heresy as it heightened the flag to a place of equality to that of the other symbols of grace. They labeled it "nationalistic heresy"; the house of God was infiltrated by a false loyalty to something other than a sovereign God. There must be a physical separation between the placement of the fixtures of the state and house of God. This distance was necessary, as an imperfect nation was in need of hearing a prophetic and redemptive word.

Paul Miller has written books and articles on Christian Nationalism and has a public platform on which he shares his opinions opposing the ideology. He has appeared in media interviews and speaks regularly on the subject. He wrote,

> I'm proud to be an American but there is a time and a place for it. There are appropriate boundaries around that, and I think the church is not the right place for that. I very much advocate for taking flags out of church buildings. Not because we hate America, but because when we're in church, we are celebrating our citizenship in a different polity in the kingdom of heaven, which is a kingdom that includes all peoples drawn from every people, language, and nation on earth. That's a wonderful thing and that's why the American flag does not belong in a church building. Similarly, I would not advocate singing patriotic songs in church. I'm a little cautious about many churches celebrating, for example, Memorial Day weekend and doing a special shout out or thank you to veterans. That's a gray area. Some churches go too far and hold big patriotic festivals on the church grounds.[2]

Closely related to the presence of the American flag is that of the Christian flag. Its origins arose in 1897 when Charles Carlton Overton stated during a Sunday school rally in the presence of an American flag there should also be a Christian flag of white, blue and red colors representing peace, faith, and the death of Christ. In January of 1942 the Federal Council of Churches of Christ in the United States of America passed a resolution that the cross is the only symbol needed to be placed in the church. Harold M. Daniels, writing on behalf of the Presbyterian Church (USA)'s Office of Theology for Worship Resources, said, "Let it be underscored that it is the cross itself, rather than a flag, which should be seen as the universal symbol of the Christian faith. because of this many church leaders affirm that neither the flag of any one nation or the so-called 'Christian flag' belong in the place of worship, because they fail to express the universality of the Christian faith and contribute to an ambiguity about loyalties."[3] Bruggink and Droppers added, "A 'Christian flag' in the front of the church is not only superfluous, it is distracting from the real, God-given symbols of the faith! Nor is there any point to placing it anywhere else, for if this questionable symbol really represents anything, it is the people of God, and they are to be actually present in the pews, and not there by way of symbol. . . It is to be hoped also that once the need for symmetry in the front of the church is gone, the 'Christian flag' may go with it. Of recent manufacture, the 'Christian flag' has no official sanction, an exceedingly doubtful purpose, and origins that can most kindly be described as 'extemporaneous.'"[4]

11

Catholics and Christian Nationalism

> He said to them, "But who do you say that I am?" Simon Peter replied, "You are the Christ, the Son of the living God." And Jesus answered him, "Blessed are you, Simon Bar-Jonah! For flesh and blood has not revealed this to you, but my Father who is in heaven. And I tell you, you are Peter, and on this rock, I will build my church, and the gates of hell shall not prevail against it. I will give you the keys of the kingdom of heaven, and whatever you bind on earth shall be bound in heaven, and whatever you loose on earth shall be loosed in heaven." Then he strictly charged the disciples to tell no one that he was the Christ.
>
> Matthew 16:15-20 ESV

The Catholic Church insists on a legacy of apostolic succession passed on from Jesus to Peter and to bishops and other apostles down throughout the centuries. Jesus commissioned twelve apostles after his resurrection to make disciples and baptize them (Matthew 28). For the Catholic Church it is the foundation for apostolic succession that bishops can trace their authority back to the apostles. The College of Cardinals elects a pope who has no term limits imposed upon the office. He can serve until death or, rarely, he resigns the office. The pope is the head of the Catholic Church and is a part of the succession of apostles and has the authority given to the apostle Peter by Jesus. What he loosens on earth will be loosened in heaven. Scholar Douglas R. A. Hare wrote in his commentary, *Matthew*,

> For traditional Roman Catholicism, this text was fundamental to the doctrine that the successive popes, as Peter's legitimate successors, constituted the foundation of the church's authority. In reaction the Reformers understood the rock to be Peter's faith, which was subsequently shared by all Christians. Recent scholars, both catholic and Protestant, are inclined to regard Peter himself as the rock but as functioning in this capacity in an unrepeatable way. In the history of salvation his role is to be seen as foundational in the emergence of the new messianic community. . . . In his strengths and his weaknesses, he represents ordinary Christians who strive, yet often fail, to be loyal followers of Jesus. Even in this passage which so strongly emphasizes his uniqueness he represents later believers who are called upon to make the same confession. And in the sequel, which dramatically portrays the limitations of his confession, he likewise represents ordinary believers who affirm their faith in Jesus but cannot quite understand why the cross was necessary.[1]

The fact that Christian Nationalism has a place of prominence in the lives of Catholic Christians may come as a strange surprise to those who assume it as a strategy of white evangelicals. And rightfully so. While white evangelical Protestants constitute over two-thirds of Christian Nationalists, fewer than a third (30%) carry similar beliefs. Less than ten percent (8%), according to PRRI's American Values Atlas, are "adherents." Members of the Roman Catholic faith (24%) stress that bills passed into law should be influenced by the Bible, even when it is in opposition to the will of the American people. Up to 23% express disbelief that Scripture does not play a determining role in scripting and implementing the laws of the land.[2] By 2024, 60% of white Catholics were associated with Republicans. According to Pew, most priests graduated from conservative seminaries, with over 80% labeling themselves as "theologically conservative/orthodox or very conservative/orthodox." This increases the chance that Christian nationalist doctrines would be appealing.[3]

Catholic support for Christian Nationalism comes in various forms, as conservative Catholics espouse issues similar to those affirmed by Christian Nationalism. Catholics do not constitute a majority of followers and hold moderate Christian Nationalist views. On this issue there is political polarization amongst Catholics who, in the recent past, were evenly split between the Democratic and Republican parties.

The church has drawn an unusual amount of recognition from both secular and religious audiences through the selection of her last two popes. Popes Francis and Leo have utilized their pulpits to challenge the viewpoint that people of faith are stagnant and intolerant. Francis's prophetic voice raised concerns about the sins of capitalism, and Leo countered the rhetoric of politicians utilizing Christian Nationalist theology. He took on Pete Hegseth who spoke of God on the side of American troops and Donald Trump calling for a ceasefire with Iran during the war initiated by the United States. He has continued the legacy of being a spiritual leader who was impartial when it came to nations or political parties. He represented a God on the side of the poor and dispossessed and has been recognized for his clarity and willingness to speak as a Christian witness to peace and just actions.

This is an interesting situation for church historians to study, as the history of popular acceptance of the Roman Catholic Church has grown in the United States over the last two centuries. Initially considered a fringe group and ostracized from American society, throughout the 19th and 20th centuries Catholics were considered to be a threat to American democracy and villainized alongside Blacks and Jewish Americans, as well as Communists. All were seen as threats to a white Christian (Protestant) nation and not "one-hundred percent American." Catholics were a unique threat as Americans feared allegiance to a foreign leader, the Pope, would water down their allegiance to the United States. Regardless, leadership was determined to play a major role in the social and political life of the nation. It was the issue of abortion that created an opportunity to partner with white evangelical Protestants in forming an ecumenical Christian right movement. The process for religious acceptance had begun.[4]

Anti-abortion and gay rights coalitions between conservative Catholics and evangelicals during the '80s and '90s have been vital in overcoming anti-Catholic bias but have also contributed to divisive rhetoric in politics. Rev. Antonio Spadaro, Catholic editor, criticized Christian nationalist mobilizations between Protestants and Catholics that have "gradually radicalized" and divided the world into good and evil opponents. They have offered theological justification for "apocalyptic geopolitics" and "spiritual war." Many characterized the election of Donald Trump as president as a "divine election."[5]

Christian Integralism

By 2024, there was a movement toward Christian Nationalism by Catholic conservatives called *integralism*. Integralists advocate for the integration of church and state. It maintains that civil authority should be subordinate to the Catholic Church. Andrea Picciotti-Bayer described integralism as "a very small group of people, not significant enough to do much. . . .They want the Church to step in and almost assume responsibility of the government lowering the Church from a supernatural mission to a temporal one."[6]

Nick Fuentes of America First, alongside Eternal Word Television, and Church Militant, embrace the term. Professor Kevin Vallier, in All the Kingdoms of the World: On Radical Religious Alternatives to Liberalism, traces the integralist movement back to the final days of the Roman Empire when the Catholic Church assumed many of the governing duties of the state. Church teachings and papal statements proclaimed that there were two divinely ordained powers, that of kings and the church. The former was in control of "temporal" matters for the promotion of "ordinary natural good" and the latter was in charge of spiritual matters that were eternal. Integralists hold that the church is above any secular authorities and has the right to dictate to governments policies that forward the mission of the church.

Integralism reemerged recently when Catholic scholars convened colleagues to converse around the topic. Patrick Deneen (Notre Dame) and Adrian Vermeule (Harvard) gathered to discuss the promotion of "New Right" and "post-liberal" themes. Like Christian Nationalism, integralists desire a Christian-dominated government to counter liberal, immoral cultural influences. Each administration should have Christian advisors as demonstrated in biblical kingships. There is some tension with Christian Nationalism as integralists reject wholesale adoption of nationalist tendencies but acknowledge that it is a better option than liberalism. They merge with CN advocates against abortion, pornography, blasphemy, and the endorsement of blue laws. Endorsement of Trump caused them to rally together as he is viewed as a reincarnation of Emperor Constantine. The Rev. Frank Pavone, a Catholic priest from Florida, served as the head of ProLife Voices for Trump.

At a 2022 conference, *Restoring the Nation*, at Franciscan University of Steubenville in Ohio, candidate J. D. Vance joined integralist leaders Sohrab Ahmari, Adrian Vermeule, Gladden

Pappin, and Patrick Deneen. The conference called for a return to those foundational components that were central to the nation's core essence. The country was on the wrong path, and only a major effort would reverse decades of leftist influence away from its Christian and Western roots. In order to correct the course there would have to be a divergence from democratic principles.[7]

Donald Trump and Catholics

Several prominent Catholics, such as Trump's VP pick J. D. Vance, former general Michael Flynn, Bishop Joseph Strickland, Laura Ingraham, Samuel D. Roberts, Supreme Court Justice Samuel Alito, and Steve Bannon, promote Christian Nationalism around the country. Flynn has paraded the country in a carnival-like revival in his *ReAwaken America Tour* and Bannon's waves his label of being a "proud Christian Nationalist" who promotes the U.S. as a "New Jerusalem." Professor Millies remarked that they have "figured out that they can appropriate a Catholic brand" and raise "a remarkable amount of money" while "selling a very patriotic-seeming message that tells a story about the happy and uncomplicated meetings between Catholic faith and the American style of constitutional government." An activist recorded Supreme Court Alito agreeing with the statement that "people in this country who believe in God have got to keep fighting for that—to return our country to a place of Godliness." His wife created controversy for the Justice when it was discovered that outside of their home an upside-down American flag and an "Appeal to Heaven" flag had been placed. Roberts is the president of the ultra-conservative Heritage Foundation and the architect of Project 2025. He describes himself as a "cowboy Catholic" who adheres to the belief that "a second American Revolution" is the present reality.[8]

Catholic Response

The Vatican has not approved of Christian Nationalist positions within the Catholic Church or the use of the brand of the church in conjunction with CN. In 2017, Rev. Marcelo Figueroa, the Presbyterian editor of the Vatican newspaper, *L'Osservatore Romano*, published an article, "Evangelical Fundamentalism and Catholic Integralism: A Surprising Ecumenism," that severely criticized the union of Catholic and American evangelicals collaborating on Christian Nationalism exploits. He charged that their "ecumenism of conflict" intertwined religion and politics, calling for a "theocratic type of state." Their angry rhetoric demonized those who disagreed with them and led to division and hatred.[9]

Bishop Michael F. Burbidge, of Arlington, Virginia, Chairman of the U.S. Catholic Bishops' Committee on Pro-Life Activities, commented on his "Walk Humbly" podcast that Christian Nationalism is inconsistent with Catholic teaching. He took a strong position in opposition to Christian Nationalism being Christian. In his podcast, he accused it of inserting "confusion" for citizens' understanding of the relationship between Christians and being American citizens. Its basic premise is that there are no separate distinctions, which is in opposition to basic Catholic Christology, delineating the proper boundaries between love of one's nation and the church. For him, Christian Nationalism confuses two distinct categories of devotion: devotion to one's nation and devotion to one's church. He distinguished between patriotism and nationalism. He defined nationalism as the selective devotion to one's country, existing only as a competitor to other nations, with exclusive devotion to it above all others. Not even one's commitment to one's faith comes even close. He said, "A Christian . . . never identifies oneself entirely with a particular nation. A Christian loves his nation, but within the broader and larger love for God and neighbor . . . . So above all, we are Catholic. We are followers of Christ, we are Christians."[10]

In an interview with *Religious News*, Bishop John Stowe, the Diocese of Lexington in Kentucky, dismissed any CN theories as being consistent with the teachings of the church and criticized any references to Catholic Christian Nationalism. Integralism had no place in America and was not aware of any congregations adopting its principles.[11]

John Stoehr, *The Editorial Board*, warned members of the Catholic faith to be wary of the dangers of Christian Nationalism. He remembered that not too long ago, anti-Catholic bias was a normalized part of the American landscape, instigated by "white conservative Protestants, who make up the core of 'Christian nationalism.'" He argued that anti-Catholic animosity still exists. Roman Catholics should understand that they are aligning themselves with those who are not far removed from anti-Catholic bias.[12] *The Catholic Voice* announced that it refused to endorse Donald Trump during the 2020 presidential election.[13]

12

Clergy and Christian Nationalism

> Here is a trustworthy saying: Whoever aspires to be an overseer [minister] desires a noble task. Now the overseer is to be above reproach, faithful to his wife, temperate, self-controlled, respectable, hospitable, able to teach, not given to drunkenness, not violent but gentle, not quarrelsome, not a lover of money. . . . The Spirit clearly says that in later times some will abandon the faith and follow deceiving spirits and things taught by demons. Such teachings come through hypocritical liars. . . . Have nothing to do with godless myths and old wives' tales; rather, train yourself to be godly.
>
> 1 Timothy 3:1-3; 4:1-2, 7 NIV

Paul's epistle, 1 Timothy 3, offers wisdom for Timothy to follow as a pastor. He must be honest, loyal in marriage, sober, peaceful, and a capable teacher. Paul through his letters warns clergy to remain diligent in teaching the truth of the gospel and not to give in to heresy or false doctrine. His advice is sorely needed in the 21st century, as ministers have adopted cultural approaches to religion more informed by societal interpretations.

Thomas C. Oden, writes:

> Qualifications of overseers, first discussed in 1 Timothy 3:2-7 and then in Titus 1:7-9, are here treated together. They range from personal excellences to competencies in financial affairs, to family life, spiritual maturity, and social skills. In the list sent to Titus, the importance of covenant sexual fidelity is mentioned first, followed by the indication of (five) vices to be avoided in church leaders and (six) virtues to be encouraged. The general requirement that an overseer must be above reproach did not imply absolute sinlessness so as to require no penitence, but rather that one's conduct would give no opportunity to critics to injure the church (Titus 1:7-8; 2:2).[1]

Clarice J. Martin, *1-2 Timothy*,

> What the writer of 1 Timothy has in view in 3:1-16 is church leaders whose behavior is irreproachable, soundness in life and work, and a good reputation before others in the 'household of God . . . the church of the living God, [is] the pillar and bulwark of the truth' . . . combating heresy, and one that reinforces ideals of Christian citizenship. . . . The author of 1 Timothy has . . . compiled a detailed list of the errors the false teachers were advancing within the Christian assembly. . . . [I]nstead of falling in line lockstep with those false teachers.[2]

Today that line is continuously crossed as preachers endorse secular philosophies and promote them as gospel truths. Clergy wrote religious apologies for societal sins from slavery to Chinese expulsion to Hispanic deportations.

During the height of American enslavement, religious scholars and congregational leaders justified bondage from a religious framework as the will of God for a righteous nation. Slavery was defended as beneficial for an inferior, superstitious race. It was the will of God and a means to civilize the African. Biblical passages such as Genesis 9 (curse of Ham/Canaan), Ephesians 6, and Colossians were seen as demanding obedience from the slave toward his enslaver. According to a 2018 *TIME* article, clergy used the words of Scripture as a foundation for the institution of slavery. Virginia's Bishop William Meade taught that slavery could be considered a means of gaining entry into heaven as current punishment for undiscovered sins: better a slave now than to spend eternity in Hell. Georgia's Bishop Stephen Elliott warned abolitionists that they were seeking to impede the work of Almighty God as attempts to Christianize Africans had failed and slavery might be God's right strategy. He stated,

> [You must] consider whether, by their interference with this institution, they may not be checking and impeding a work which is manifestly Providential. For nearly a hundred years the English and American Churches have been striving to civilize and Christianize Western Africa, and with what result? Around Sierra Leone, and in the neighborhood of Cape Palmas, a few natives have been made Christians, and some nations have been partially civilized; but what a small number in comparison with the thousands, nay, I may say millions, who have learned the way to Heaven and who have been made to know their Savior through the means of African slavery! At this very moment there are from three to four millions of Africans, educating for earth and for Heaven in the so vilified Southern States—learning the very best lessons for a semi-barbarous people—lessons of self-control, of obedience, of perseverance, of adaptation of means to ends; learning, above all, where their weakness lies, and how they may acquire strength for the battle of life. These considerations satisfy me with their condition and assure me that it is the best relation they can, for the present, be made to occupy.[3]

The 1960s gave a televised boost to the efforts of evangelists to get their message across to the American populace, as well as growth in the size of their congregations. Not only did they grow in recognition, but also in cultural and political influence.

Today, there is much more intentionality in promoting what should be considered violations of separate but equal. Ministers are the primary violators finding it difficult to navigate between ecclesiastical and secular roles without intertwining the two. It has never gotten to this point of engagement. Clergy around the country are assuming responsibility for things not under their authority, some even inform members for whom to vote. Some do the work of campaigns and even join staffs. The Johnson Amendment prohibits such actions and can remove a nonprofit's tax-exempt status. Periodically Christian ministers have been avid supporters of efforts to merge church and state. Christian Nationalist clergy attempt to influence church members, in both subtle and not so subtle ways, for whom to vote as a reflection of their Christian principles. Some pastors have strongly encouraged their members to volunteer for selected campaigns for candidates who stand for a so-called conservative agenda. The country must be recaptured from humanists who desire to implement change based on reason and ethics without adherence to religious dogma or belief and reclaimed for God. Spiritual salvation comes from political participation.

The 1960s produced a new category of clergy, televangelist, a combination of the words of television and evangelist. Their actions led ultimately to a Christian Nationalist movement that still resonates in the 21st century. The 1962 Supreme Court ruling, *Engel v. Vitale*, caused an eruption in evangelist rage over the court determining that state-sponsored prayer in public schools was unconstitutional. It galvanized the Christian right, giving them an issue that laity could protest.[4] One of the premier influencers was televangelist Jerry Falwell, pastor of Liberty Baptist Church. In 1970 he wanted to gain a seat at the table with the world's leaders and to impact American culture and values. His first step was to create a new organization, the Moral Majority, to implement his vision. It was supremely successful in creating what became known as the Christian Right, and Christian fundamentalism. It was the most public pronouncement by members of the clergy to promote Christian Nationalism as a component of the Christian faith. It popularized Christian Nationalism for millions and normalized the merger of a Christian identity alongside an American one.

The 1970s ushered in a reversal of roles and strategies. A new influx of conservative leaders saw a path to combine their efforts in the war against secularism and Christian liberals. Previously, white evangelical ministers were alienated by doctrinal differences and largely uncooperative with one another. Prior to this time, largely due to the public profile of the Civil Rights revolution, it was liberal clergy, even those in the conservative Southern Baptist Convention, who were more likely to engage in political activism. Christian conservatives in all denominations followed a call to evangelism, church doctrine, and advocated for individual morality. Labeled "the civil gospel," it maintained American origins as a Christian nation that had lost its way. Only by asserting religious values and beliefs through political activity would morality be restored and the rights of Christians protected. The Christian Right united evangelicals around cultural and societal issues. It brought them together in action and in purpose, urging that they gravitate toward politics as the forum to prevent society's fall. The nation was headed in a wrong direction away from being a pious nation and correction was needed.[5]

A perceived threat to racially segregated schools has been a *cause célèbre* of Christian Nationalists. Throughout the 1970s, religious schools were in danger of losing their tax-exempt status if they did not accept African American students. Under the guise of fighting abortion, Christian conservatives joined together. This was normally not considered a Protestant issue, but rather one of the Catholic Church. Resistance increased after the 1954 Supreme Court ruling in *Brown v. the Board of Education*. In *Green v. Kennedy* (1970) and the follow-up case, *Green v. Connally* (1971), tax-exempt status was to be withdrawn from segregated academies. President Richard Nixon sent a memo to the IRS to enforce the ruling. Weyrich, a staunch opponent to the rulings, mobilized evangelicals to convince voters that the fight was one of curbing abortion rights, while their real intent was to secure the right to discriminate in private schools, keeping them all-white. Bob Jones became the litmus test when the IRS withdrew its tax-exempt status in 1976.[6]

Jerry Falwell founded the Moral Majority (MM) in 1979 to combat what many considered gains. For decades he preached in support of segregation and the separation of church and state by telling members to avoid politics. Political victories by African Americans in the courts, the decision on school prayer, and other progressive actions were decisive factors for him to reverse his position. He was incensed by liberals who were deemed enemies of the faith and wrong on political issues. He joined with conservative activists like Paul Weyrich, co-founder of the Heritage Foundation, to usher in a new period of engagement between politics and religion. By 1980 Falwell reported that the MM had chapters in 47 states and worked to register four million voters. The organization lobbied politicians, did voter registration, and raised funds, to gain political power and influence to redirect the country's course. It was less an organization and more a coalition of culture-warrior pastors around the country who acted in unison following the lead of Falwell and other conservative fundamentalists. Falwell launched the "I Love America" tour and before thousands declared that America was a Christian nation. "This is a Christian nation. What has gone wrong? What happened to this great republic? We have forsaken the God of our fathers. The prophet Isaiah said that our sins separate us from God. . . . The Bible is replete with stories of nations that forgot God and paid the eternal consequences. . . . The destiny of our nation awaits your answer."[7]

The rise of the religious right was associated with the *Roe v. Wade* decision. Rather, it was the perceived threat to racially segregated schools that was feared even more. It was a major motivating incident and there was an effort to curb the growth of integration, especially as it related to school desegregation. By 1980 the movement had considerable momentum, and efforts were cited as being one of the reasons Jimmy Carter lost the presidency to Ronald Reagan. Evangelicals voted against one of their own in huge numbers despite the fact that Reagan had signed into law one of the most pro-abortion laws into existence as governor of California. The movement was born.[8] In his book, *Democracy Matters,* Cornel West dissected the related Christian fundamentalist movement that started in the 1970s. He charged that the Christian church, since the days of Constantine, has been corrupted by the power of the state. Christian fundamentalists have sided with the empire against the poor and dispossessed. They have chosen the status and power and constantly utilize the very words of faith to justify the goals of the empire for conquest over weaker people. He contrasted prophetic Christians and Constantinian Christians being in a battle for the soul of America. The former seeks to proclaim universal healthcare, a living wage, and tolerance. The latter is boun d to three dogmas: "'free-market fundamentalism, aggressive militarism, and escalating authoritarianism.' The battle for the soul of American democracy is, in large part, a battle for the soul of American Christianity."[9]

Televangelist Pat Robertson founded the Christian Coalition in 1989 as a birthchild of the Moral Majority. It assumed its mantle of leadership and promoted Christian Nationalism as a political and religious program for the country. His creation of the Christian Broadcast Network (CBN) provided messages that consisted more of conservative propaganda than messages of the Christian faith.[10] He was an ardent Christian Nationalist advertising God's "Law of Reciprocity" where nations are held responsible for their acts against God. In 1987, Robertson ran for president under the banner, "Restore the Greatness of America Through Moral Strength."[11]

The Coalition grew into the largest Christian Right organization with the greatest amount of political effectiveness. For the first time, conservatives voted as a coalition for Republican candidates with whom they felt affiliation. For all intents and purposes, they became a wing of the Republican Party. Leaders motivated religious conservatives to work for the election of candidates who legislated conservatively. As a result, Christian Nationalist clergy, and the movement, filled the ranks of the Republican Party. Robertson never attempted to hide the fact that he intended the Christian Coalition to work directly and only with the Republican Party. "We want . . . to see a majority of the Republican Party in the hands of pro-family Christians by 1996." It relied heavily upon laity and not clergy, unlike Falwell's Moral Majority. Its stated mission was to unify evangelicals with each other and also with other ecumenical partners desiring to engage in effective political action on issues focusing on the well-being of the family. It trained Christians for engagement in politics.[12] He openly criticized interpretations of the Constitution promoting separation of church and state. During his 1987 presidential campaign, Pat Robertson argued that only Christians and Jews were eligible to serve in government and rallied against church and state separation. After his campaign folded, his supporters flooded Republican campaigns and influenced platform policies. In Arizona, the United States was declared a Christian nation and the Constitution was the founding document for "a republic based on the absolute laws of the Bible, not a democracy."[13]

James Dodson, the founder of *Focus on the Family*, became a major conservative influencer during the 1990s. By 1998, there were 34 branches containing more than two million members.

He urged that Christians should influence policy and legislation in the fight against abortion, evolution, and homosexuality. He supported increased defense spending, free enterprise, lower taxes, and churches' charitable ministries. He was especially vehement in his war against cultural humanism and its societal influence. His *Family Research Council* became the most powerful Christian Right lobbying organization in Washington, D.C., with a Christian Nationalist mindset.[14]

Its stated goals were to reverse the country's corruption of values through the spread of cultural depravity. It attacked the Women's and Gay Rights movements, lobbied for the return of government prayer in schools, and sought to reverse *Roe v. Wade*, which legalized abortion. It went beyond traditional issues important to the conservative faith community but shuffled into foreign policy. It supported efforts to defeat communism around the world, an increase in defense spending, and pushed for strong support for the State of Israel."[15]

It was not always the case where conservative Christians opposed abortion rights or legislation. After the *Roe* ruling, many conservative religious leaders and organizations applauded access to abortion. A 1968 symposium of evangelicals refused to label abortions as sinful, rather justifying the right to end an abortion in support of "individual health, family welfare, and social responsibility." A 1971 Southern Baptist Convention resolution called for "Southern Baptists to work for legislation that will allow the possibility of abortion under such conditions as rape, incest, clear evidence of severe fetal deformity, and carefully ascertained evidence of the likelihood of damage to the emotional, mental, and physical health of the mother."[16] The same resolution was reaffirmed in 1974 and 1976. Former president, W. A. Criswell stated, "I have always felt that it was only after a child was born and had a life separate from its mother that it became an individual person."[17] The surprise supporters of the court in *Abington v. Schempp* were Southern Baptists who applauded the consistency of the court as it upheld religious freedom, one of their cherished constitutional guarantees. The case involved a prayer written in a broad fashion to appeal to interfaith sensibilities and approved by a coalition of Protestant, Jewish, and Catholic clergy. It read, "Almighty God, we acknowledge our dependence upon Thee, and we beg Thy blessings upon us, our parents, our teachers and our Country."[18] Surprisingly, only the Catholic Church disapproved of the ruling. Evangelicals wrote in their publications that the state should not promote school prayer, and the prayer served no purpose in expressing the sentiments of true religion. It was a mostly forgotten ruling the following year that created an uproar.

In December 2019, Christian Nationalist minister Sean Feucht and other worship leaders were invited to hold a worship service inside the White House.[19] He is a vaccine denier and criticized protest movements such as Black Lives Matter as "violent, destructive, and in opposition to Christianity." Rev. Robert Jeffress, pastor of First Baptist Church in Dallas, Texas, identified America as a "Christian nation" in his church sermons and in the public square. During a 2017 July 4th Independence Day program, "Make America Great Again," the church's choir sang an original song produced for the event. There were several references to Trump's campaign slogan but there was no mention of the Christian faith or God.[20] Rev. Paula White emailed clergy in support of Donald Trump and chaired the National Faith Advisory Board (NFAB).[21]

While progressive Christian leaders and some leaders within evangelical Christianity were highly critical of Trump's presidency, Franklin Graham, president of the Billy Graham Evangelistic Association and Samaritan's Purse, maintained staunch support. On his Facebook he praised the president's actions and defended him against attack.[22] He believed that it was not by accident that Trump became president. "I don't think he came to be president by mistake or by happenstance, I think, somehow, God put him in this position. Because he's not a politician. He seemed to do everything wrong as a politician, he offended many people, did the wrong things, but somehow, he became president and I just have to think that . . . God put him in that position for a purpose. . . . And we need to . . . support him."[23]

13

Politicians and Christian Nationalism

> "You are the light of the world. A city set on a hill cannot be hidden. Nor do people light a lamp and put it under a basket, but on a stand, and it gives light to all in the house. In the same way, let your light shine before others, so that they may see your good works and give glory to your Father who is in heaven."
>
> Matthew 5:14-16 ESV

Matthew 5 is one of the most impactful chapters in the Gospels, even the entire Bible. The Sermon on the Mount contains teachings that have given inspiration to Christians throughout generations. In his "light/city on a hill" metaphor Jesus instructed his disciples that their mission was to be a sign to the world of God's love and grace. They were to signal to the world what it meant to be in a relationship with God for the benefit of others. They were chosen not because they were special, but because God called them to share with others God's message of divine redemption. God is a God of covenant who calls the world to faith through humility and peaceful engagement. Before God, no nation, not the United States or Israel, is great or more beloved than all the others. The prophets chastised the "chosen people" for becoming like other nations, selfish and oppressive, and, in essence, neglecting its covenant with God. If God has endowed America with a special status, it is for the benefit of the entire world.

Scholar Douglas R. A. Hare writes in *Matthew*,

> Each Christian is individually called to be such a light, but in Matt. 5:13-14 the community as a whole is challenged to fulfill its corporate mission of serving as salt and light for the world. Such a task cannot be accomplished by independent individuals. It is one we must work at together. . . . It is only as the church genuinely proclaims Christ as Lord . . . that the church can truly be the light of the world. The church needs to remember constantly that it is in fact not the light itself but only the window through which the light is to be seen. . . . [I]t is called to visibility. . . . The church's good works are to function in the secular world as indelibly etched pictures of the Father's love. . . . The God who is praised more highly by acts of generosity to the poor and by kindnesses performed for enemies than by the most eloquent prayers is better conceived as a caring parent than as an impersonal force.[1]

The American City on a Hill

Since its founding, Americans have heard Christian Nationalist oratory from the mouths of her elected leaders, from local representatives to presidents. Politicians openly transgressed the separation of church and state doctrine with Christian Nationalist proclamations and legislation.

Governor John Winthrop, the future governor of the Massachusetts Bay Colony, pronounced the earliest political reference to a "city on a hill." In 1630, delivered a speech, "A Model of Christian Charity," aboard the ship *Arbella*. He has been given the title, "the Puritan Moses" and the deliverer of the "most famous lay sermon in American history." He compared the settlement to a "city upon a hill," in "covenant" with God, serving as a beacon to "all people." He was quoting Jesus's Sermon on the Mount (Matthew 5:14). Winthrop called for the establishment of a "Holy Community," where the ship-bound migrants were to be charitable to one another. If they complied, they would receive God's blessings, but they would incur God's wrath if they strayed from being such a beacon. It was a call for moral living under a religious mandate.[2]

The phrase "city on a hill" has been appropriated by politicians who falsely interpreted Jesus's service commandment into one of self-glorification. Rather than a redeeming, sacrificial love being the hallmark of God's call, politicians redirected Jesus's purpose into braggadocio for the United States. American greatness is manifested in its divine mission to lead the world. America has been commissioned by God to be a light upon a hill that cannot be hid, and poignantly, a "city upon a hill."

It was picked up in 1961 by candidate John Kennedy in his candidacy for the presidency of the United States. Succeeding presidents utilized it including Lyndon Johnson, Richard Nixon, Jimmy Carter, Ronald Reagan, George H. W. Bush, Bill Clinton, and Barack Obama.[3] Echoing Kennedy in 1989, President Ronald Reagan centered several speeches around the concept. His running theme was of American exceptionalism with a divine mandate for the promotion of freedom and democracy:

> I've thought a bit of the 'shining city upon a hill.'. . . I've spoken of the shining city all my political life, but I don't know if I ever quite communicated what I saw when I said it. But in my mind, it was a tall, proud city built on rocks stronger than oceans, wind-swept, God-blessed, and teeming with people of all kinds living in harmony and peace;

> a city with free ports that hummed with commerce and creativity. And if there had to be city walls, the walls had doors and the doors were open.[4]

Christian Nationalist Politics

The American public has adjusted its opinions on church engagement with politics. In 1968 a poll revealed that 53% of Americans did not want churches to engage in politics. By 2007, 51% said it was okay, contrasted by 46% who did not. Half of both Black and white Protestants agree that Christian principles and the Bible should exert major influence on the governance of the country. Catholics (60%) fall in line with these beliefs.[5]

Scholars previously thought that demographics offered a regional measurement to determine voting patterns; Southerners voted Republican while Northerners were Democrats.[6] There is a need to differentiate between different races. Fewer Blacks (32%) view Republicans in a pro-religion lens than Hispanic Catholics (47%). Most white evangelicals (64%) held that Democrats were aggressive toward religious institutions and members.[7] Contrary to white and Hispanic Christian Nationalists, Blacks are not generally associated with Republican Party politics nor do they voice support for Donald Trump.[8]

Christian Nationalist legislators have passed a series of laws around the country to force religion upon public institutions. In 2018, six legislative bodies passed laws that reflect Christian Nationalist rhetoric that mandated that every public school prominently display the national motto "In God We Trust." Arkansas passed the first legislation mandating public schools to publish the quote in 2017, followed by Alabama, Florida, Arizona, Louisiana, and Tennessee. Minnesota made the posting optional and in North Carolina the Department of Motor Vehicles was required to produce "In God We Trust" specialized license plates. In 2024, the governor of Louisiana signed into law a bill that required that every public building in the state post, in large letters, the Ten Commandments.[9]

In 2021, New Hampshire, Arizona, Florida, and Oklahoma made illegal so-called "Divisive Concepts," that banned teachers and school systems from discussing "age, sex, gender identity, age, sexual orientation, race, creed, color, marital status, familial status, mental or physical disability, religion or national origin."[10] During the pandemic, Christian Nationalist adherents stood against the healthcare prohibitions forbidding church gathering and decried the regulations as against the will of God. Caleb Campbell summarized that collectively the thought was that "Refusal to adhere to public health guidelines was portrayed as allegiance to God."[11]

In 2024 the Louisiana state government ordered the posting of the Ten Commandments in every classroom. It mandated that every school, from public schools to the state universities, post a poster sized 11 by 14 inches with legible print. The law was passed and signed by Governor Jeff Landry and endorsed by Attorney General Elizabeth Merrill. It was openly labeled as an effort to insert religion into the classroom for the initiation of students into the Christian faith. Other states have produced efforts with similar intent. Florida legislators approved the insertion of chaplains into school district classes and Oklahoma's education leader mandated the use of the Bible as a tool of instruction. Texas, Oklahoma, and Utah have followed Louisiana's lead and introduced bills to post the Ten Commandments. The law was deemed unconstitutional by U.S. district judge John W. deGravelles who considered it as a violation of the First Amendment. He refuted the position of the state that the basis of the law was to commemorate the Ten Commandments as foundational to the country's system of law. A similar decision was reached in a 1980 Supreme Court ruling that a Kentucky law was equally unconstitutional as an endorsement of state-sponsored religion. The 2019 platform of the Republican party of Texas purported that the United States of America was a Christian nation.

Christian Nationalist legislators continue to insist that America is a Christian nation and seek to govern implementing its precepts. One of the staunchest Christian Nationalists was Senator Jesse Helms (R-NC). First elected in 1972, he consistently opposed "abortion, gay rights, racial equality, arts funding, and aid to what he calls 'foreign rat holes.'" He stated that "secular humanism" ran throughout the halls of Congress.[12] He said during a speech to the North Carolina Christian Educators Association, "Christianity is not only true, it's much higher than religion. It is the meaning of America as far as I'm concerned."[13]

At the Republican convention Senator Sam Brownback (KS) proposed in 2004 that his party should move for the reconsideration of the separation of church and state position. Tom DeLay, Republican majority speaker in the House, gave a full endorsement on the significance of the Christian faith: "Only Christianity offers a comprehensive worldview that covers all areas of life and thought, every aspect of creation. Only Christianity offers a way to live in response to the realities that we find in this world—only Christianity."[14] Alabama's former Chief Justice, Roy Moore, was fanatical in his attempts to locate on state property marble monuments with the Ten Commandments carved upon its surface.

Lauren Boebert, Republican congresswoman from Colorado, confirms her Christian nationalist credentials. Congressman Josh Hawley (R-MO), July 10, 2024, spoke at the National Conservative Conference, and assured America that he was a Christian Nationalist.[15] U.S. Representative Marjorie Taylor Greene said pretty much the same thing in an interview. She affirmed and reaffirmed her self-definition of being a Christian Nationalist, "We need to be the party of nationalism, and I'm a Christian, and I say it proudly, we should be Christian nationalists."[16] Speaker of the House for the 118th Congress,

Republican Mike Johnson, an avowed Christian, has associations with Christian Nationalists. An Appeal to Heaven flag hangs outside of his office. It was adopted by the New Apostolic Reformation (NAR) as a symbol of the new revolution for spiritual values and a signal for an apocalyptic age where God's rule is established.[17]

What makes this period in American history so pivotal is that, for the first time, believers with Christian Nationalist ideologies have seats at the tables of power. They are not seeking to influence legislators and presidential policy, they are making policy and determining the political positions of the government. During Trump's first term as president, his cabinet was filled by Christian Nationalists. Attorney General Jeff Sessions, a United Methodist, used the words of Scripture to assert the authority of the administration to enforce its immigration policies and laws. To question the administration was to challenge God's authority to set up rulers to implement God's will. Then vice president Mike Pence, in his speech at the 2020 Republican Convention, inserted references to the flag where Scripture referenced Jesus.[18]

The second presidency of Donald Trump as the 47th president of the United States was ripe with Christian Nationalist adherents in his cabinet. CNN reported in January of 2024, "Under Trump, Christian nationalists will have unprecedented access to the power of the federal government. Trump's GOP has unified control of Congress. And a conservative supermajority, which has already blurred the line between separation of church and state in a series of decisions favoring Christian interests, controls the US Supreme Court."[19] For many, their goal is a religious one, to install a government led by Christians intent on domination of the United States and global conquest, peaceful or through the implementation of violent actions. Many are part of Christian Nationalist organizations that promote radical beliefs with the understanding that American politics is the instrument that God will use to usher in

Christian domination over the nation and world. The Freedom from Religion Foundation stated that his nominees "read like a 'Who's Who' of Christian nationalists and Project 2025 creators."[20]

White Christian Nationalist televangelist Paula White was appointed the director of the White House faith office. She faithfully campaigned for candidate Donald Trump by regularly sending out emails to pastors and laity urging that they support Trump. Peter Morocco served as the Director for Foreign Assistance at the State Department during the first Trump administration. He met with Christian Nationalists in the Balkans, including Milorad Dodik, in 2018 to conspire to bring an end to USAID programs. In 2025 he met with the House Foreign Affairs Committee and questioned the constitutionality of foreign aid.[21] Stephen Miller served in both Trump administrations. A member of the Jewish faith, he has nonetheless adopted political policies ripe with Christian nationalist goals.[22] Robert Kennedy, Jr., was confirmed as the head of the nation's health services despite being an anti-vaxer. He echoed the chants of Christian nationalist groups who insist that trans people are "unreal."[23] Trump's Secretary of Defense, Pete Hegseth, was the poster boy for the movement with a body tattooed with Crusader tattoos. He had membership in a Christian nationalist church, Christ Church, headed by Pastor Doug Wilson and wore Christian nationalist tattoos. He preached a masculine, patriarchal message and called for an elimination of any barriers barring full church participation in politics. His intention was to establish a theocracy dominated by white Christian men. Facing criticism he tweeted, "Anti-Christian bigotry in the media on full display. They can target me—I don't give a damn—but this type of targeting of Christians, conservatives, patriots and everyday Americans will stop on DAY ONE at DJT's DoD."[24] Hegseth stated that Republicans should focus less on religious liberty and more on Christian Nationalism. He led voluntary Bible studies in the Pentagon each week and delivered Christian Nationalist statements that the war with Iran was sanctioned by God who protected American troops.[25] Former South Dakota governor Kristi Noem, is a committed Christian Nationalist and was Trump's director of Homeland Security before being fired in 2026. Upon being elected state governor, she sponsored an "Inaugural Worship Service with Governor Noem" in the Capitol rotunda. During her time in office, she promoted school prayer and worked to ban abortion in the state. John Ratcliffe, CIA, makes constant usage of Christian Nationalist themes and utilized Christian imagery throughout political phrases and speeches.[26] Republican presidential candidate Vivek Ramaswamy, appointed to the Department of Government Efficiency, is Indian American and a Hindu and declared that he was a "nonwhite nationalist."[27] Linda McMahon, Department of Education, collaborates with CN pastor Tim Dunn to establish a theocracy with a privatized public school system. Others with either Christian nationalist or Project 2025 identifications include Janette Nesheiwat (Surgeon General), Dave Weldon (Centers for Disease Control and Prevention), Lee Zeldin (Environmental Protection Agency), Tom Homan (Border Czar), and Marty Makary (Food and Drug Administration).[28]

Presidents and Christian Nationalism

Presidents are the face of a nation where citizens want to believe that they are good at heart and their nation is a force for right in the world. Americans want to believe that their form of government is the best the world has ever seen, and it is their destiny to spread democracy around the world as a mission from God. They believe in God and want their president to be a faithful believer as well.

Americans want a president with religious faith but not one who makes policy based solely on those beliefs. Publicly, at least in the beginning, presidents stated their commitment to uphold the Constitution. Many were moderate to strict constitutionalists pledging the semblance of a wall of separation. Thomas Jefferson, the "Father of the doctrine of separation between church and state," was consistent in his admonitions that the government should not endorse any one religion nor exercise any control over the institution.

Presidents felt politically obligated to walk a political tightrope. On one hand, to align themselves to the constitutional boundaries in the First Amendment's separation clause while reflecting the nation's religious beliefs. Many felt compelled to fulfill their vow to defend the Constitution but still reflect the religious attitudes prevalent in their day.[29]

Many affirmed a Christian Nationalist sentiment that connected the founding of the nation by God including Theodore Roosevelt and Warren Gamaliel Harding. In an October 22, 1932, speech, Herbert Hoover regularly spoke of America being founded as a Christian nation. Franklin D. Roosevelt mentioned God in all four of his inaugural addresses, asking for divine guidance through difficult times. In his second speech, he inferred that he was the political Moses tasked with the responsibility to lead his people to the Promised Land.[30] As president, Harry S. Truman frequently united religion and Christianity. America was a "Christian nation" and it "was established by men who believed in God. "You will see that our Founding Fathers believed that God created this nation. And I believe it, too."[31] Ronald Reagan spoke of America's mission emanating from a "divine plan." He quoted Pope Pius XII, "Into the hands of America God has placed the destinies of an afflicted mankind."[32]

Several confirmed that God was directly responsible for their election. Several sensed a divine hand guiding them to run for the office and once elected stated a closer relationship with God through an enhanced dependency. There was a sensation of being *called*, using language similar to that of clergy called by God into ministry.

Presidents often expressed that America was God's New Israel in a special covenant relationship with God. President Dwight Eisenhower blended his religious and political beliefs seamlessly. He believed that recognition of God in the public sphere was necessary and should be made at every opportunity. He was committed to making *America Religious Again* and directed much of his domestic energy to evangelizing the country. God was directly responsible for American greatness and if the country turned away from God, disaster would ensue. For him, American citizenship and Christian faith in God were two sides of the same coin. He declared: "Without God, there could be no American form of government nor an American way of life." In 1952 Eisenhower promised that his presidential campaign would be a "great crusade for freedom." He frequently inserted scripture into his stump speeches Upon winning the presidency he equated it with a call to usher in a religious revival. He commented, "I think one of the reasons I was elected was to help lead this country spiritually. . . . We *need* a spiritual renewal."[33]

His inauguration ceremony was as much a religious consecration as a secular event. That morning, he attended two church services: a brief one at St. John's Episcopal Church and a special service at National Presbyterian Church. His swearing-in was filled with religious symbolism. The newly elected president was sworn in on two Bibles. His first act as president was to lead the nation in prayer.[34] He was the first president to be baptized while in office, at National Presbyterian Church, and attended the first ever National Prayer Breakfast under the theme, "Government Under God."[35]

In February of 1954, he attended a service where the Reverend George Docherty, pastor of New York Avenue Presbyterian Church, Washington, D.C., urged him to insert the words "under God,' in the Pledge of Allegiance. On June 14, 1954, Flag Day, the president authorized the words "under God" to be inserted into the Pledge of Allegiance.[36] In 1956, he adopted the phrase "In God We Trust" as the United States' official motto. He also labeled American currency with the phrase "In God we Trust."[37]

President Eisenhower achieved his goal as American church attendance grew in the decades before and after his presidency. The president's goal was to be achieved as "piety and patriotism became one and the same, love of God and love of country conflated to the core." According to Kruse, "His administration succeeded in sacralizing the state, swiftly implementing a host of religious ceremonies and symbols and thereby inscribing—quite literally, in many ways—an apparently permanent public religion on the institutions of American government. Eisenhower managed to merge the two into a wholesome 'government under God.' The state was now suffused with religion, and so it would remain."[38]

Christian Nationalism motivated the support of evangelicals in their selection, and rejection, of candidates for the office of president. The original poster boy was Jimmy Carter, a Southern Baptist, born-again Christian. They voted for him in overwhelming numbers but soon soured upon him. Once in office, he was much too progressive for their tastes.

White evangelicals found their hero in the person of Ronald Reagan. He should have been much more controversial in their eyes due to his past record on abortion, but he said all the right things. On July 17, 1980, his acceptance speech for the Republican Party's nomination gave testimony to a God who favored the United States. After he asked for a moment of silent prayer, he said, "God bless America." At the end of his 1984 State of the Union address, Reagan was the first to end his annual SOTU speech with the words. The saying has become a standard in the mouths of politicians. To little acclaim, President Richard Nixon had previously littered speeches with the phrase.[39]

The presidency of George W. Bush reignited Christian Nationalism as the darling of evangelicals as he was everything evangelicals had hoped Reagan would be. Christian

Nationalism dominated his presidency, and after 911 he abandoned any pretense and openly affirmed his belief that God was on the side of the U.S. Bush's presidency called for participation in "Christian politics."[40] Bush invoked references that the righteous country, America, the "city on the hill" was unjustly targeted and compelled into a holy war against the forces of evil, an "Axis of Evil" (Iran, Iraq, and North Korea). God had issued a holy call to wage war and that "God [was] not neutral between them. . . . We have a calling from beyond the stars to stand for freedom."[41,42]

Bush's administration lifted the Christian Right to levels of Christian Nationalist activism that dwarfed that of the Moral Majority. Critics charged that the boundaries separating church and state were obliterated. He motivated Christian participation by claiming that up until the 20th century the United States was a Christian nation. Congregations recruited and trained members for campaign work utilizing church directories. His most blatant offenses were by the financial distributions to faith-based organizations, violating IRS standards.[43]

His "Compassionate conservatism" led to the creation of the White House Office of Faith-Based and Community Initiatives. He lifted the ban forbidding religious institutions and congregations from receiving federal dollars through "Charitable Choice."[44]

Religious conservatives failed to criticize him, as the CIA committed heinous acts of torture under "enhanced interrogation." The *Christian Century* wrote, "What is alarming is that Bush seems to have no reservations about the notion that God and the good are squarely on the American side."[45,46]

The president most hated by Christian Nationalists was Bush's successor, President Barack Obama. He was the worst possible nightmare of white evangelicals and tea party radicals, who disapproved of him by 75 percentage points for reasons that are unexplainable. Like Bush, he should have been an ideal candidate as both were openly religious, faithful husbands, and fathers. They openly discussed their Christian faith and neither initially supported gay marriage. Obama was a model Christian example, but many white evangelicals remained skeptical and openly opposed his programs and policies. Blacks argued that his race brought out the worse in religious conservatives. Many gravitated to various conspiracies and refused to give him their vote.

With the election of Donald J. Trump, an amplified version of white Christian Nationalism was on display. Comically, the most unchristian representative was President Donald J. Trump. He was elected president while uttering Christian Nationalist pomposity with unhealthy doses of racist, transphobic, and misogynistic slurs. Donald Trump always walked a fine line between faith, no faith, and convenient use of Christian Nationalist rhetoric. In his first term in office, Trump invited a group of clergy, all evangelicals, into the Oval Office. A picture was later taken that showed the president sitting at his desk surrounded by the ministers who prayed and laid hands on him. The photo was circulated to imply that the president has not only the blessing of the clergy, but of God who anoints him as president. Christian Nationalists saw a president who was placed in office by the hand of God and who was implementing the will of the Almighty. For the clergy, the desire to have access to the president granted the ability to influence government policy.

While standing on the White House lawn, he once referred to himself as "The Chosen One." Christian Nationalists became even more convinced of their political choice for president once he delivered upon his promises to nominate staunch conservatives to the Supreme Court who would overturn *Roe v. Wade* through Dodd's decision.

PART 3

What Are Christian Nationalist Issues?

14

Christian Nationalism and Abortion

> Then God said, "Let us make humans in our image, according to our likeness, and let them have dominion over the fish of the sea and over the birds of the air and over the cattle and over all the wild animals of the earth and over every creeping thing that creeps upon the earth."
>
> So God created humans in his image,
> *in* the image of God he created them;
> male and female he created them.
>
> God blessed them, and God said to them, "Be fruitful and multiply and fill the earth . . ."
>
> Genesis 1:26-28

Genesis presents a beautiful picture of the creation of human beings in the image of God, *imago deo*. As such, people reflect the moral, spiritual, and intellectual nature of a creator God. God has touched humanity with God's presence and connected God's spirit with the human spirit. The fight against abortion has become a priority issue for Christian Nationalists. The fight against abortion is perceived as an urgent call from God for the protection of the life of the unborn child. It is argued using the most stringent and virulent religious language. According to Walter Brueggemann, in *Genesis*, "The creator is humanized as the one who cares in costly ways for the world. . . . The creature is seen as the one who is entrusted with power and authority to rule. The text is revolutionary. It presents an inverted view of God, not as the one who reigns by fiat and remoteness, but as the one who governs by gracious self-giving. It also presents an inverted view of humanness. The man and woman are not the chattel and servants of God, but the agents of God to whom much is given and from whom much is expected (cf. Luke 12:48)." Through the act of creating and blessing, a "generative power of life, fertility, and well-being that God has ordained within the normal flow and muster of life . . . God's life-giving work is not extrinsic to creation as though it must always intrude. Rather, it characterizes the world. Creation is itself life-giving in the image of the God who gives all life."[1]

Pro-Life or Pro-Choice

Abortion must be the most important issue in the history of the world with all of the attention dedicated to it. Christians are obsessed with either eradicating it from the face of the earth or protecting a woman's right to choose. Historically, abortion had not previously been a hot-button issue for Christian Nationalists. What started as a *cause célèbre* for the Roman Catholic Church has been adopted by Christian Nationalists. Historically, the eradication of abortion rights was primary for the RC church as an extension of prohibiting any means of birth control. The church associates it with a contradiction of God's command to "be fruitful and multiply."[2]

Rebecca Todd Peters, *Trust Women*, wrote in 2018 that abortion is a high-priority issue involving morality primarily to Christians. Nationally, only 25% of Christian Nationalists support the right to reproductive healthcare for women. Evangelicals and Roman Catholics voice the strongest objections based on issues of sexual morality and the moral status of the "prenate." She argued, "For centuries, Christianity has been used and abused to shape how people think about women, sexuality, and families. Uncovering Christianity's deep and abiding role in how we think and talk about abortion is essential, whether we are Christian or not."[3]

The History of Abortion in the United States

Since the 1960s, the Roman Catholic Church has campaigned against the use of contraception, including a 1968 papal encyclical by Pope Paul. For the first time the issue of abortion rose to being a political issue in the states. Beforehand, abortion attitudes were politically moderate as the procedure modernized and became safer. Advances in medical technology ensured a woman's safety combined with a growing desire for smaller families. State laws increased accessibility, with California and Colorado allowing abortions in cases of rape, incest, and danger to the mother's health. By 1972, 18 states had legalized the procedure or eased restrictions. The Supreme Court's passage of *Roe v. Wade* in 1974 guaranteed a woman's right to an abortion as a "right to personal privacy." The decision granted access as a constitutional right during the first six months of pregnancy. There was limited access during the second trimester determined by the mother's health. For the first time, opposition to *Roe* galvanized across denominations as Protestants joined the fight and the pro-Life movement was born.

Roe remained the law of the land until the 2023 Supreme Court *Dobbs v. Jackson Women's Health Organization* decision ruled that abortion was not guaranteed by the Constitution. It overturned fifty years of protection for a woman's reproductive rights and was celebrated as a major CN triumph.

The Nation reported, "[*Dobbs]* is the crowning achievement of a Christian Nationalist movement that has come to dominate American politics, consolidating its power in the Trump era. . . . *Dobbs* not only fulfills the Christian right's decades-long ambition of overturning *Roe* but very explicitly gives them license to enact the harshest regime they can imagine to defend what they claim are the biblical values of a Christian nation."[4]

Another Christian Nationalist victory was won in 2024 when Alabama Supreme Court Judge Tom Parker ruled that destroyed embryos were children when he utilized religious language to underpin his ruling. He invoked the prophet Jeremiah, the book of Genesis, with references to 16th- and 17th-century theologians. He determined that "Human life cannot be wrongfully destroyed without incurring the wrath of a Holy God. . . . Even before birth, all human beings bear the image of God, and their lives cannot be destroyed without effacing his glory." This view is a loose misinterpretation based upon the writings of John Calvin and Thomas Aquinas that the fate of humans can either reflect or diminish the glory of God. His legal ruling, based upon biblical interpretation, confounded those who criticized his usage of Christian Nationalist justifications.[5] Julie Ingersoll, a University of North Florida religious professor, wrote, "He framed it entirely assuming that the state of Alabama is a theocracy, and that that is a legitimate way of evaluating laws and policies. . . . It looks like he decided to just dismiss the history of first amendment religious freedom jurisprudence at the federal level, and assume that it just doesn't apply to Alabama."[6]

Right to Life Terrorism

Few Americans, including members of the Roman Catholic Church, support the insistence that birth control is sinful, nor do they share the ferocity of the outrage. It is astounding that not only the determination of the opposition, but the threatened hostility against providers has risen to a level that is disrupting society. Several Christian Nationalists express that their anger at the availability of abortion justifies violence; some even advocate for the murder of abortion providers. Protestant academic Matthew Taylor at the Institute for Islamic, Christian and Jewish Studies summarized that Christian Nationalists define abortion as murder, therefore violence is permitted to stop it. Taylor wrote, "Christian nationalists are roughly twice as likely as other Americans to believe that political violence is justified.[7]

Ministers have been a major disruptive force in the fight for abortion rights. After September 11, 2001, Christian Nationalist rhetoric was uttered by Falwell and Robertson, who blamed God's wrath on secular humanists. In 2024, ProPublica reported on the activities of a Wisconsin pastor, Matthew Trewhella, of Mercy Seat Christian Church in Milwaukee. He called for churches to form militias, that being gay is criminal, and that abortion providers should be murdered. He called for the establishment of a Christian theocracy based on the Old Testament. He denigrated his enemies as "wicked dogs, whores, and tyrants." He supports secession and believes laws of the country should reflect the laws of God and the teachings of the Bible. Based on that he has called for the criminalization of homosexuality calling for the death penalty for "the filth of sodomy." He wants women to stay at home serving as mothers and wives. For over 20 years, Trewhella denounced *Roe v. Wade* while railing against abortion and gun safety regulations. He blockaded abortion clinics and called for the formation of church militias. He defended the murder of abortion providers, causing two state chapters of Right to Life, the anti-abortion group, to condemn him. During the 1990s, he became one of the nation's most militant anti-abortion activists. His organization, Missionaries to the Preborn, organized members to chain themselves to cars parked in front of clinic entrances. By 2007, the group had taken credit for permanently closing down six of eight Milwaukee clinics. After an activist killed an abortion provider in 1998, he signed a document describing the murder of these doctors as "justifiable." His followers have been accused of committing violent crimes against abortion providers and clinics.[8]

The Future for Reproductive Justice

Rebecca Todd Peters seeks to change the nature of the debate. She argues that the starting point for the discussion goes beyond one concentrated solely on ethical behavior. She discussed the misappropriation of morality as a reason to oppose a woman's right to have an abortion. The issue is not the right to or sinfulness of an abortion; the starting point must focus on the life of the woman and her relationship with the prenate.

> "By focusing public attention on the morality of abortion, the justification paradigm has eclipsed the much more morally significant reality of women's sexual and reproductive health. When we recognize that the moral question begins when a woman is faced with the problem pregnancy, we see that the starting point of our ethical conversation should be women's lives."[9]

Society must develop a new moral understanding of both pregnancy and abortion, defined by the relationship between the woman and the prenate. And she must provide her assent and her willingness to enter into the stated relationship. She must also have the right to end the pregnancy based on conditions that bring in new realities during the course of the pregnancy.[10]

Candidate Barack H. Obama, formerly an opponent to abortion rights, criticized the arguments of religious conservatives against abortion:

"I may be opposed to abortion for religious reasons, but if I seek to pass a law banning the practice, I cannot simply point to the teachings of my church or evoke God's will. I have to explain why abortion violates some principle that is accessible to people of all faiths, including those with no faith at all."[11]

15

Christian Nationalism and LGBTQIA

> When David had finished speaking to Saul, the soul of Jonathan was bound to the soul of David, and Jonathan loved him as his own soul. . . . Then Jonathan made a covenant with David because he loved him as his own soul. Jonathan stripped himself of the robe that he was wearing and gave it to David and his armor and even his sword and his bow and his belt. . . . Jonathan made David swear again by his love for him, for he loved him as he loved his own life.
>
> 1 Samuel 18:1-4; 20:17

Christian Nationalism and Homosexuality

This passage with David and Jonathan portrays an intimate relationship between two men, one who is obviously in love with the other. Jonathan dedicated everything he possessed as an expression of his love for David, who obviously had feelings for him as well. The Bible states that in response to the death of King Saul and his son Jonathan that David stated, *"[Y]our love to me was extraordinary, surpassing the love of women"* (2 Samuel 1:26 ESV). Walter Brueggemann, author of *First and*

Second Samuel, wrote: "The term 'love' may refer to both an emotional attraction and a political commitment." Later we read that "David swears by his love for Jonathan, for David loved Jonathan, as David loved David's own life. David is utterly committed to Jonathan, and this love will survive.[1]

Christian nationalism is strongly linked to opposition against LGBTQ+ rights, with 52% of its adherents opposing nondiscrimination laws and only 22% supporting marriage equality. This ideology fuels anti-trans legislation, efforts to restrict school curriculum, and religious exemptions allowing discrimination, aiming to align U.S. law with conservative, traditional views of gender and sexuality.

Christian Nationalists point to Scripture for their position on the issue of sexual identity and opposition to LGBTQIA rights. They are not alone, as every Christian denomination has a history of persecutions against gays and lesbians. For centuries, the church has justified its stance of the Word of God believing that the Bible condemned homosexuality. Christian Nationalists have been vehement against members of the LGBTQIA community. They consider a gay lifestyle to be a human aberration and a choice to live a homosexual lifestyle.

Christian Nationalists recite and interpret Scriptures that condemn homosexuality in the Old and New Testaments. Yet there has not been a robust discussion on the totality of Scriptures that reflect and offer insight into what might be considered spiritual attitudes considering human sexuality. There is ample evidence to counter popular anti-LGBTQIA interpretations. For Christians, the teachings of Jesus are pivotal. First off, Jesus never condemned same-sex love. There were plenty of opportunities for him to do so. His criticism concerning sexual sins is centered around heterosexual adultery (Matthew 5:27-30). He condemned divorce on the grounds that it violated the sexual purity of the couple (Matthew 5:31-32). Some would argue that his condemnation of "sexual immorality" includes homosexuality, but they are interjecting their own exegesis to replace that of Jesus. The Lord condemned heterosexual lust, adultery, and fornication. He condemned sex outside of marriage between a man and a woman. In John 8, he was confronted by men who brought a woman charged with the sin of adultery. Knowing their real intentions were to foil him, he told those with stones ready, that only the sinless could condemn a sinner: *"Let the one who is without sin cast the first stone at her"* See John 8:7). One another occasion he provided a list of sins: *"evil thoughts, murder, adultery, sexual immorality, theft, false witness, slander"* (Matthew 5:19 ESV). Homosexuality is conspicuously absent. Even more pointedly, there were homosexuals in his community and acknowledged in the Torah. Every society has had a gay presence, publicly and privately. He made no effort to highlight it as an abomination before God, contrary to Leviticus (18:22). The Roman Catholic Church, one of the historic leaders in the condemnation of homosexuality, centuries ago, listed seven deadly sins: pride, envy, gluttony, lust, anger, greed, and soothe. Homosexuality is not amongst them.

Religious dogmas passed down from our parents are ingrained into our unconsciousness and influence our behavior. The church taught members that homosexuality is a sin, and members have passed it on to their children. Many feel that if there is any connection to the Bible or our heritage of religious teachings, prejudicial beliefs can be applied to life in the 21st century. It is ironic that justifications for discrimination are viewed as defensible by the claim of religious freedom. Similar rationales were done in the past as the Bible was used to validate support for the institutions of slavery, white supremacy, apartheid, anti-Semitism, misogyny, and colonialism.

The United States and The History of LGBTQIA

The United States has a long history of persecution of gays and lesbians. Members of the LGBTQIA community faced

Christian Nationalist discrimination from all quarters. Social and political repression undergirded by religious teaching. For centuries, it was illegal to come out of hiding and announce one's sexuality to the world. It was to jeopardize your relationship with your family, community, and not only have you fired, but permanently barred from professional fields.

In the 17th century, New England laws that targeted homosexuals were labeled as sodomy charges. The penalty was the death penalty. The Immigration Act of 1917 banned persons with "constitutional psychopathic inferiority," a term used to discriminate based on sexual orientation. From the late 1940s and until the early 1970s interrogations bullied and threatened employees in the thousands with many losing their jobs as threats to national security. It was the perfect combination of a political agenda carried out based on religious prejudice.[2]

The 1950s initiated new Christian Nationalist fears: the dread of communism and the threat of homosexuality. Both were seen as un-American, a danger to American Christian society, and ungodly. Not only did Christians piously partner with the government to condemn the community, it endorsed its illegality, labeled it a perversion and a mental illness. Churches were silent and approved of harsh police brutality. Kevin M. Kruse wrote that in the 1950s there was an intensive effort to wrap American life around the flag and faith. A third entity, the entertainment world, worked to promote religion. "When it came to the role of religion in American life, political culture and popular culture sang from the same hymnal."[3]

In 1953 President Dwight D. Eisenhower issued Executive Order 10450 that prevented the hiring of homosexuals in government positions as security risks. Frank Kameny lost his job and became a gay activist. In 1954 Senator Lester Hunt, whose son was gay, was blackmailed by associates of Senator Joe McCarthy to withdraw from his reelection campaign. After withdrawing, he committed suicide.[4] FBI Director J. Edgar Hoover measured applicants by their all-Americanism displayed by reverence for God, love of country, and honor for the flag.[5]

Christian Nationalist persecution of the LGBTQIA community in the mid-20th century was political repression under a religious justification. The Lavender Scare resulted in the cleansing the ranks of the State Department of gays and lesbians referred to as "immoral, scandalous, dangerous, and perverts." In 1952, the American Psychiatric Association published its *Diagnostic and Statistical Manual of Mental Disorders* and described homosexuality as a sociopathic personality disturbance. There was pushback when a decade later psychologist Evelyn Hooker challenged gay prejudice. Her paper, "The Adjustment of the Male Overt Homosexual," offered that no differences existed between male heterosexuals and homosexuals. In 1973 the American Psychiatric Association removed homosexuality from any category listing it as a mental illness. In 1958 the Supreme Court ruled in *One, Inc. v Oleson*, ruled that homosexuals had the guarantee of First Amendment rights. Illinois became the first state to repeal its discrimination laws in 1962.

The modern LGBTQ+ rights movement began on June 28, 1969, when police raided an underground gay bar in New York City, the Stonewall Inn. It sparked a response from the gay community and activists and provided energy for the modern LGBTQ+ rights movement. After decades of advocacy, there was a win in 1994 when the federal government initiated "Don't ask, don't tell." Gays and lesbians could serve in the U.S. military as long they did not publicly identify their sexual identity. Congress refused to provide federal endorsement of homosexual marriage when it passed the *Defense of Marriage Act* (September 21, 1996). Massachusetts led the way when on November 18, 2003, it became the first state to legalize same-sex marriage. In 2011, "Don't ask, don't tell" was repealed. On June 26, 2015, the United States Supreme Court legalized same-sex marriage, declaring that same-sex marriages could no longer be denied to those who desired it.[6]

On June 26, 2015, the Supreme Court declared that same-sex marriages could no longer be denied to those who desired it. The court ruled that religion lay at the base of objection to same-sex marriage.

The Church and LGBTQIA

Of those who affirm Christian Nationalism and register hostility toward the LGBTQIA community, preachers lead the way. Texas pastor Jack Graham tweeted, "We can bend our knee to Christ in faith and stand for our flag in freedom."[7] Atlanta pastor Eddie Long preached sermons on how healthy heterosexual relationships result in "Godly men." His partnership with the daughter of Martin Luther King, Jr., resulted in a 2004 "Reigniting the Legacy" march in opposition of same-sex marriage. They led a parade of over 24,000 people, mostly Black, on Atlanta streets.[8] Christian Nationalist sermons made news for being preached in Tennessee, Texas, and Arizona. In North Carolina, Lieutenant Governor and pastor Mark Robinson said that being gay or transgender is "filth," "garbage" and "perversion." He was the Republican candidate for the governor of North Carolina in 2024. He lost. According to *NOW*, "Several preachers across the country have called for the execution of LGBTQ people. This summer, thirty-one members of the Patriot Front were arrested in Iowa before they could invade a Pride gathering shortly after a preacher there said from the pulpit: 'God told the nation that he ruled . . . Put all queers to death.'"[9]

Christian denominations failed to provide any quantitative leadership in advocating for the rights of the LGBTQ+ community. In May of 1996, Episcopal Bishop Walter C. Righter was tried for heresy in a trial for ordaining an openly gay deacon. He was acquitted. The Presbyterian Church (USA) found the

Rev. Jane Spahr guilty (August 27, 2010) of misconduct on the charge of officiating same-gender weddings. In 2013 The United Methodist Church tried and convicted the Rev. Frank Schaefer after he performed his son's wedding to another man in 2007. In April of 1972, The United Methodist Church approved a statement of *Social Principles*. It proclaimed contradictory statements. It declared that the "practice of homosexuality . . . [was] incompatible with Christian teaching" while affirming that "persons of homosexual orientation are persons of sacred worth." On June 25, 1972, the United Church of Christ ordained William R. Johnson as the first openly gay minister.[10] The 1979 Episcopal Church General Convention followed a similar path as the United Methodists, with a dual resolution. On one hand, it is "not appropriate for this church to ordain a practicing homosexual or any person who is engaged in heterosexual relations outside of marriage." On the other, homosexual people have an equal claim on the church's love and acceptance. In 1984 The UM General Conference declared that "self-avowed practicing homosexuals are not to be accepted as candidates, ordained as ministers, or appointed to serve." The 1996 Presbyterian Church (U.S.A.) General Assembly reached a compromise. Gays could be ordained as officers as long as they lived a celibate lifestyle; in "fidelity within the covenant of marriage between a man and a woman or chastity in singleness." In 2024 the Presbyterian Church in America passed an overture at its General Assembly saying those who identify as gay were not qualified for ordination.[11]

Denominations have moved in the last decades to reversing prior anti-LGBTQ discrimination against individual gays and lesbians and advocated for gay rights. Beginning slowly in the 1980s, denominations acknowledged the humanity of LGBTQIA persons and began to empower their serving as clergy and allowing the same-sex ceremonies.

In the latter half of the 20th century, denominations accelerated their support. The Moravian Church declared in 1974 that gays and lesbians were full members of the Christian community. The Mennonite Church has several LGBT-affirming denominations. Black denominations, the Catholic Church, and evangelicals refuse to do so. Members of Black traditions were less restrictive. In 2004, Coretta Scott King objected to a constitutional amendment banning same-sex marriages as a form of "gay bashing." She argued that it would do nothing to protect traditional marriages. Julian Bond stated, "With so many problems affecting black Americans . . . what harm is done by people in love?"[12] No Mennonite Churches in North or South America have officially endorsed same-sex marriage, but several have discussed greater moderation on church positions.

By the 21st century, progress and acceptance increased. On July 4, 2005, the United Church of Christ General Synod legalized all marriages, irrespective of genders. In 2009, the Evangelical Lutheran Church in America's Churchwide Assembly ordered the ordination of gay and lesbian pastors. On May 10, 2011, the Presbyterian Church (U.S.A.) eliminated the previous lifestyle celibacy stipulation. In 2015, the Church redefined its constitution by legitimizing marriage "between two people," expanding it beyond one man and one woman. In 2015, the Episcopal Church allowed any couple to be married. In 2024, the United Methodists disavowed their anti-LGBTQ policies and teachings and lifted bans on same-sex marriage and gay clergy. The Evangelical Lutheran Church in America, the largest Lutheran church body in the United States, allows for LGBTQ+ marriage and ordination of LGBTQ+ clergy. The United Church of Christ (June 25, 1972) ordained its first gay minister, William R. Johnson. The Episcopal Church elected Gene Robinson as their first openly gay bishop on June 7, 2003. The ELCA did likewise on May 31, 2013, when R. Guy Erwin was ordained as bishop. The United Methodist Church's first openly lesbian bishop was Karen Oliveto (July 16, 2016).

In 2021, Megan Rohrer was the ELCA's first openly transgender bishop.

But not everyone was on board. The Seventh-day Adventist Church opposes same-sex relationships stating that "sexual intimacy belongs only within the marital relationship of one man and one woman" on biblical framing. Baptist denominations, Southern Baptist and the American Baptist Churches USA (ABCUSA), neither affirm a gay lifestyle nor same-sex marriage and inconsistent with biblical teachings. In 2013 the Disciples of Christ endorsed the ordination of LGBT clergy while leaving the decision to local congregations. None of the historical African American denominations have moved to endorse LGBTQ rights to marriage nor acceptance including the National Baptist Convention nor the national Al Baptist Convention, USA, Inc. The Jehovah's Witness, Church of Latter-Day Saints, Lutheran Church-Missouri Synod, do not ordain homosexuals or permit same-sex marriages. Pentecostals are not in a formal relationship with one another, rather in close relationship. Most hold that homosexuality is a sin including the Assemblies of God and the Church of God in Christ.

The Roman Catholic Church does not ordain gay men, but under Pope Francis has moderated its stance from sin to disorder. It opposes same-sex marriage, but the pope voiced an openness for homosexuals to receive the Sacrament of Holy Communion, hospital visitation, and a blessing for same-sex couples. Eastern Orthodox Churches oppose same-sex marriage. Muslims forbid homosexual couples, and many countries make it illegal. The Jewish community is split, with some Reformed and some Conservative Jews offering support, while Orthodox Jews do not. Hindus and Buddhists have a mixture of support and opposition amongst members.[13]

It is ironic that there have been instances where the most homophobic rants were made by those who were closeted gays themselves. Many Christian Nationalists ignore the evidence that people are born gay and that, as long as humans have existed, there have been men who are gay and women who are lesbian. Regardless, they consider it to be wrong and sinful, even as children born into their families and communities state that they have a different sexual orientation than what they might consider to be biblical.

16

Christian Nationalism and Gender Justice

I commend to you our sister Phoebe, a servant of the church at Cenchreae, that you may welcome her in the Lord in a way worthy of the saints, and help her in whatever she may need from you, for she has been a patron of many and of myself as well.

Greet Prisca and Aquila, my fellow workers in Christ Jesus, who risked their necks for my life, to whom not only I give thanks, but all the churches of the Gentiles give thanks as well. Greet also the church in their house. . . . Greet Rufus, chosen in the Lord; also his mother, who has been a mother to me as well. Greet Asyncritus, Phlegon, Hermes, Patrobas, Hermas, and the brothers who are with them. Greet Philologus, Julia, Nereus and his sister, and Olympas, and all the saints who are with them. Greet one another with a holy kiss. All the churches of Christ greet you.

Romans 16:1-16 RSV

Women and the Bible

The Apostle Paul confuses us when it comes to issues of gender justice in the life of the church. His messages concerning women are contradictory and without explanation when one considers the total of his communications. It would appear that he experienced tremendous change in his attitudes toward the acceptance of women in leadership positions in the church. During the time of his writing the letters to the church in Corinth, he reflected his Jewish training and called for the subordination of women and to not even allow women to speak during services. He wrote in 1 Corinthians 14:34 that women should have no voice within the confines of the church. They bring about shame upon themselves, their family, and the church itself. Under a command of submissiveness, they should direct inquiries to their husbands when at home. But by the end of Paul's ministry, he was commending women as colleagues and partners in the service of Christ. In Paul's long list of personal greetings in chapter 16 he commends Phoebe as "our sister, a servant of the church at Cenchreae" (16:1). Paul recognizes Phoebe as a respected disciple of the Lord. Paul instructs the believers in Rome to "welcome her in the Lord in a way worthy of the saints" (ESV). And for her to be relieved equally as a fellow leader in the church. In 16:3-5, he greets Aquila and his wife, Prisca, as a team, describing both as "my fellow workers in Christ Jesus." Both equally share in the ministry in "the church in their house." He also greets "Mary, who has worked hard for you" (16:6 ESV) with equal reference as the men and with mutual and equal responsibilities. A second husband and wife team, Andronicus and Junia also have virtual significance in the work of ministry. Thomas L. Hoyt, Jr., wrote, "That Phoebe was called a deaconess, the only person so named in the New Testament, suggests that the church office of that name was emerging. She was from Cenchrae, the eastern seaport of Corinth. Paul warns her to be welcomed, because she belongs to the Lord. Members of the church, as 'saints,' have a duty to show hospitality, and she has helped him in many of their fellow church members. In mentioning Prisca and Aquila, Paul's Roman readers would have noticed that the woman's name came first. The ordering suggests that her missionary role was more important than that of her husband."[1]

A lack of support for gender justice is not just a part of the CN story, but Christianity as a whole has fallen short on advocacy and only recently within the last half century promoted the rights of women and girls. This is interesting because in antiquity religious beliefs were interspersed with both male and female gods and goddesses. Egyptian, Mesopotamian, Greek, and Roman mythology were filled with dynamic female figures who for some, were dominant in importance and worship. Modern Western culture tended to downplay various gender roles elevating males to prominence while downgrading women to support roles. By the Victorian age customs dictated that women be reserved for motherhood and as wives. Today's quest for equality is attempting to recapture ancient equality.

Christian Nationalism is strongly linked to traditionalist gender ideologies and patriarchy. Research demonstrates that adherents favor a male-dominated society. It insists on a social order for society, the church, and the home where men are the heads of households, maintaining an authoritarian autonomy. Heterosexual marriage, hindered roles, and patriarchal hierarchy originate in the pages of Scripture and are divinely ordained. If this model is not maintained, society will soon deteriorate into chaos.

American society has been harmed by becoming emotionally soft and its members unprepared for the rigors of life. The male psyche has been damaged by femininity and wokeness, resulting in damaged boys and men who struggle to find their place in society. Women having stepped out of their roles of motherhood and being wives bring disrepair to the stability of the family.

Christian Nationalists with a history in the evangelical portion of the church more than likely were nurtured in a patriarchal institution with an emphasis on masculinity. Men were natural leaders whose primary role was to protect women who were natural caregivers for their children. Brian Levin, director of the Center for the *Study of Hate and Extremism* at California State University, San Bernardino, said that the spread of xenophobic prejudice and bigotry online has helped make intolerance "transnational and transethnic. . . . Misogyny, a fascination with fascism, weapon fetishization are things that, I think, define aggressive masculinity. That cuts across a variety of ethnicities and subcultures."

Kristin Kobes Du Mez, in *Jesus and John Wayne*, described the impact of dysfunctional masculinity and its impact on evangelical churches, many of which subscribe to CN. Patriarchal theology ascribes to the male testosterone-driven impulses to aggression and dominance as being derived from his being created as such. Therefore, he is just following his creatureliness when he asserts himself in the family and wider society. "Within this framework, men assign themselves the role of protector, but the protection of women and girls is contingent on their presumed purity and proper submission to masculine authority. This puts female victims in impossible situations. Caught up in authoritarian settings where a premium is placed on obeying men, women and children find themselves in situations ripe for abuse of power."[2]

While Christian Nationalists focus on early Paul to deny women a place of leadership in the church and seek to lower their service to that of positions of servitude, there are other voices and many other points of scriptural reference. Genesis 1:26-31 reads:

> Then God said, "Let us make humans in our image, according to our likeness, and let them have dominion over the fish of the sea and over the birds of the air and over the

> cattle and over all the wild animals of the earth and over every creeping thing that creeps upon the earth."
>
> So, God created humans in his image,
> in the image of God he created them;
> male and female he created them.
>
> God blessed them. . . .
>
> God saw everything that he had made, and indeed, it was very good. And there was evening and there was morning, the sixth day.

The story of the subordinate position of women is supplied by the story of the creation of humanity as found in Genesis. Interestingly enough, the most popular version is told from the second version found in Genesis 2:18-25. God creates Adam in isolation and mentions that he is alone and needs a "helper as his partner." God puts him to sleep and removes one of his ribs to form a woman. But in Genesis 1, the creation of women and men occurs simultaneously and they are equally blessed. Generations of Christians have only been told of the creation of Adam as the dominant figure and Eve as his "helpmate." But in the eyes of God they are equal as children of God's act of creation.

Primary is the illustration demonstrated by Jesus in his relationships with women. Jesus has a ministry with women in significantly instrumental roles and as leaders in ministry. He never subjugated women and broke social taboos, allowing women to engage with him on an equal basis as men. Even the argument that he only called male disciples is buffered by his being ministered to by women in the gospel of Luke. Mary and Martha were personal friends of his and offered him hospitality in Martha's home and confronted him due to his late arrival when their brother Lazarus died. Despite not being listed amongst the disciples, they are the first to witness his resurrection and informed the disciples that he was raised from the dead.

Christian Nationalism as a Feminist Issue

Protestants have made strides over the past decades in accelerating the role of women in positions of authority and rejecting past patriarchal roles. There has been an outright rejection of patriarchy as women have taken the lead in producing statements on equality and disrupting gender bias in local congregations. In 2026 the heads of several communions were led by women, in particular, women of color. Rev. Jihyun Oh served as the Stated Clerk of the Presbyterian Church (USA), the highest elected position in the PC(USA). Rev. Teresa "Terry" Hord Owens is the General Minister and President of the Christian Church (Disciples of Christ) in the United States and Canada. Rev. Dr. Karen Georgia Thompson serves as the General Minister and President of the United Church of Christ (UCC).

Secular organizations such as the National Organization of Women (NOW) stand in opposition to Christian Nationalism as an obstacle to the advancement of the rights of women and exist as a feminist issue. CN influences a host of political decisions, lobbying for policies and laws that restrict the rights of women: reproductive justice, LGBTQ+, and voting rights. NOW argues that these issues are interconnected. It is alarmed by the decisions that limit a woman's autonomy over her body and her reproductive choices. The Dobbs Supreme Court ruling that overturned the landmark *Roe V. Wade* decision was applauded by CN endorsers. Similar approbation resulted from the later Arkansas decision. "Christian nationalism, which often seeks to impose a particular set of values and beliefs that can directly contradict the principles of gender equality and individual autonomy. . . . With the belief that God has designated the United States to be a beacon of hope rising among the nations, it is not surprising to witness the continued integration of biblical imagery into American politics. . . . Advocating for a civic religion, particularly Christianity, involves practices such as placing crosses in public spaces, mandating prayer in public schools, and displaying religious texts like the Ten Commandments in courtrooms. Christian nationalism, endorsing and propagating violence in the name of religion, represents a distorted interpretation of the essence of Christianity."[3]

17

Christian Nationalism and White Supremacy

The sons of Noah who went out of the ark were Shem, Ham, and Japheth. Ham was the father of Canaan. These three were the sons of Noah, and from these the whole earth was peopled.

Noah, a man of the soil, was the first to plant a vineyard. He drank some of the wine and became drunk, and he lay uncovered in his tent. And Ham, the father of Canaan, saw the nakedness of his father and told his two brothers outside. Then Shem and Japheth took a garment, laid it on both their shoulders, and walked backward and covered the nakedness of their father; their faces were turned away, and they did not see their father's nakedness. When Noah awoke from his wine and knew what his youngest son had done to him, he said,

> "Cursed be Canaan;
> lowest of slaves shall he be to his brothers."

He also said,

> "Blessed by the LORD my God be Shem,
> and let Canaan be his slave.
> May God make space for Japheth,
> and let him live in the tents of Shem,
> and let Canaan be his slave."

Genesis 9:18-27

This narrative in Genesis 9 has been used over the centuries to justify African slavery by both religious and secular enslavers. According to this interpretation, Canaan, the ancestor of the African races, was cursed by his father's father to be the servant of his uncles, the ancestors of other races. This story was used to connect race and slavery in ways unintended by the biblical writer. This misuse still echoes today as the Bible is provided as evidence that slavery had biblical antecedents and sanction.

Christian Nationalism and the Birth of White Supremacy

The history of the country has been consistent in demonstrating the link between Christian Nationalism and white supremacy. Christian Nationalism has been conspicuously present as it related to race. Racist theories taught toleration for whites but racial subjugation for others. Freedom was a right reserved for whites while Blacks and Native Americans were for enslavement or extermination. Gorski and Perry, authors of *The Flag and The Cross*, examined the history of white Christian Nationalism and its implications for American democracy and the ways in which it limited the freedoms of racial-ethnics. "For a new racial order was emerging in the New World, an order in which 'white' meant 'free,' 'Black' meant 'slave,' and 'red' meant neither bound nor free but 'savage.'. . . [T]he price of the Constitution was the perpetuation of slavery."[1]

Christian Nationalist apologists utilized every justification, religious, political, and social, to maintain white supremacy and the institution of slavery. The enslaved were fed a daily regimen of Christian Nationalist rhetoric of racial inferiority with religious foundations. Benjamin Quarles, author of *The Negro in the Making of America*, wrote,

> Once slavery had become a dominant feature of Southern life, it became necessary to defend it. Hence a pro slavery argument developed, with southern opinion makers—congressman, clergyman, newspaper editors, and college professors—contending that slavery was a positive good. One of their arguments was that the Negro was biologically inferior to the white—that race determined mental and moral traits. The Negro, as a member of an inferior race, was meant to be a slave, his normal and natural condition.[2]

The enslaved suffered under one form of Christian Nationalist discrimination after another as both the religious community and political establishments entrenched legal bondage through racist politics grounded in flawed interpretations of Scripture. Churches provided the theological justification for human bondage readily accepted by white enslavers. During the colonial period, the white church sided with oppression and white supremacy against biblical teachings on justice and unconditional love. Confusedly, contrasting themes were intertwined often in the same doctrinal tracts and preached from the same pulpits. The church provided scriptural justifications concerning the ownership of Christian slaves by Christian slaveholders. For example, they argued it was supported by Scripture as not one of the Old Testament prophets witnessed against it. In the New Testament, they pointed to Paul advising the servant Onesimus to return to his master. Southern clergymen comforted themselves with the thought that obedient slaves would gain their freedom in heaven. Catchphrases were repeated that "slavery is an ordinance of God" and is "Scriptural and right."[3] Christian theologians and clergy developed one ideology for whites of liberty and freedom while the enslaved were instructed of God's wrath for all who sought deliverance from slavery.[4]

Christian enslavers derived racist interpretations from biblical sources. Slavery was a legitimate economic enterprise based on an array of suspicious interpretations. Since Jesus never openly condemned the institution, they could consider it acceptable.[5]

Christian theologians continued to provide slavery with theological undergirding as economic exploitation was protected by the federal policy and laws. The church provided answers for any question concerning the ownership of Christian slaves by Christian slaveholders. William Warren Sweet, in *The Story of Religion in America*, connected the theology of Christian Americans as being chosen by God to dominate other races. "The New England Calvinist considered that he was God's elect and that to him God had given the heathen for an inheritance, and by enslaving the Indians and trading them for Negroes he was doing nothing more than entering into his heritage."[6]

Christian silence and complicity were proof of the paradox of a Christian nation holding human beings in bondage. Many of the most influential congregational ministers were slave owners, as were John Davenport of New Haven, Ezra Styles, president of Yale, and even Jonathan Edwards."[7] Presbyterian clergy were among the main proponents of justifiable exploitation. The Reverend John H. Witherspoon, the only minister to sign the Declaration of Independence, wrote to his wife, "I believe African Slavery, lawful & not unchristian, and that it is better for them, on the whole, than liberty without a due preparation for the reception of the blessing."[8] Old School Presbyterians were rabid defenders justifying slavery based on the words of Scripture and that it was morally justifiable. Rev. Dr. J. H. Thornwell, in South Carolina, placed the responsibility for its existence at the metaphorical feet of God, citing its apparent acceptability in both the Old and New Testaments.[9]

Black Opposition Voices

Blacks opposed the Christian Nationalist justification for slavery that America was chosen by God to enslave Blacks for their betterment. They challenged a Christian Nationalist mentality and proposed that racist greed was the real cause for bondage and not God. Both freedmen and the enslaved refuted the use of the Word of God to justify the nation's commitment to slavery. Blacks had a reverse theory that stated definitively that God was on the side of the oppressed. They saw their own fight for liberation exemplified in the story of God's intervention and subsequent liberation of the Hebrew slaves. They prophesied that the same God was on their side and would intervene in their fight for freedom. Jesus, the Suffering Servant, identified more with them than with their oppressors.[10] Eugene D. Genovese, author of *Roll, Jordan, Roll*, wrote,

> [W]hites of the Old South tried to shape the religious life of their slaves, and the slaves overtly, covertly, and even intuitively fought to shape it themselves. . . . Africans eventually provided their own version of this interpretation of Christianity's political role. . . . However much Christianity taught submission to slavery, it also carried a message of foreboding to the master class and of resistance to the enslaved. . . . Afro-American slaves, drawing on both Euro-Christianity and their own African past, combined the two and in the process created a religion of their own while contributing to the shape of Christianity as a whole.[11]

The 1831 Nat Turner rebellion resulted in discriminatory laws prohibiting the religious practices of the enslaved and many had to go underground, preaching one sermon to whites and another to Blacks. Eugene D. Genovese wrote, "The preachers did not typically call for revolt and violence, for conditions overwhelmingly discouraged insurrectionary ideas among sober Black men. But many could turn into revolutionaries if conditions changed. . . . [M]any had to be judged by the slaveholders as dangerous men of unpredictable political tendency."[12]

The Black community raised a prophetic voice and challenged proslavery rhetoric as crass hypocrisy and anti-Christian. Black Christians challenged the limit of theological discourse limiting Black freedom to spiritual salvation while limiting the liberty of one's body as being reserved for whites. They saw through the shallow theologizing of white clergy who offered weak scriptural justifications for the enslavement of other human beings, white supremacy, and Black inferiority. Frederick Douglass moaned that he would much rather be enslaved by a nonbeliever than the most church-going Christian. "For of all slaveholders with whom I have ever met, religious slaveholders are the worst. I have ever found them the meanest and basest, the most cruel and cowardly, of all others. It was my unhappy lot not only to belong to a religious slaveholder, but to live in a community of such religionists."[13]

Abolitionists were active, mouthing charges of hypocrisy at those who supported systemic oppression with religious sentiment. Slavery would not exist without the sanction of religionists whose sanction made it reputable. No area of society was safe from abolitionists' ire as they criticized the government, churches, businesses, and individuals for complicity. Churches were harbors for robbers who stole children, murderers of the enslaved, and those who committed adultery against God's liberating grace. With the passage of the 1850 Fugitive Slave Law, William Lloyd Garrison tore up and they burned a copy of the Constitution as an act of protest against the country's legitimization of slavery. He disavowed the Constitution as a document endorsing slavery as "a covenant with death and an agreement with hell."[14]

Religious activism increased in the conflict over slavery, especially the intertwining of political action and the abolition of slavery.

The Civil War brought to a head the contradictions of pro-slavery Christian Nationalist ideology. Contradictions abounded as the churches preached a God of love on Sunday but embraced Christian Nationalist beliefs throughout the week. Racist theories persisted expounding upon Black inferiority. Gorski and Perry wrote, "By the time of the [Civil] war, three theories were dominant: Blacks were slaves due to the curse of God and for having black skin. . . . Slavery was a blessing to the Black race as it introduced them to civilization and Christianity. In colonial Virginia. . . . the curse of Ham won out over the image of God. As so often happens, the theology followed the money."[15]

Native Americans: Church and State Imperialism

It must be acknowledged that in the history of the United States, there was another race of people much more numerous, with towns, villages, and governments of their own. Indigenous nations had developed highly sophisticated cultures that coexisted with nature, maintaining high levels of conservation. Their ability for religion and governing authority to coexist without either controlling the other was novel for Europeans.

Indigenous people of the Northern Hemisphere experienced the genocidal zeal of Christian Nationalism. Indigenous peoples were demeaned as savages whose lives nor culture were worth preserving. The Trail of Tears was carried out by a president, Andrew Jackson, who as a Presbyterian acted in accordance with his religious beliefs of white supremacy. White politicians, clergy, and settlers made no attempts to grant the rights of native sovereignty to indigenous peoples. Any vacant lands could be encroached upon under the doctrine of *vacuum domicilium*. It was considered lawful to respond to native resistance with extreme measures of violence against women, children, and the elderly. Manifest Destiny gave them the religious justification that God was responsible for their actions and provided land for those who knew how to manage and produce a harvest.[16]

It is significant that the fight for American independence was justified by a religious dogma that freedom was the right of all people. Indian Wars were fought as religious battles to extend Christianity, as white politicians and missionaries expressed a mandate from God to Christianize a savage people by any means necessary. But the real goal was to take the land under any justification. Under the domain of religious and political ideology the American government, aided and abetted by the American people, waged unfiltered war on Native Americans, and then forced the survivors to relinquish their religion, identity and culture. Native Americans were reticent to adopt Christianity and forgo their indigenous beliefs due to any evidence of any moral benefit it offered their white neighbors.[17]

In the Northeast the sons of William Penn, known as the Paxton Boys, murdered hundreds of Native Americans in their genocidal campaign, justified by Scripture aberrations. The night before a massacre, Reverene John Elder, Paxton Presbyterian Church, led them in Psalm 137 ("Happy shall he be, that taketh and dasheth thy little ones against the stones" KJV). This is one of the most disturbing calls for violence in Scripture and was used to justify the murder of their native neighbors. Elder Saunders Kent read 1 Samuel 15 to justify genocide.[18] Ben Franklin confronted the Paxton Boys with words of severe disapproval. Their actions found no justification in Christian ideologies. Franklin reprimanded them,

> [This is] a Horrid perversion of Scripture and of Religion! The people of Pennsylvania pretend to be Christians. . . . [The] Conestoga massacres could have been perpetrated 'by no civilized nation in Europe. . . . The Conestogas would have been safe in any part of the known world . . .

> except in the neighborhood of the Christian white savages of texting and Donegal![19]

The United States accumulated territory that was to become the states of New Mexico, Utah, Nevada, Colorado, Wyoming, and California. The losers were Native Americans and Mexico. By the time it was over, most of the indigenous tribes living in California had lost both their lands and their lives. If any refused to become Christian and culturally American, they were not fit to live. As Europeans established their own towns, they sought to dominate and control indigenous people and destroy their culture. They established "praying towns" as precursors to boarding schools. In 1638, the first reservation in the U.S. was established on the Quinnipiac homelands in Connecticut, covering 12,000 acres. John Elliott, a Puritan, wanted a place for Native Americans who had adopted the Christian faith and created a set of "praying towns." These were the first reservations set aside for their quarantine, for the purpose of "civilizing" the residents. It was controversial from the very beginning as Native leaders protested the towns as inadequate and not something they ever demanded. Colonials applauded with congratulations for the effort to protect and domesticate tribes by eradicating their cultural identity within colonial missions and schools. Those confined within the boundaries lost their freedom, culture, and identity.[20]

President Abraham Lincoln, known as the Great Emancipator, was emphatic about ending American slavery and his desire to reunite the broken nation. He often quoted Scripture, such as when he stated that a house divided against itself cannot stand. But his policy toward Native Americans was uninformed and often brutal.[21] As usual, politicians and ministers led the way. In his Indian policy, President Lincoln is considered to have been more lenient than previous American presidents and the public at large. Nevertheless, he believed that the best policy toward Native Americans was one of "civilization" through forced assimilation, the adoption of white customs, and the removal of tribes to reservations. He approved forced removal from tribal lands and the Homestead Act; he broke tribal treaties and authorized the execution of 37 Dakota warriors in the Dakota Uprising of 1862. He granted pardons to 264 who were originally condemned to death. Lincoln was president during the start of the boarding school era, between 1819 to 1969. Hundreds of thousands of Native American children were taken from their families and repatriated to 523 boarding schools in 38 states. The *National Native American Boarding School Healing Coalition* documented the location of boarding schools mostly located in Oklahoma and the Four Corners region of the Southwest in the Navajo Nation.[22]

Christian denominations partnered with the federal government to implement a policy of cultural extermination underwritten by a religious rationale. The boarding schools cemented a relationship between church and state to Americanize Native Americans by destroying every component of their cultural traditions, especially religion. The 1883 Code, Rule Six is informative: "Indigenous healers and healing practices were viewed as not only an obstacle to the adoption of Christianity but also as an active threat to the boarding school system."[23] Religious organizations that participated included the American Missionary Association of the Congregational Church, the Board of Foreign Missions of the Presbyterian Church, the Board of Home Missions of the Presbyterian Church, the Bureau of Catholic Indian Missions, and the Protestant Episcopal Church. The University of Chicago Divinity School posted online the nefarious partnership between Christian denominations and the government. American colonizers had two related goals: cultural assimilation and religious conversion. It was thought that if indigenous identity was suppressed by the overwhelming superiority of American culture, resistance to the theft of land would be minimal. Religious justification and the judiciary partnered on the side of the conquerors as native children had few defenders. The doctrine of church and state was set aside as religious people were paid and received native land.[24]

Despite barely surviving the onslaught, Native Americans sought to retain as much of their culture as possible. They did this by adopting a hybrid belief system agreeing to adopt American religious and cultural beliefs but performing a syncretistic lifestyle. Hybrid religious theologies combine native teachings and Christian beliefs to create a Native American Church. Anglos refused to compromise and demanded that all remnants of traditional beliefs be abdicated. John Lame Deer, Sioux, attempted to bury his mother in the way of his people in 1920. He complained, "They wouldn't even allow us to be dead in our own way." Much grief would have been prevented if Native people were allowed to assimilate through retaining elements important to a defeated people, but compromise was not the American way.[25]

The Psychology of Christian Nationalism

The period following the end of the Civil War culminated in religiously themed white supremacy under a Christian Nationalist foundation. It has been said that while the South lost the war, it won the peace. The South re-created itself from the myth of the Resurrected People who rose from the dead, similar to that of Jesus, to be redeemed. It created its own form of therapy through the creation of myths of a noble people in a noble land. A Lost Cause theology was fashioned from the biblical story of the Exodus where they, too, were tried and tested by the hand of God. They were the prototype of the suffering servant in Isaiah who, rather than being wrong in their secession and enslavement of African Americans, were just, honorable, and faithful. As Kevin Phillips puts it:

> In some respects, the South did not lose the Civil War: Southerners eventually resolved the dissonance between the world as it was and the world as they had wanted it to be by securing enough of their war aims—states' rights, white supremacy, and honor—to permit them to claim their share of the victory.

All with a religious and theological basis as the will of God for the white race to subjugate.[26]

Black inferiority was justified and terror a way of life. African Americans were portrayed as reprobates who had to be controlled in order to suppress their natural inclinations. Once released from the shackles of slavery, Black men were viewed as an existential threat to white women and American society. These views did not belong to a few extremists but were mainstream and unopposed in every segment of white society. As a way of convincing itself and the world of its purity and choosiness, Southerners began a process of building monuments to itself through the region. Statues, monuments, and memorials of the slain Confederate soldier were engraved with Christian symbols to symbolize the righteousness of the Lost Cause. The memorials were placed on public lands for all to see as evidence that they were a people called by God to reclaim their rightful place in the world as triumphant children chosen by God. Southerners were God's New Israel, and the chosen ones baptized by war and blood. The final act of their redemption was the removal of federal troops in 1877 and the end of Reconstruction. Confederate monuments also served the purpose to quell any efforts for equality on the part of African Americans as many were constructed long after the end of the war closer to a growing Civil Rights Movement.

As late as the 1900s, Christian Nationalism infected every aspect of society in every region including industry, literature, agriculture, commerce, and morals with pro-slavery endorsements still being uttered.

Christian Nationalist Defender: The KKK

The KKK sought to establish America as a Christian nation through violence. It was unique in that its particular brand of Christian Nationalism declared war on racial outsiders, especially Blacks. It is the oldest hate group in the U.S. with several reappearances: first after 1865 and again between 1920 and 1930. They used both political and religious symbols, such as the wearing of robes, burning crosses, and waving the American flag. All represented their proclamation of a gospel of white supremacy. Their goal was to maintain a white Protestant America under the banner or racial and religious intolerance. History professor Randall Stephens (Northumbria University) wrote,

> Christians in America may not like to acknowledge how influential the Klan was or how the group made strong connections between faith and racial/ethnic purity and God and country. "Religion remains a prominent part of the Klan," though many would like to pretend that it's not.[27]

The songs and creeds of the Christian church were the model for Klan literature. Billy Sunday, a predecessor to Billy Graham, received donations from the Klan as he toured the country preaching sermons endorsing white supremacy. Throughout the 1920s the terrorist organization directed its hatred toward Blacks, Catholics, Jews, immigrants, "union organizers," "birth-control advocates," "internationalists," "village reprobates," and "fallen" women.[28]

Kelly J. Baker, author of *The Gospel According to the Klan: The KKK's Appeal to Protestant America, 1915-1930*, gave an interview to the *New York Times* in 2021 labeling Christian Nationalism as a core belief of the Klan. She said the two were connected and not isolated incidents but a part of the Christian Nationalist trend that has been part and parcel of the American experience. She commented on the 1925 KKK parade through the streets of Washington, D.C. under a banner reading, "America First: One God, One Country, One Flag."[29] She described the organization as the largest in Klan history in all 48 states with almost five million members. It was comprised of both men and women holding positions as pastors, politicians, bankers, and dentists. She summarized it as a marriage between white supremacy and religion.

> "They stood for, explicitly, white supremacy and white Protestantism. Arguably, it is an evangelical movement too. For membership you were supposed to be a white Christian. You had to be supportive of nationalism and patriotism. They actively encouraged members to go to church. Their language was definitely influenced by evangelicalism, the way they talk about Jesus Christ as their Lord and Savior."[30]

18

Christian Nationalism and Religious Freedom

> "All things are permitted, but not all things are beneficial." All things are permitted, but not all things build up. Do not seek your own advantage but that of the other. . . . I mean the other's conscience, not your own. For why should my freedom be subject to the judgment of someone else's conscience? If I partake with thankfulness, why should I be denounced because of that for which I give thanks?
>
> So, whether you eat or drink or whatever you do, do everything for the glory of God. Give no offense to Jews or to Greeks or to the church of God, just as I try to please everyone in everything I do, not seeking my own advantage but that of many, so that they may be saved.
>
> 1 Corinthians 10:23-33

In the United States, there is an ongoing debate on the religious freedom of Christians. Should a Christian participate in activities, or even engage in business, with persons whose lifestyles they disagree with and find morally objectionable? In chapters 9 and 10 of 1 Corinthians, the Apostle Paul seeks to add clarity on the rights of Christians as they seek to live a life of obedience to the word of God. Earlier he sought to clear up a controversy brewing in the church over the sacrament of Communion. Legitimate questions arose concerning when one should withdraw from the table due to acts of sin committed during the week. Likewise, should one eat food sacrificed in the worship of idols, or does such consumption defile one before God? Paul advised the church to take into consideration the feelings of others and the injury our actions might make on both believers and nonbelievers. If you are invited to a dinner with sacrificed food, rather than satisfy one's conscience, eat so as to not offend the host. He advises that it is not our own conscience that is the only consideration when making decisions in engaging with others, but the offense Christians might give.

Christians should not use their liberty as a means to hurt others, even if they think they are following God. Ultimately, we are to be more focused on glorifying God by the manner in which we treat other human beings, even when it offends us. Jesus taught his disciples that they will have to make sacrifices in their service and mission. He even described his mission as one of service to others as the "Son of Man came not be served, but to serve." At the heart of Christian discipleship is a call to not follow our own conscience but to do the will of God regardless of the discomfort it might bring to us. "Give no offense to Jews or to Greeks or to the church of God, just as I try to please everyone in everything I do, not seeking my own advantage but that of many, so that they may be saved" (verses 32-33).

History of Religious Freedom

Religious freedom is upheld as a sacred gift of both American democracy and Christianity guaranteed by the Constitution. In the New Jersey State Capitol, a tablet celebrates religious freedom as a founding principle: "This tablet is placed to honor the Pilgrims of the Mayflower. In an age of intolerance and of bigotry, the Pilgrims of the Mayflower laid the foundations of this mighty nation wherein every man, through countless ages, shall have liberty to worship God in his own way."[1] On the other hand, Charles C. Haynes, in *Religious Freedom in America*, argued that religious freedom alone did not motivate European settlers coming to America. Quite the contrary, as state churches were the norm in Virginia, Maryland, North Carolina, South Carolina, and Georgia.[2]

The first two clauses of the First Amendment declare an endorsement of religious liberty. The Establishment Clause prohibits the government from establishing an official religion of the United States and guarantees the right to an individual's religious beliefs and the expression thereof. George Washington was quite visionary when it came to the new republic and the rights it should protect. He stood firm for the religious rights of all people regardless of the faith they practiced. The new country should be a place where religion, regardless of the faith, was not a barrier to success or opportunity. He opposed any positions where one religion stood in a superior position above all others.[3]

For a country constitutionally founded upon the rejection of restrictions on religion, it has effectively continuously inched away from the founder's intent. Primary to the cause of Christian Nationalism is safeguarding the right of religious freedom as defined within the ideology.[4] The Center for American Progress is concerned about the direction of the country, away from First Amendment rights of freedom of religion. As the debate continues, many are paying attention to the ways in which popular opinion is shaping the political landscape with many leaning in Christian Nationalist directions."[5]

The Supreme Court and Religious Freedom

The Supreme Court has been called upon to decide the limits of religious freedom in the nation, and it has taken the lead in redefining the meaning of religious freedom. Christian theologians argue that this is contrary to the teachings of Jesus in the New Testament. SCOTUS ruled in the *Masterpiece Cakeshop v. Colorado Civil Rights Commission* in favor of a Christian business owner, baker Jack Phillips. He had refused service to a gay couple who wanted him to bake a wedding cake for their same-sex ceremony. Phillips stated before the decision, "I'm being forced to use my creativity, my talents and my art for an event—a significant religious event—that violates my religious faith. . . . Because of my faith, I believe the Bible teaches clearly that it's a man and a woman. Making a cake to celebrate something different, causes me to use the talents that I have to create an artistic expression that violates that faith."[6]

The Court has sided with legalized discrimination. During the 1960s and '70s, the Supreme Court decided that prayer led by school officials was unconstitutional and only students could engage in leading religious services. In 2000, in *Santa Fe Independent School District v. Doe,* ruled similarly that coach-led prayers during football games was not permissible. In *Shurtleff v. Boston* the court discounted the religious implications and debated it as a free speech argument.[7] In 2014 the *Hobby Lobby* Supreme Court ruling determined that an employer could deny his employees health care coverage for contraception based on religious objections. The *Braidwood Management* case ruling went much further to stretch the meaning of religious freedom to the point that the employer did not have to provide coverage for a drug, prophylaxis (PreP), that prevents the spread of HIV. He did not rely upon religious objection other than the fact the drug would "encourage homosexual behavior, prostitution, sexual promiscuity and intravenous drug use."[8]

Amanda Tyler, of the Baptist Joint Committee for Religious Freedom (BJC), spoke on the current judicial philosophy of the Supreme Court concerning religious freedom. "Christian nationalism is antithetical to the constitutional ideal that belonging in American society is not predicated on what faith one practices or whether someone is religious at all."[9] She told the Center for American Progress that Christian Nationalism is "single biggest threat" to religious freedom. She dissected the ways that the First Amendment grants religious expression on two fronts. The citizen is protected from any government establishment of a national or state religious preference. And guarantees the right of religious expression free from government oversight. She explained that recent decisions by the Supreme Court run counter to the intent of the First Amendment. It is much too deferential to the rights of individuals, thereby creating a crisis for the overall religious freedoms of everyone. It has misinterpreted the principles of the Establishment Clause in what it defines as government sponsored discrimination against the religious rights of a few.[10] Protecting religious freedom is not just important for those in the minority and their religious practices, but the majority is impacted as well. As the wall between church and state continues to crumble, so will the rights of all.[11]

Robert P. Jones, in *The End of White Christian America*, observed that the right to discriminate under the guise of religious freedom was being expanded to all manner of businesses: bakeries, wedding photographers, bed-and-breakfasts, pharmacists, pediatricians, front-line service providers, county clerks, and social workers. If they could put forth an objection to serving same sex couples, it was now their right, according to the recent rulings of the Supreme Court.[12]

Different Faiths and Religious Freedom

The Presbyterian Church's Advisory Committee on Social Witness Policy (ACSWP) produced the 2018 policy statement, "Religious Freedom Without Discrimination." It decried the efforts of religious leaders and politicians to define religious freedom as the right of businesses to discriminate in hiring and in limiting their services. The 2018 223rd General Assembly voted to affirm the declaration and implicit actions. The statement declared that religious freedom does not grant a Christian the right to discriminate against others. It is a failure to understand that the essence of religious freedom does not mean the right to impose one's views upon the lives of others. To follow Christ means to stand on behalf of those who are targeted for discrimination and oppression, to defend their God-given dignity against the false privilege of false piety. Religious freedom is a shield of defense against oppression, not a sword of suppression. "Such practices of inequality perpetuate second-class citizenship in the name of religion, a violation of the First Amendment's prohibition of government establishment of religion."[13]

I testified before the HOR Committee on Education and Labor (2019) in support of the *Do No Harm* bill. It was intended to correct the misuse of the *Religious Freedom Restoration Act* where Christians denied services due to the sexual identity of perspective customers. In my testimony I said the following:

> "Policies adopted under the guise of religious freedom are in reality nothing more (or less) than a targeted attempt to promote a singular religious viewpoint that does not believe LGBTQ individuals are entitled to the full scope of human rights to employment, healthcare, and parenting rights. These policies give businesses, service and healthcare providers, government workers, and private citizens engaged in commercial activities the unfettered right to discriminate against others, deny them needed services, and impose their own religious beliefs on others, so long as they cite their religious or moral belief as the reason for doing so."[14]

Religious Freedom in the 21st Century

Silver Springs, Maryland, has a dense concentration of religious institutions unlike any other location in the country. It is referred to as "Embassy Row of Religions" and locally as "Highway to Heaven." The Public Religion Research Institute (PRRI) describes it as the country's most religiously diverse county. In the same community, not only is there a collection of Christian congregations, but also a Kingdom Hall of Jehovah's Witnesses, a Cambodian Buddhist Society, a Muslim Community Center, the Maryland Hindu Milan Mandir, and a psychic. PRRI's CEO Melissa Deckman highlighted qualities contained within similar neighborhoods. They are densely populated by racial and ethnic diversity. Whites, while constituting a majority of residents (40%), reside with a Hispanic population of 20%, along with disproportionate percentages of African Americans, Asian Americans, and members of the Hindu, Buddhist, and Islamic faiths. Other counties include Kings County (New York); Suffolk County (Massachusetts); and San Francisco County California.[15]

19

Christian Nationalism and The War On Christians

> "I am a Jew, born in Tarsus in Cilicia, but brought up in this city, educated at the feet of Gamaliel according to the strict manner of the law of our fathers, being zealous for God as all of you are this day. I persecuted this Way to the death, binding and delivering to prison both men and women, as the high priest and the whole council of elders can bear me witness. From them I received letters to the brothers, and I journeyed toward Damascus to take those also who were there and bring them in bonds to Jerusalem to be punished."
>
> Acts 22:3-5 ESV

The Apostle Paul, while not being one of the original twelve, claimed the title by his being called personally by Jesus to discipleship on the Damascus Road. He was a persecutor of the church and was an accomplice to the stoning of Stephen for proclaiming Jesus as Messiah. After his conversion, the disciples feared accepting him due to his past actions in tormenting Christians. This fear of persecution continues in the 21st century and is very real around the world. But not so much in the United States with a Christian majority. In his book *Acts*, William H. Willimon calls attention to Paul's past relationship with persecution:

> "Note that Paul uses the present tense to describe his relationship to Judaism. 'I am a Jew.' Whereas those who have beaten him are zealous for the tradition and law and order, Paul describes himself as a zealot for God, (v. 3). Paul knows what it means to persecute others in the cause of religious righteousness, but this is exactly what he did to 'the Way' (v. 4). By language, upbringing, and zealotry Paul has established a link with his audience. If someone does not believe him, all he has to do is to ask the chief priest and the council (v. 5).[1]

The War on Christians

A deep motivation for Christian Nationalists is a trepidation of being persecuted for their Christian faith. This is rather difficult to fathom, as the religion has been the majority faith in the U.S. since its beginning. Philip S. Gorski and Samuel L. Perry highlighted the complaints of Christian Nationalists who list grievances of discrimination. "White Christian nationalists sincerely believe that whites and Christians are the most persecuted groups in America. . . . The United States cannot be both a truly multiracial democracy—a people of people and a nation of nations—and a white Christian nation at the same time."[2]

The Guardian reported that American Christians portray a "sense of victimhood in a secular culture."[3] Many believe that Christians in the 21st century face higher levels of discrimination than do Muslims, whose rights supersede their own. All aspects of American life, and life in general, consists of a cosmic contest of spiritual warfare of good versus evil. Their language and speeches are filled with references to warfare against the forces of evil. One of their tools is to use the agencies of government to implement the change their desire. In order for the world to be remade into God's original purpose, Christians must engage in the battle for the sake of Jesus by being politically and socially engaged. Professor Matthew Taylor, the Institute for Islamic, Christian, and Jewish Studies, grew up evangelical and commented, "There's been a tectonic shift in how the leadership of the religious right operates. . . . These folks aren't as interested in democracy or working through democratic systems as in the old religious right because their theology is one of Christian warfare."[4]

Prophetic warnings issued by the Moral Majority were adopted by the Christian Coalition. Pat Robertson warned that a "new world order" would cause a rearrangement in world hierarchies where Christians would be hunted down and persecuted.[5] As noted in *The Evangelicals,*

> (Pat) Robertson went on to report that only a vital, economically strong, Christian United States' could 'prohibit a worldwide Satanic dictator from winning his battle.' Satan's strategy was to make 'a frontal assault on Israel'—and that was the plan of 'the presently-constituted new world order.' Satan would also 'launch a war against the Christian people'—and already the very techniques the Nazis had used against the Jews were being used against Christians.[6]

America's Catholic bishops, some aligned with Christian Nationalism, have characterized those who disagree with their policy positions as engaging in a war against Christians and promoting their persecution in their fight for religious exemptions from gay marriage laws and other measures they consider immoral.[7]

Tim Alberta's *The Kingdom, the Power, and the Glory: American Evangelicals in an Age of Extremism* explored how President Trump capitalized on conservative trepidation that there existed a war on Christians by the Democratic Party. During his 2016 campaign, he promised that when he won, "Christianity will have power." During the 2020 effort, he warned that his opponent Joe Biden would "hurt God" and target Christians for their beliefs. Embracing dark rhetorical and violent conspiracy theories, the president seized upon notions of an American apocalypse, enlisting evangelicals to help frame a cosmic spiritual clash between the God-fearing Republicans who supported Trump and the secular leftists who opposed the 45th president. Their goal was the overthrow of the country's Christian ethics.[8] Once elected in 2024, he established a two-year task force to study and eradicate the anti-Christian bias of the Biden administration. When he spoke at the 2025 National Prayer Breakfast, he stated, "The opposing side, they oppose religion, they oppose God." Ryan Bangert, of the *Alliance Defending Freedom*, applauded the creation of the task force as being long overdue, as he castigated the Biden administration for "deliberately targeting Christian beliefs through discriminatory policies." The U.S. Conference of Catholic Bishops echoed his endorsement of the task force and spokesperson Chieko Noguchi commented, "We are hopeful in hearing the news that the Administration is seeking to address anti-Christian bias and incidents, and we stand ready to offer our own insights into how we might ensure that all people are able to fully exercise their religious freedom."[9]

Franklin Graham claimed in 2018 that Christians were faced with global persecution, and particularly in the United States. For him, Trump was the only politician defending Christians and the Christian faith.

> The world is attacking Christians because they hate the name of Christ. And President Trump has been defending Christians. I find this refreshing to have a president who's not afraid to say Jesus, he's not afraid to have prayers where people end in the name of Jesus. We've never had

> this, not in my lifetime, and he defends the Christian faith more than any president in my lifetime.[10]

President Trump formed a federal task force to investigate and combat the "persecution against Christians in America."

Jason Whitlock created a new category, Christianityphobia, as he accused the media of conspiring against Christians. He expounded upon his belief that to maintain a Christian identity puts one's reputation and safety at risk. "I've poured a lot of energy into establishing my identity as Christian. . . . Why isn't my self-professed identity worthy of protection and respect? Is corporate media Christianityphobic?"[11] Candace Owens did a series on interviews pushing back on charges that Christian Nationalism was a danger to the country. She argued that threats from crime and other issues are doing more damage to the nation. She charged that it was an attempt on the part of the left to weaponize the term. "Now, I'm sure when you consider the myriad of issues facing our country today, what you're really concerned about is that there might be some Christians who are also in love with our country. They are Christian nationalists. When you see drug dealers, illegal immigrants, crime rates, gang violence, I'm sure you're thinking, it's the Christians we should be afraid of."[12]

One of the earliest manifestations of this fear was the "War on Christmas." Early in the 21st century Fox news anchors complained about Christian persecution in the media and wider American society. The charge was that each December stores greeted customers with "Happy Holidays," rather than the more appropriate greeting, "Merry Christmas." It is regarded as an affront and threat to the sanctity of Christmas. There is some validity to the decrease in religious connection to Christmas, but no rational person would say that a change in greetings is the cause. A 2017 Pew Research study revealed that Christmas was celebrated to a lesser degree as a religious holiday in public and in private as belief in the spiritual aspects of the season has waned. In 2013, 59% of Americans participated in religiously orientated Christmas celebrations. By 2017, only 55% celebrated it with any religious thought. Few Americans think that religious displays, such as Nativity scenes, should be allowed on government property. According to Pew, "A growing share of Americans say it does not matter to them how they are greeted in stores and businesses during the holiday season—whether with 'merry Christmas' or a less-religious greeting like 'happy holidays.'"[13]

Counter Viewpoints

Paul Miller, in an article for *Christianity Today,* described Christian Nationalist supporters as living in a world of fear that they are threatened by cultural foes who want to destroy their way of life and usher in secular humanism. Their only recourse is to fight back, literally.[14]" Minister Matthew Trewhella wrote in his 2013 book, *The Doctrine of the Lesser Magistrates*, that people of faith have divine justification to fight against political oppression. He stressed that "government officials have a divine 'right and duty' to defy any laws, policies or court opinions that violate 'the law of God.'" Godfearing men have the right to push for making illegal abortion and prohibiting same-sex marriage. If it comes to it, violence can be used to enforce the laws of God even if it means violently overthrowing the government. There are times when men "must redden their swords." All this from a man who claims to be a minister of Christ Jesus.[15]

Matthew Taylor, the Institute for Islamic, Christian, and Jewish Studies (Baltimore), expressed concern over the creation of the task force and the contention that Christian persecution is widespread in the U.S. His 2024 book, *The Violent Take It By Force: The Christian Movement That Is Threatening Our Democracy*, cautioned that rarely is the majority religious community persecuted by the minority. On the contrary, he warns that it can lead to minority persecution. "It's a bit absurd to claim that there is widespread anti-Christian bias. When a majority begins to claim persecution, that is often a license for attacks on minorities."[16]

20

Christian Nationalism and Islamophobia

"Teacher," said John, "we saw someone driving out demons in your name and we told him to stop, because he was not one of us."

"Do not stop him," Jesus said. "For no one who does a miracle in my name can in the next moment say anything bad about me, for whoever is not against us is for us. Truly I tell you, anyone who gives you a cup of water in my name because you belong to the Messiah will certainly not lose their reward."

Mark 9:38-41 NIV

Jesus called twelve disciples as his followers. Their response was to assume a sense of privilege and desired to exclude outsiders from a sense of intimacy with Jesus. They even argued with one another on who was the greatest of their number. Christian Nationalists have an insidious fear of outsiders, especially from the Islamic community. There has been a historically elevated level of tension between Christians and Muslims since the days of the Crusades. Christians have been the aggressors, projecting that Islam was a threat to the

Christian faith. September 11 renewed the animosity as Christians described this as an attack on Christianity and a sign of the apocalypse. Christian Nationalists have been extremely vocal in their attacks on the faith.

Commenting on the Scripture passage above from Mark, Lamar Williamson notes:

> The point at issue is whether or not to welcome a charismatic prophet who calls on the name of Jesus but does not belong to the apostolic group. . . . The problem as presented here is not that the man was not following Jesus, but that he was not following the Twelve. . . . Jesus' answer is categorical: 'Do not forbid him.'. . . [I]ntroduced by a solemn 'Amen, I say to you,' pronounces a blessing on all who give physical aid and comfort, as a cup of water, to a traveling evangelist or any needy person who belongs to Christ. The giving and receiving which characterizes disciples is not to be limited to some in-group, but should be common to all who bear the name of Jesus Christ.[1]

Islamophobia

In the aftermath of 911, American hostility toward Islam increased dramatically. The first half of the second decade of the 21st century saw a rise in the number of attacks directed at people of the Islamic faith. Hussam Ayloush, executive director of the Council on American-Islamic Relations, commented,

> Twenty-one years after the attacks, Muslims continue to face the threat of targeted violence. . . . [9/11 presented] a perfect storm of the American people and its government needing a common enemy. . . . The unfortunate reality is there are people and organizations that benefit from perpetuating Islamophobia, bigotry, and war.[2]

Muslims have been stereotyped as terrorists and profiled as the enemies of America within. The fact is that they have been very loyal to the United States and law enforcement. Gallup reports that they have been the eyes and ears on the ground and provide the greatest percentage of tips in the prevention of two out of every five threats from al Qaeda. Despite their attempts to live peaceably, a large percentage of Muslims, in the United States and abroad, report that they do not feel respected in Western societies. Fifty-two percent of American and 48 percent of Canadian respondents believe that the West is hostile to members of the Islamic community. Though in smaller percentages, citizens from Italy, France, Germany, and Britain agree. The reasons listed are politics, religion, and culture; but the prime reasons for conflict between Islamic and Western societies are either cultural or religious, or both. In the United States there is both prejudice and discrimination broadly spread by misinformation against the Islamic community.

Religious hatred in the United States echoes much of the world, ever-present but being challenged as unacceptable. It becomes even more difficult to evaluate as there is often a racial component to the acts of intolerance. Islamophobia certainly falls under this complication, as both race and religion often are intertwined in the hateful reactions experienced. Erik Love, in his book *Islamophobia and Racism in America,* argued that America has a long history of refusing to acknowledge the presence of racism, especially in many of its variant forms. American aversion to acknowledging anything that damages its international image has caused a short circuit in its transparency on its faults and sins. He writes,

> Islamophobia, frankly, is a popular form of racism. . . Racism affects those who fit the racial profile of Middle Eastern, yet there is scant recognition that Islamophobia is racism. This is the racial paradox at the core of Islamopho-

> bia in America. . . . (T)he refusal to see racism is a recurrent trend in American history.[3]

Baptist minister and professor at Wake Forest University, Charles Kimball, wrote of the damage done by American Christians who spurted hateful rhetoric about Islam. He pinpointed the remarks on *60 Minutes* by minister Jerry Falwell who said that "Muhammad was a terrorist." Earlier Falwell equated the destruction of the twin towers in New York City as the result of God's anger at the United States for a growing secularization. Kimball warned that comments made in the U.S. had negative, and often violent, consequences around the world.

> These kinds of verbal assaults on Islam and the prophet of Islam do far more damage than most Americans realize. They feed extremism among Muslims who want to frame conflict as being between Christians and Muslims. Such hateful statements literally put Christian missionaries and humanitarian aid workers at risk all over the world. Pompous proclamations undermine or destroy efforts many Christians and other people of goodwill make to build bridges of understanding and cooperation, often in the midst of very difficult circumstances. . . . In the process, negative stereotypes about Christians and Christianity are reinforced precisely at a time when we must all be working toward better understanding and cooperation in our increasingly fragile and interdependent world community.[4]

The Center for American Progress produced a report, "Fear, Inc," that determined that the spreading of untruths about Muslims led to feelings of prejudice around the country. Surveys found that almost half of Mormon, Protestant, Catholic, Muslim (60%), and Jewish (66%) persons responded that they believed that most Americans were prejudiced toward Muslims and Islam. Muslims (48%) who reported acts of overt discrimination directed toward them fall in line with the percentages of Hispanics (48%) and African Americans (45%) giving similar sentiments. Those who expressed a greater likelihood of prejudice toward Muslims were more than likely to have knowledge about Islam. Americans who stated that they are not bothered by Muslims still report a negative image of Islam. Knowing someone who is Muslim reduces overall prejudice, although in smaller percentages.[5] In May 2022, the Council on American-Islamic Relations (CAIR) reported that between 2020 and 2022 there was a 9 percent increase in the number of attacks aimed at U.S. Muslims. The 6,720 complaints ranged from a variety of issues: "immigration and travel, discrimination, law enforcement and government overreach, hate and bias incidents, incarceree rights, school incidents, and anti-BDS/free speech."[6]

Hinduphobia and Sikh Phobia

Hindus and Sikhs face much of the same xenophobic threats and violence. *The Washington Post* reported that Hinduphobia was a growing menace occurring more and more often in the United States. The year 2022 saw growing incidents of violence and confrontation incidents targeting Indian Americans and Hindu temples. The FBI registered 110 anti-Muslim incidents, 89 anti-Sikh conflicts, and 11 offensive actions they listed under "anti-Hindu bias." Rutgers University's Network Contagion Lab did a 2022 study that confirmed that hateful attacks against the Hindu community occurred and were increasing. Racist slurs were directed at members of the community, including being "dirty." There were similarities to those targeting the Jewish community only through the use of memes portraying tilaks, swastikas, and bindis as representative of Hindu culture.[7]

On March 15, 2022, the General Assembly of the United Nations passed a resolution proclaiming the "International Day to Combat Islamophobia (IDCI)." The U.S. House of

Representatives passed H.R. 5665 to combat Islamophobia across the globe. Senator Corey Booker reflected, "We've witnessed in recent years an alarming rise in Islamophobia both in the United States and globally that has threatened the religious freedom, well-being, and lives of Muslims."[8] At both the UN and the Capitol, members of the Hindu community raised objections that members of the Abrahamic religions were not the only groups to be persecuted. The first section of the third decade saw a rise in the number of violent attacks directed at members of the Hindu faith. In the fall of 2022, a number of Hindu temples and persons were physically defaced or harmed. Krishnan Iyer was confronted at a Taco Bell, called a "dirty Hindu" and "ugly Hindu," and spat at. In Plano, Texas, a similar incident occurred. A statue of former Prime Minister of India, Indira Gandhi, was toppled over, on two occasions, in front of a temple located in Queens, New York. It is felt that much of the disdain originated in India and spread to the U.S. by way of the Internet. There is little publicity on the acts of hostility across the country, and the term Hinduphobia is seldom used. There is rising sympathy and acknowledgment to the rise in violence perpetrated toward the Hindu community. In April 2021, a former FedEx employee targeted and murdered four Sikh Americans in Indianapolis, Indiana.

Hindus have a history of welcoming and inviting into their community people who are persecuted from everywhere in the world: Syrian Christians, Jews, the Parsis, and Tibetans. Yet, despite their having an open door to others, they have not found a similar welcome from others. In 2016, Francois Gautier, writing for the *Times of India*, noted:

> Hindus have been the most persecuted people in the world, they have been invaded, raped, enslaved, converted by force, killed, their temples razed and colonised by many nations, from Alexander the Great to the Moghols and every European nation took its pound of gold and flesh.

> It has been calculated that 100 million Hindus died at the hands of Muslim invaders, from the Hindu Kush to Mumbai 2008, without a doubt, the greatest holocaust of humanity.[9]

Christina Jimenez, in *United We Dream*, submitted strategies on how to combat Islamophobia and discrimination against people of the Islamic faith. Organizing must begin in local communities against efforts to divide people against one another based on religion or race. Movements developed must be along intersectional lines across diverse communities. "We must strategize together because our futures are intertwined. Black, white, Muslim, immigrant, LGBTQ, AAPI communities—all people must build a multiracial movement of love to confront the hateful headwinds we are expecting in the years to come. Now is the time for white people, people of color, and people of conscience to link arms with Muslims and undocumented people to build a protective network of love between these communities."[10]

21

Christian Nationalism and Christian Zionism

Then I saw an angel coming down from heaven, holding in his hand the key to the bottomless pit and a great chain. And he seized the dragon, that ancient serpent, who is the Devil and Satan, and bound him for a thousand years, and threw him into the pit, and shut it and sealed it over him, that he should deceive the nations no more, till the thousand years were ended. After that he must be loosed for a little while. . . .

I saw the souls of those who had been beheaded for their testimony to Jesus and for the word of God, and those who had not worshiped the beast or its image and had not received its mark on their foreheads or their hands. They came to life, and reigned with Christ a thousand years. The rest of the dead did not come to life until the thousand years were ended. This is the first resurrection. . . . [T]hey shall be priests of God and of Christ, and they will reign with him a thousand years.

Revelation 20:1-6 RSV

Christian Nationalists have always held a sense that God was directing their nation. Therefore, they have been watchful for evidence of prophecy being fulfilled. Christian groups zealously watch for signs of the Second Coming of Jesus. They adopt similar yet differing doctrines of belief systems about the final days. Most focus upon the books of Daniel, Ezekiel, and Revelation and their revelations about God's plan for the end of existence. The Seventh Day Adventists (William Miller) and Jehovah's Witnesses (Charles Taze Russell) were founded in attempts to decipher Christ's Second Coming. Regardless of the fact that Jesus warned against doing so.

Rev. Dr. Brian K. Blount, in *Revelation*, wrote of three methods of analyzing the apocalypse. Fundamentalists read the text literally. For one thousand years, Christ and the church will govern before the end of time at his Second Coming. Spiritualists maintain a spiritual vantage point. Jesus will return, and one thousand years will pass before the final judgment. There are two resurrections, a spiritual one at baptism and a final one in bodily form. A political viewpoint paints the millennial as paradise for the faithful actively engaged in the struggle for justice regardless of the form oppression might take. For one thousand years there will be a reign of Christ for all the church where the present reality is transformed. "Millennial, then, 'is not about the end of the world, but about a reign of God that ends the idolatry and criminality of empires in this world.' It is not a passive utopia. It depends upon the witnessing activity of those who believe in it. It also cannot be spiritualized. It takes place in history. It gives direction to present history, guides human action, and marshals human witness."[1]

One of the major issues Christian Nationalists face in attempting to predict or bring about an eschatological event is largely ignored. The effort to bring about or otherwise affect the Second Coming contradicts the teachings of Jesus. Those who ascertain biblical literacy ignore the passages that contradict their desire to control God and God's mission of salvation. Our actions will only make things worse and impact the most vulnerable in horrific ways. Wars in the Middle East and the Israeli extermination of the Palestinian people will not force Jesus to return. And if it does, the response probably won't be that which is hoped for. He predicted that many who will call upon him in those days he will fail to recognize if our actions are not those of God.

Christian Zionism

Christians in general have an emotional connection with Israel due to it being the birthplace of Jesus and the spiritual homeland of Christianity. Christians of every denomination (Evangelicals, Protestants, Pentecostals, charismatics, and Holiness) have sought to discern evidence of biblical prophesies that predict Armageddon and the eschaton (last days).[2]

Public Religion Research Institute (PRRI) determined that "Christian nationalists are also more likely than other Americans to see political struggles through the apocalyptic lens of revolution and violence."[3] A TIME/CNN poll revealed that Americans are were generally more aware of biblical predictions about the end of the world and signs of its appearance in the wake of the September 11 attacks. Guided by a combination of faith, fear, and apocalyptic visions, 59% were looking for the fulfillment of the book of Revelation. Almost 25% associate the September 11 destruction of the World Trade Center to be similarly predicted.[4]

Based on biblical predictions, the Middle East has been identified as the central location where God's action will take place. The state of Israel will play the prominent role in the end of the world. Christian Zionists have identified the state of Israel as the key location. The word *Zionism* is derived from "Zion," the name of a mountain in the Bible that represented the city of Jerusalem and the Promised Land. The Zionism movement started at the end of the 19th century. Theodor Herzl, an Austro-Hungarian journalist, is considered the father of modern Zionism. He articulated a vision for the creation of a Jewish nation to deter global anti-Semitism and violence against the Jewish people. He was convinced that unless the Jewish people had their own homeland, they would always be faced with rejection in whatever country they presided. He wrote, *Der Judenstaat* (The Jewish State) in 1896 as a call for the right of Jewish self-determination by the establishment of a Jewish state. The First Zionist Congress occurred in Basel, Switzerland, in 1897 and led to the establishment of the World Zionist Organization (WZO). Its stated goal was the creation of a Jewish homeland in Palestine.[5]

The move toward full-throated endorsement of Christian Zionism is a fairly recent development. Prior to the 1970s, it was the liberal establishment that offered unlimited support for the state of Israel. Evangelicals opposed political activism in favor of the evangelical mission to spread the gospel. It was spiritually over activism. As the 1960s progressed, so did the advance of the Christian Right and their war on secularization. The 1967 war communicated a message that Israel's victory signified Christ's Second Coming as dictated in the book of Revelation. Jerry Falwell told the world that the win only occurred due to "the intervention of God Almighty." It was an eschatological sign of the last days that prompted the development of Christian Zionism with strong regional support in the American South. By the end of the century, evangelicals reversed their lukewarm embrace of Israel, and the security of the Jewish state became paramount. Support grew within the ranks of the Republican Party concurrently.

Several influential books promoted apocalyptic theories from the shadows. Hal Lindsey's *The Late Great Planet Earth* is one of the most prominent. Pivotal to all doctrines of the end times has been the highly anticipated return of the Jewish people to Palestine as their ancestral homeland. Despite the political justifications after the end of World War II and the attempted genocide of the Jews by the German state, the creation of the state of Israel has been interpreted through a religious lens, as prophecy fulfilled. In 1998, John Hagee, an unrepentant dispensationalist, wrote: "We are racing toward the end of the time, and Israel lies in the eye of the story. . . . Israel is the only nation created by a sovereign act of God, and He has sworn by His holiness to defend Jerusalem, His Holy City. If God created and defends Israel, those nations that fight against it, fight against God."[6] The *Left Behind* book series by Tim F. LaHaye and Jerry B. Jenkins pointed to apocalyptic predictions based on the Matthew 24:36-37 response by Jesus to the disciples' question: *"What will be the sign of your coming and the close of the age?"* (Matthew 24:3). Despite Jesus's determination to refuse to provide any definite answers to the exact moment of his Second Coming, interpreters have nevertheless persisted to provide clues. The series used narrative fiction to detail the biblical rapture through unfolding events when suddenly, miraculously, half of the world's population consisting of Christian believers and children under the age of 12 disappear. Those left on the earth are to fight against the Antichrist throughout the ten books.

Time magazine did a cover story in 2002, "Apocalypse Now." It focused on the importance of Jerusalem to Jews, Muslims, and Christians. The article summarized the evidence upheld by Christian Nationalists, as well as Christian Zionists, to link biblical predictions with events from the present as proof of their beliefs.

> [T]he subsequent return of the Jews to Israel after 2,000 years and the capture of Jerusalem's Old City by the Israelis in 1967, were taken by devout Christians and Jews alike as evidence of God's handiwork. Israel once again controlled the Temple Mount, a site so holy to Islam and Christianity as well as Judaism that Israeli Prime Minister

> Ariel Sharon's simple act of visiting the mount was sufficient to ignite the current Palestinian uprising. The Temple Mount is the location of al-Aqsa Mosque, one of the holiest sites in Islam, and is also the very place where Christians and Jews believe a new temple must one day be rebuilt before the Messiah can come.[7]

During a 2024 House hearing on religious extremism, a series of texts went between committee members, Rev. Rick Allen (R-GA) and Mark Meadows. Content focused on the January 6 insurrection and a call for boldness and determined resolve to overcome forces of darkness threatening the nation. They would be victorious because God was on their side. Allen texted, "Tell the President to hang in there, so many are praying for God's revelation and a miracle! . . . Our Nation is at war, it is a Spiritual War at the highest level. . . . This is not a war that can be fought conventionally, this is God's battle and He has used President Trump in a powerful way to expose the deceit, lies and hypocrisy of the enemy." Both contended that it was God's will for Trump to emerge victorious. Allen continued, "This is his opportunity to confess that he can no longer fight this battle alone, he must give it to Christ, . . . and Gid (sic) almighty will show him the way to victory." Meadows responded, "God bless you." It was apparent that there was agreement that Christians were confronted with evil principalities and must win the "spiritual battle" against Democrats challenging Trump. Only Trump, as God's appointed warrior, could prevent defeat.[8]

Mike Huckabee was appointed by Trump to be the ambassador to Israel in 2025. He has a long history of placing priority upon the primacy of Israel being the sole inheritor of the Holy Land. Jews are God's chosen people and modern-day situations are inherited according to an Old Testament vantage point. To the point of denying that there is any "such thing as a Palestinian." His foreign policy positions are biased based on his reading of biblical prophecies highlighting Israel as being pivotal to God's plan for end-times conquest. His motive is not peace and security in the Middle East nor Israeli continued existence, rather to usher in the Second Coming of Jesus through Armageddon. His Christian Zionist hope is that the Jewish people will ultimately convert to Christianity. Former U.S. ambassador Luis Moreno, after having visited the Holy Land with Huckabee, criticized Huckabee's selection as ambassador: "I unfortunately was exposed to him during his visits to Israel back in the day. Full blown (and knowledgeable) fanatic of the End of Times, Apocalypse, Israel's destruction, etc. A true and utter nut case. Couldn't be a more dangerous selection."[9]

Apocalyptic Ideologies

Americans are enamored with the idea that their country is the global defender of democracy and the rights of the poor and helpless. They have always had an eye on the Middle East searching for signs of the return of Christ and the end times. Various ideologies that explain how, when, and why God will bring about a new era of existence beyond the present reality have been put forth over the centuries. Theories about the last days and how it will occur revolve around the use of the word *"millennial."* It is related to the Latin word, *chiliasm*, or *chiliastic*, meaning "thousand." It is in reference to a tightly held belief that Jesus will fulfill his promise to return during the lives of his first disciples. Since the first century, followers have been anxiously awaiting his prophesy to be fulfilled.[10] According to author Jeffrey B. Webb, "[Millennialistic] belief complicates efforts to find a negotiated settlement between Israelis and Palestinians: Many evangelical Christians have a highly particular notion of what Jewish control of this land (the Holy Land) will mean for the future; for them, it is a signal of the imminent Second Coming of Jesus Christ."[11]

Premillennialism reveals that Jesus will return before the 1,000 years of peace and prosperity. A false messiah, the Antichrist, will mislead people into following him, or her. As a result, a politician, the Beast, will become head of an effort to unify all of the nations of the world under one government. Common references are to the United Nations, the World Council of Churches, and even the Pope. For seven years, known as the Tribulation, there will be death and destruction as sickness, plague, famine, and other natural and human catastrophes ravage the world and annihilate one-third of the earth's population. It is then that Christ will return and as a first step, will rescue Christians by removing them from the earth into heaven. He will then restore order by defeating the Antichrist and the Beast during the Battle of Armageddon. The Middle East is of vital importance as the location where the conquest will occur. Premillennialists see the signs of this occurring with the creation of the state of Israel and is partially responsible for the tremendous level of support for Israel by evangelists and conservative Christians. Only a literal interpretation of Scripture is acceptable. Evidence is found in the biblical prediction that Jesus will return after 1,000 years of global peace. Gayraud Wilmore pinpointed that is a highly pessimistic apocalyptic prediction that calls for the fulfillment of biblical prophecies. But they can only be ushered in by the return of Christ descending from heaven to rule Jerusalem. The first resurrection happens during "the Rapture," as all true believers are granted eternal life as trumpets blow in a new heaven and a new earth. He lists several categories: Pretribulation or Rapture premillennialists stress that Christ will remove his church prior to pretribulation. Post-tribulationists deny that Christians will be safe from the devastations of the Rapture but will encounter the risen Lord in the midst of the chaos. Then will come the thousand years of peace and the ensuing battle with the devil, who, upon losing, will endure eternal suffering.[12]

Believers in Postmillennialism stress that after 1,000 years of justice and righteousness being established on the earth there will be the Second Coming of Christ. He will bring about the resurrection of the dead and sentence humanity to either heaven or hell. A secondary factor is the conversion of the Jew people to Christianity. Daniel Whitby (1638-1726) predicted that for Christ to return Christians would have to take the initiative to establish the kingdom of God here on earth by resolving the pains and suffering of the masses. Only once there is a peace on earth will Jesus return. There is a conflicting doctrine that reverses the order of events.[13] For postmillennialists, the period could be one thousand years, or it could occur sooner. Regardless of when, Christ will return. Until then, the mission of the church is that of the *Great Commission* to preach the gospel to the ends of the earth (Matthew 28).[14]

Related to millennialism is the doctrine of Dispensationalism. History is divided into seven dispensations with a different response from God toward each one. It starts with the Jewish people who have not been faithful to the covenant they received from God. It culminates with a seventh dispensation that belongs to the Christian church and is ongoing. "It offers the hope that all true Christians, 'the spiritual people' will be 'raptured' and meet Christ in the air before the tribulations begin." For Dispensationalists, the establishment of Jewish Settlements on the West Bank in either Judea or Samaria in conjunction with the rebuilding of Solomon's Temple exiling Muslims who also hold it to be a holy place, is one of the first steps.[15] Wilmore understands dispensationalism as God's judgment of creation occurring in a highly organized fashion. Each period in time is judged either with favor or dissatisfaction that is neither random nor without divine intention. God dispenses justice in a systematic manner. Most adherents interpret the Bible through a literal lens, holding on to each word literally. Cyrus I. Scofield (1843-1921), the editor of the famous Scofield Reference Bible, promoted seven dispensations or periodic covenants between God and his creation: Innocence; Conscience; Human Government; Promise; Law; Grace; The Kingdom of Heaven. Yet, there is disagreement about the correct interpretation of the symbolic narrative of the end times. Theories propound differences in the number of end periods and the timetable of events. Some advocate for a literal interpretation while holdouts call for a spiritual reading. Wilmore warns of the culpability of those who teach end-of-the-world theologies to their followers. Imposters have misled followers and exploited their fears. Many have had their bank accounts emptied, possessions acquired, or been manipulated to satisfy sexual fantasies. The innocent have been subjected to abuses and even death.[16]

Anti-Semitism and Anti-Zionism

The charge of anti-Semitism must be taken seriously due to the violence faced by the Jewish community. Anti-Semitic language and violence have escalated in the United States. The dangers faced by Jews around the world are not based on paranoia; it is real. The Jewish community in the United States is under the threat of attack each and every day. Synagogues are targeted for mass shootings and buildings are defaced. The Tree of Life Synagogue shooting reveals the hostility from a small but dangerous element of American society that is a continuous threat to the Jewish community. The actions of billionaire Elon Musk to allow banned actors such as Donald Trump and Kayne West (Ye) back on the X (formerly Twitter) platform raised concerns that his ownership would increase hate. West got booted off when he tweeted "Death Con 3 on Jewish People." His account of 32 million followers increased after the tweet. Musk reinstated Andrew Anglin from a ten-year ban wherein he had admitted that the best way to recruit neo-Nazis was to attack the Jewish community. He attempted to unite followers under the banner of anti-Semitism, saying,

"All enemies should be combined into one enemy, which is the Jews."[17]

In August of 2017, white supremacists marched in the streets of Charlottesville, Virginia, after coalescing in a Unite the Right rally to prevent the removal of a Robert E. Lee statue being threatened with removal. During the night, many marched holding flaming torches while shouting, "Jews will not replace us." Tragically, a young life was ended when someone drove a car into a crowd and killed Heather D. Heyer, a 32-year-old paralegal marching for racial tolerance. Thirty-five counter protesters were injured as the car plowed into unaware marchers. Brandeis University interviewed Jewish historian Deborah Lipstadt who explained that the Charlottesville chant expressed centuries-old fears that Jews, in league with peoples of color, are engaged in a nefarious plot to destroy the white Christian civilization, the "great replacement" or "white genocide." She stated, "In its simplest and most straightforward interpretation, that chant can be understood to say Jews will not replace 'us,' i.e., white Christians in our job or our dominant place in society."[18] The killer in the Pittsburg synagogue posted that Jews were "bringing in invaders to kill our people."[19]

Second gentleman Doug Emhoff hosted a roundtable in December of 2022 with members from the Reform, Conservative, and Orthodox denominations. He opened the conversation by warning, "We're seeing a rapid rise in antisemitic rhetoric and acts. . . . Let me be clear: words matter. People are no longer saying the quiet parts out loud—they are literally screaming them." Susan Rice remarked, "There's nothing more vicious than what we are seeing today, out of the mouths of our leaders, our public figures, our celebrities, our elected officials. . . . (The US has to) do battle here with equal vigor and passion against it."[20]

The Anti-Defamation League reported that anti-Semitic attacks were up 34 percent as 2,717 incidents of assaults and vandalism occurred.[21] The U.S. Department of State outlined a difference between anti-Semitism and legitimate criticism of the state of Israel. "Antisemitism is a certain perception of Jews, which may be expressed as hatred toward Jews. Rhetorical and physical manifestations of antisemitism are directed toward Jewish or non-Jewish individuals and/or their property, toward Jewish community institutions and religious facilities. . . , targeting the state of Israel, conceived as a Jewish collectivity. However, criticism of Israel similar to that leveled against any other country cannot be regarded as antisemitic."[22] In 2022 the Department of Homeland Security issued a dire warning that domestic terrorist groups were utilizing the Internet to encourage attacks on the Jewish community and surmised a connection between online anti-Semitism and offline violence. Juliette Kayyem commented to *The Washington Post*, "The idea that there is a difference between online chatter and real-word harm is disabused by a decade of research." Former Representative Denver Riggleman said, "This type of escalation and hate and dehumanization, the hatred of the Jewish population—it's a really directed target. Violence is inevitable."[455]

The magazine *Sojourners* reported in 2003 on a letter signed by 43 leaders in the evangelical church contesting universal support by evangelicals for Israel. Ron Sider (Evangelicals for Social Action), Serge Duss (World Vision), and Don Wagner (Center for Middle East Studies) stated that evangelicals are discerning actions that are biblically and ethically correct when done by the state of Israel.[456] In that same edition, Jewish student Josh Healey criticized the efforts of some to label any criticism of the Jewish state as anti-Semitism and called for honest examination of the occupation of the Palestinian people. "Criticism of Israel is not inherently anti-Semitic. . . . Some have argued that although criticism of Israel may not be anti-Semitic in its intention, it is so in practice. . . . The only way for there to be a meaningful peace in the Middle East is for Israel to face repercussions for its human rights violations."[23]

No one must allow their right to protest the violence of Israel to be smothered by a desire not to be painted as an anti-Semite. The public needs to be active and vocal in defending the rights of Palestinians to a life free from oppression. Far too often, criticism of the state of Israel is greeted by the unfair charge of anti-Semitism. The United States is unequivocal in its support of the state of Israel. Presidential administrations rarely vote out of step with the interests of Israel and in the United Nations vetoes any positions that criticize or promotes sanctions against the Jewish state. The support is also high amongst American citizens as support for the nation is without relation. Whenever there is criticism of the actions of Israel in relation to the Palestinians there is the charge of anti-Semitism. One can criticize the actions of the state of Israel and support the Jewish community at the same time. Investigation into the lives of Palestinians reveals immense suffering, containment by the state of Israel, repressive policies and laws, and continual loss of land to unlawful settlements.

American Christians are in an emotional struggle with their feelings about Jewish people and their perceptions of the state of Israel. How does one stand with the Jewish community to ensure that violence is not a threat to individual lives, synagogues, or the community, while at the same time, be vigilant to rally behind an oppressed Palestinian people fighting for basic human rights? It is important to separate the two issues, criticism of Israel and acts of anti-Semitism. One must not conflate the two. When defending Palestinian rights, we must not hold the actions of a nation as the actions of every Jewish person. Don't assume that every Jewish person supports or defends the actions of the state of Israel. Many of the college protesters on campuses were of the Jewish faith. Jews calling for a ceasefire held rallies in the nation's capital. Don't direct your anger at the Jewish people. NBC News reported on a tweet by a Palestinian against anti-Semitism, "Our struggle is for justice, liberty, and life and it can't be tainted by hatred."

The article concluded, "Far from (being) offensive, criticizing the Israeli government should be viewed as an act of love that could help make everyone more safe and more free. The freedom and safety of Jewish Israelis and the freedom and safety of Christian and Muslim Palestinians are not mutually exclusive—in fact, they are secured through co-existence."[24]

22

Christian Nationalism and Capitalism

"Do not store up for yourselves treasures on earth, where moth and rust consume and where thieves break in and steal, but store up for yourselves treasures in heaven, where neither moth nor rust consumes and where thieves do not break in and steal. For where your treasure is, there your heart will be also. . . . No one can serve two masters, for a slave will either hate the one and love the other or be devoted to the one and despise the other. You cannot serve God and wealth."

Matthew 6:19-21, 24

In the Gospel of Matthew, the writer has a catalog of sermons by the Lord dealing with the ethics of the faith. The Beatitudes are found in Matthew 5 issuing a series of blessings for those spiritually seeking to be in relationship with God. Going forward to Matthew 6, teachings on anger, adultery, divorce, retaliation, love for enemies, and prayer turn our attention to our loyalties, either God or money. Jesus plainly says, "You cannot serve two masters." You will either hate one and love the other, be devoted to one and despise the other. Followers must choose their allegiance carefully and deliberately.

F. F. Bruce, in *Hard Sayings of Jesus,* in an exegesis of Matthew 6 determined that the word *mammon* was a rather common term used by religious teachers in the Jewish community to denote wealth. Jesus adopted its usage, but not necessarily in a positive way, rather to denote its usage in ways not beneficial to the user or community. Especially in consideration of the attitudes of those who sought its accumulation for their individual use. He contrasted the prayers of the poor and the wealthy, and the former prayed with an emotional intensity that the rich man never experienced as his needs were already met. When someone who is impoverished prays, "give us this day our daily bread" (Matthew 6:11), he means in a way that is heartfelt. He wrote, "Since the service of mammon is presented in this saying as an alternative to the service of God, mammon seems to be a rival to God. Service to mammon and service of God are mutually exclusive. The servant of mammon, in other words, is an idol worshipper: mammon, wealth, money has become his idol."[1]

Christianity and Capitalism

Christian Nationalists adore the capitalist system and refuse to criticize capitalism as an ideology. Loyalty to the nation is aligned alongside patriotism and capitalism, both of which are mutually equated as vital components of American democracy. For all Americans, but especially for Christian Nationalists, the mission of 21st-century Christianity has become relegated to the mission of the empire that executed Jesus, as his teachings have become assimilated into the goals of the capitalist system. Capitalism has become so normalized for Christians that there is hardly any critical thought to political conflicts between the two pursuits, either in differing ideological foundations or either's purpose for being. It is deemed to be un-Christian, un-American, and un-Patriotic to offer critical analysis of capitalism's failures. There is scant public criticism of its inability to enhance the lives of those suffering under immense poverty, while tremendous wealth is held in the hands of the few, with no strategies to promote economic equality.

Prosperity theology has special appeal for poor Americans as an avenue for personal and social advancement, security. This theology promotes capitalism. Blacks and Hispanics have been uniquely attracted to its orbit, especially for immigrant communities. It offers a feeling of belonging through a gift-exchange system. The believer gives to God in exchange for a gift, either from God, a fellow church member, or a believer. There are different specificities in the definition: "health and wealth gospel, gospel of success, seed faith gospel, capitalist wealth dogma, gospel of greed, American gospel of pragmatism, individualism, upward mobility, commercialized gospel," and "another form of Pentecostalism." Adherents refer to it as "Word of faith, positive confession, prosperity theology, the law of reciprocity, gospel of greed" and "prosperity." Some teachers maintain that life on earth should be filled with an abundance of good health, financial success, material wealth, and happiness. It is the will of God and the undeniable right of believers who live in obedience to God's commands. The death of Jesus means victory over illness, poverty, and sin. The poor are impoverished due to the poverty of their faith. Those who "name it and claim it" receive the bounty of God through financial blessings. God has a surplus to be granted to those who truly adhere to this theology of wealth. Often tied to faith is a positive confession of faith and the constant payment of financial tithes and offerings.[2]

This radically different message started under the auspices of such men as Kenneth Copeland, and Kenneth Hagin. It teaches that the purpose of faith in Christ is to grant you a financial blessing of money and wealth. It affirms that God's promise for faith is of wealth and health. If you believe and pray in the name of Jesus, you will live a life of good health and prosperity. This is contrary to the teachings of the Bible, especially those of Jesus.

Christian ministers placed their institution in service to capitalism. Christianity was made subservient to industry by fusing the goal of religion with that of monetary profit. This corrupt theology justified the acquisition of wealth in the hands of the few at the expense of the many was ushered into the mainstream by the preaching of mainline clergy. As a result, Elizabeth Bruenig, in *The New Republic*, argued that in the United States, Christianity has been made submissive to the goals of capitalism as leaders justified greed as godly. She described Christianity as "capitalism's most impressive conscription. . . . [I]f the Christian ethos has suffered any great harm from its recruitment in support of capitalism, it has been the tamping down of a uniquely anti-capitalist, revolutionary sentiment in the Gospel." She asserted that American Christianity must free itself from this "oppressive relationship" and must rediscover its foundational grounding. This involves a rediscovery of a "a genuinely revolutionary Christian politics: one that neither seeks to bolster capitalism blatantly nor offer meager patches for its systemic problems."[3]

Corporate and religious leaders conspired with each other in the 1940s for the purpose of eliminating New Deal programs that combated the poverty of the Great Depression. This was a special irony in that Christian ministers served as a teacher who defined poverty as a sin that oppressed God's children. Jesus told the rich young ruler to sell all that he had, give the money to the poor, and come, follow him. The result of the alliance was the emergence of an American capitalist Christianity with Christianity and capitalism being joined at the hip. To proclaim one is to proclaim the other as they share similar social characteristics.[4] James W. Fifield, Jr., made it his personal goal to destroy the gains of the New Deal and prevent its growth as a national policy. His was the primary innovator and stated to the wealthy that capitalism could be preached as a component of Christian truth. The government and its social programs of uplift for the impoverished distorted and diminished both ideologies. These and similar efforts, such as the Social Gospel movement, poised a threat to the well-being of a Christian-capitalist system. He reshaped the conversation about the primary role of government, corporations, religion in society. The tyranny of the Franklin Roosevelt New Deal campaign would be ended as businesses would be free from government regulation and profit limitations. He acted through a network of Protestant pastors and the organization he founded, *Mobilization for Spiritual Ideas*, or *Spiritual Mobilization*. He promoted a Jesus whose teachings did not oppose the goals of business to make a profit. No, Jesus was the best friend business and capitalism had. It was the government that opposed God's way and hampered the goal of profit. The goals of a welfare state stood in direct opposition to the teachings as found in the Bible, especially the eighth of the Ten Commandments. The government, through the New Deal, sought to steal from the wealthy and give to the poor contrary to the way God intended for poverty to be addressed. But in reality, he became the spokesperson for the tycoons who generously plowed money into his ministry. Corporations such as Sun Oil, Chrysler, and General Motors saw him as the perfect pitchman to oppose Roosevelt's programs of uplift for the poor. In return for their financial contributions, he popularized a theology of graft and greed with the intention to generate less regulation and destroy the New Deal. Labor unions were a target and denigrated as a tool of evil.[5]

There followed a constant string of preachers who merged the principles of capitalism with those of American Christianity. By 1954, Oral Roberts formulated a prosperity gospel doctrine, "seed faith theology," that promised a sevenfold return on financial investments in God's "divine economy." More economic in nature than theological, it described a God whose primary desire for believers was material prosperity, which could only be generated through a life of sowing and reaping God's harvest. According to David T. Adamo,

> The law of seed-faith is based on three main principles: (1) Believers should turn their lives completely to God and recognize that God is the source of all their needs and if they bless any one person, they are not the source of the blessing but God. (2) The principle of sowing and reaping: according to him, whatever any believer gives freely to God will be returned to him or her in many folds. (3) The seed of anything, such as compassion, talent, time, love, money and kindness, will be received back from God.[6]

Kenneth Hagin, sickly throughout his childhood, introduced health alongside wealth as a benefit of the Christian faith through his Word of Faith Movement. Alongside the Word of Faith movement, there exists two other Protestant traditions closely associated ideologically with prosperity gospel; they are the Black Spiritual Movement and the Unity School of Christianity.

Multimillionaire capitalists funneled wheelbarrows of money into the ministries of Billy Graham and later Jerry Falwell, clergy who failed to side with the struggles of the poor who existed amid an oppressive economic system that was not receptive to their needs. Graham promoted the salvation of free enterprise equally with preaching the message of the gospel. He argued against any type of government assistance to the poor either domestically or internationally. The poor did not need "more money, food, or even medicine; it is Christ. Give them the Gospel of love and grace first and they will clean themselves up, educate themselves, and better their economic conditions."[7]

Today this spiritual immoralism is evidenced in the "moral therapeutic deism" apparent in the mass-produced ideology of self-help gurus selling models of self-improvement and actualization displayed under faith aspirations. Ministers who cheapened the faith by convincing the wealthy that their success was a blessing from God and due to virtue rather than vice, contrary to biblical teachings. They sell the false promise of prosperity to the poor, but only if they buy into a corrupt theology of wealth and health as the word of God. Leaders of the faith offer no criticism of the corruptions and greed of today's robber barons and applaud the desire for wealth and power by people exploited by heresy and economic idolatry. A quasi-spiritual manifesto that emphasized the accumulation of personal happiness and wealth. Norman Vincent Peale was a controversial "prosperity gospel" preacher and Wayne Allyn Root was a conservative extremist, conspiracy theorist, and self-described "capitalist evangelist." He stated that Jesus was the "CEO of the Christian religion."[8]

During the 1980s Christianity intermarried not only with politics but also industry. Spiritual power became equated with economic and political power and the messages of preachers, industrialists, and politicians became inseparable. One prominent example was a small devotional booklet that invaded the corporate world to teach a connection between faith and increasing one's territory (wealth). *The Prayer of Jabez* (1 Chronicles 4:9-10), is based on only two verses in 1 Chronicles, illustrating that Jabez prayed for God to grant him an increase in his assets. This small booklet makes its rounds in the business community and church Sunday schools. Its promise was that those who prayed this prayer on a daily basis would be astounded by the magnitude of God's blessings being outpoured on their behalf. God has financial blessings waiting to be delivered, but they remain in place if they are not requested. Believers are in control of the divine who cannot act until they do.

The *ReAwaken America* tour, a traveling roadshow featuring self-declared Christian nationalists, brought some 50 speakers into Miami declaring the necessity for a second term for former president Donald Trump. Conservative podcaster Stacy Whited promised supporters an imminent "transference of wealth from the wicked to the righteous" that would make those in the audience rich.

To complicate the results of such a false belief system, Christian entrepreneurs have sought to profit from their faith without any adherence to the gospel message. Businessmen target customers with merchandise containing Christian themes and logos. T-shirts, hats, clothing, and even amusement parks are decorated with Christian themes. For-profit commercial enterprises are marketed as public faith statements hoping to create the illusion that what they are doing is a genuine expression of their faith. It goes beyond sharing the good news of the gospel as profits are rarely tithed to charitable causes.

By the 1940s, there was a concerted effort on the part of American businesses, especially advertising agencies, to promote church attendance as a normal part of American life. Kevin Kruse detailed the history of religion utilized for political purposes to influence public opinion. "Political leaders and religious reformers led the way in fomenting the religious revival of the Eisenhower era, but their counterparts in Hollywood and on Madison Avenue proved to be indispensable allies. Prompted by both patriotism and an eye for profits, entertainers and advertisers did a great deal to promote public expressions of faith in the era. Prominent advertising agencies promoted religious observance as a vital part of American life and religion as an essential marker of the national character. . . . When it came to the role of religion in American life, political culture and popular culture sang from the same hymnal."[9] The 1949 Religion in American Life (RIAL) campaign by the Advertising Council was launched to emphasize the unique and important role that religious institutions played in American life. It stressed the importance of church and synagogue attendance. The campaign lasted for over a decade and was promoted in newspapers, magazines, radio, and television. Its success was attributed to the overt message that religion was a foundational component in American life and the nation's commitment to "human rights and individual liberty, as suggested in our national motto, 'In God We Trust.'" Newspaper editors received scripts with the statement, "democracy is a system of government derived from religious principles." This effort on the surface promoted the value of a religious lifestyle, but its primary intent was the promotion of economic and political interests. Many of the campaign's leaders worked on the Eisenhower presidential campaign and utilized the theme: "Faith in God and Country. That's Eisenhower! How about you?"[10]

At the same time, the nation was about to erupt in a civil rights revolution to destroy the shackles around the necks of African Americans that American religiosity had failed to address or combat. The public that was extremely receptive to mottos uniting Christianity with political themes promoting liberty and justice, did not blink an eye when these same freedoms were denied to people of color. The country was immersed in crass hypocrisy accepting the inferiority of Blacks as a part of God's divine creation. Congregations and their ministers stood on the side of the legality and morality of Jim Crow laws and policies. Racial violence occurred in the same neighborhoods where RIAL's positive imaging billboards stood when Blacks attempted to move in. It is noteworthy that the South has been viewed as the region where religion was of unique importance and impact. The South also was the region where the most barbaric policies and practices occurred. The United States has forever demonstrated a split personality when it came to what its standards were to define what it meant to be a Christian nation. On one hand, it meant keeping Blacks in their rightful place as God intended, as the subordinate servants of whites. On the other hand, it meant glamorizing the wonder of American society as the land where democracy was born as a sign for all men to live free.

This surface religio-economic symbiosis has intensified as it has been accepted as a harmless form of civil religion. But its impact has nulled any critical critique of the orthodox meaning of Christian identity and the answer to the question, "Are Christianity and capitalism compatible?"

Churches of Color and Capitalism

This heretical belief is spreading throughout the country and is experiencing inexplicable growth in the Black church. Since enslaved ancestors originally adopted Christianity, African Americans have maintained the highest percentage of any racial demographic. The promise of liberation from the biblical story of Exodus and the image of a God of deliverance and justice attracted followers. But recently, from Christian Nationalism to prosperity ministry, heretical ideologies have taken root in the African American church, threatening to eliminate its prophetic voice. According to *Dissent* magazine, "After the heyday of the freedom movement passed in the 1970s, two contrasting paths gradually emerged in black churches: one stayed true to the message of social justice while the other turned to an emphasis on individual morality and a gospel of prosperity. Most rising religious leaders took the latter approach."[11] John Blake, *CNN*, wrote, "Forty years after his death, King remains a prophet without honor in the institution that nurtured him, some black preachers and scholars say. They also say King's 'prophetic' model of ministry–one that confronted political and economic institutions of power–has been sidelined by the prosperity gospel."[12]

The prosperity gospel is very appealing to those who have financial difficulties, as the messages are linked to improving one's situation in life simply by expressing faith in Jesus. Church historian Edward Wheeler claimed that Black prophetic pastors rarely fill the pews like other pastors because their message is so challenging and often enrage people because they proclaim God's judgment on powerful nations, especially the United States. "It's dangerous to be prophetic. I don't know many prophetic preachers who are driving big cars and living very comfortably. You don't generally build huge churches by making folks uncomfortable on Sunday morning."[13]

Prosperity pastors have become amongst the most popular preachers in the Black evangelical church. A survey by YouGov revealed that race plays a decisive role in how prosperity preachers are viewed. Blacks were much more likely to state a "very favorable" or "somewhat favorable" perspective than either Hispanic or white evangelicals. Similar expressions associated wealth as a "sign of God's favor: Blacks (34%); Hispanics (24%); and whites (9%)." Blacks (70%) expressed favorable views of T. D. Jakes with lower percentages stated by Hispanics (24%) and whites (10%). Non-Black prosperity preachers were viewed with greater positivity by Blacks. Questions about the impact of prayer on one's wealth revealed that Blacks (42%) connected the two more strongly than Hispanics (25%) or whites (15%). Twenty-five percent of Blacks assumed that it was ok for preachers to acquire wealth through their service to God while only one-in-seven whites believed similarly.[14]

Such preachers have become brands, building megachurches and business empires with the prosperity message. Creflo Dollar has been a leader for decades. In the 1990s, Bishop T. D. Jakes was labeled as "America's Preacher." His "Women Thou Art Loosed" conferences promised release from suffering and promoted prosperity through vulnerability. His sermons, speeches, and books promoted moral and financial uplift utilizing personal faith. He said little about a gospel of justice in line with the teachings of the Bible and Jesus. Bishop Eddie Long, New Birth Missionary Baptist Church, in Atlanta, Georgia, was a prominent proponent. God will deliver tremendous financial blessings if members tithe 10% of their income utilizing Proverbs 3:9-10.[15]

In his 2020 book, *Prosperity Gospel Latinos and Their American Dream*, sociologist and Presbyterian minister Tony Tian-Ren Lin said that the prosperity gospel "shows immigrants how they may thrive in a late-capitalist society." In 2020, the Trump reelection campaign launched "Evangelicals for Trump" with a visit to El Rey Jesus Global, a Latino megachurch in Miami led by pastor Guillermo Maldonado. El Rey is part of the Word of Faith network, a subset of the Pentecostal movement that espouses a form of the prosperity gospel.[16]

Jesus and Capitalism

The problem is that this theology is in direct conflict with the teachings of Jesus. Jesus taught about prosperity, but as a danger to those who seek it as their primary goal. He told the parable of the Rich Old Fool who desired to retire with his wealth and prepared to store his goods in barns to live on in luxury. During the night, God visited him in a dream and told him that his soul was required of him and asked who would acquire his wealth for their use. Jesus also told the parable of the rich man and Lazarus. They both died, and the rich man went directly to hell, and poor Lazarus went to heaven, where he was comforted. Those who endorse prosperity ministries are limited in their use of Scripture, as there are few, if any, references in the Gospels. The teachings of Jesus offer a counter perspective as the elements of faith, love, and sacrifice are at the top of his teachings.

The Christian faith is based upon faith in Jesus Christ as the Son of God who was crucified on a cross and resurrected on the third day. Christians believe that he is the unique Son of God who died for the forgiveness of our sins. Christianity has as its Savior a poor, carpenter's son from a meager village named Bethlehem. Rather than offering justification to the wealthy for selfishness and greed, he criticized religious leaders who were supporters of the status quo, where the social problems of the poor were treated as normal. Professor Elizabeth L. Hinson-Hasty, in her book *The Problem of Wealth*, argues for a reframing of the way wealth inequality is studied, measured, and remedies sought. Often, studies are directed at the impoverished; she maintains that it is the wealthy who need to be studied for solutions to a global problem. The problem is not poverty, but wealth. It must be addressed with a theological lens. A Christian social lens does not condemn wealth, but greed. She doubts whether the accumulation of unlimited wealth by a few benefits the entirety of the global human family. "The early followers of Jesus introduced an alternative social logic and economic reality. Their faith and understanding of their role within the economy rose from a very different set of values. The primitive Christian catechism contains teachings from the Hebrew Bible and the sayings of Jesus concerning the dangers of wealth and the obligation to share. The early followers' understanding was that in times when God's intervention in human history was apparent to them, God repudiated the rich and chose people in poverty as instruments of salvation."[17]

There is an inherent conflict between the nature of capitalism and Christianity. The goal of the former is the pursuit of wealth through the buying and selling of goods, while the latter calls for a life of faith in a sovereign God who provides for every need. One calls for acquisition while the other sacrifice. To label oneself a Christian capitalist is a contradiction in terms. America is flush with signs in store windows indicating a Christian business. Its message is that the proprietor lives by the teachings of Jesus and is faithful, honest, and just. Rather than being governed by the principles of Christianity, often the owner is guided by the rules of free enterprise. Ken Ham founded *Answers in Genesis* to run the entertainment venues *Noah's Ark* and the *Creation Museum* in Northern Kentucky. In 2022, 1.5 million tourists visited the *Noah's Ark Park*. It is marketed as a religious experience to instill "young-earth" theories that humans and dinosaurs existed at the same time 6,000 years ago. Ham described it as a "Christian business" and mandates that employees sign on to a statement of faith and abstain from intercourse, if unmarried, alongside anti-gay and anti-transgender policies. It receives a tax-break and advertises bourbon on its facilities.[18] *True Religion* is a clothing brand that does not appear to have any religious intent other than its name.

Religious freedom is lifted up as the ultimate manifestation of faith rather than service and love. Freedom to practice discrimination toward any who do not fit into a rigid religiosity that defines who is acceptable and who is not, whose lifestyle is worthy of service. This is done despite the fact that the Bible teaches that God is not partial to the rich or the poor and is a God of steadfast, unconditional love.

Theologian Shirley C. Guthrie, the author of *Christian Doctrine,* labels the pursuit of wealth as one's life goal to be idolatry. Anything that becomes a substitute for dependence on God redirects one's attention from the creator to that which is created. Money, personal relationships, professional mobility, should never become priorities in our lives and displace God as our first pursuit. Guthrie pointed to lessons learned from the words of Jesus as to a Christian's attitude toward the possession of wealth. "The teachings of Jesus warn both the wealthy and his Christian followers concerning any capitulation to the accumulation of wealth as one's life goal. He overturned the tables in the temple for the primary reason that business had invaded the house of God for the purpose of profit. Christianity is on the side of the poor and the dispossessed and calls the wealthy to use their wealth for the benefit of those whose lives are burdened by poverty and despair. This still goes for those who seek to follow Jesus in today's world."[19]

Capitalism has assumed the religious significance of Christmas and big business is in charge of Christmas in America.

The biggest threat to the integrity of Christmas is capitalism. Its primary menace is the commercialization that has led to the complete lack of any religious significance. Corporations have hijacked the season and turned it into one big buying and selling frenzy. There is more conversation about "Black Friday" and "Cyber Monday" than Jesus. Pastor Smith-Pollard reflects,

> Big business is the leading force of our nation during Christmas and throughout the year. It's not ethics. It's not faith. It's not morality, and it's not values. Even though we want to believe these things lead us, when it comes to the bottom line, Santa Claus and all things commercially Christmas is a genius business strategy, and that is the leading force.[20]

D. R. McConnell, in *A Different Gospel*, claimed as his brothers in the faith those who founded the prosperity gospel of health and wealth. He rejected their teachings as unchristian and contrary to the teachings of Jesus. "Christianity is not a healing cult, and the gospel is not a metaphysical formula for divine health and wealth." He condemned any teaching that equated the gospel with the promise of wealth as a reward and preachers who chastised members who suffered under illness as lacking adequate faith. Christians are victimized by immoral and guiltless teachers who declare that with adequate faith their financial and biological problems will be solved. With the proper faith, they will never have to worry about having enough money to meet their needs or endure sickness. If you find yourself lacking, it is not because it is the will of God, but you don't truly believe. McConnell concluded, "[T]he most inhumane fact revealed about the [prosperity] faith movement is this: when its members die, they die alone."[21]

Christians should present a challenge to citizens of the richest country in human history with resources that could change the lives of millions to utilize its capacity to do good in the world, and not simply focus on personal achievement. It represents the loss of a spiritual purpose. It matters when the true meaning of Christianity is distorted into conveying a message that is in contradiction to the teachings of its founder. Jesus called followers to live a life of unselfish love where giving is done because we live in a world where millions of children don't have fresh drinking water, enough food to eat, nor a home to live in. And to do it consistently (Luke 6:1-4). Jesus called people to not focus merely upon themselves but to acknowledge the interconnectedness of all of humanity where the last are first and the first are last. Jesus calls not just for charity, but for societal change as believers are called to share messages of joy, love, and peace through actions to enhance the lives of others (Matthew 23:23). He challenges the act of giving presents to the impoverished as a once-a-year act of charity but must be year-round and lifelong. He calls us to go beyond the act of giving a present or two but to correct the systems that deny living wages, healthcare, and equity. It is not a matter just for those of the Christian faith but has greater significance for the world. Whether you are a believer or not, we live in a world of disparity and a focus on sacrificial sharing would help change the world.[22]

23

Christian Nationalism and Militarism

In days to come,
  the mountain of the LORD's house
shall be established as the highest of the mountains
  and shall be raised above the hills;
all the nations shall stream to it.
  Many peoples shall come and say,
"Come, let us go up to the mountain of the LORD,
  to the house of the God of Jacob,
that he may teach us his ways
  and that we may walk in his paths."
For out of Zion shall go forth instruction
  and the word of the LORD from Jerusalem.
He shall judge between the nations
  and shall arbitrate for many peoples;
they shall beat their swords into plowshares
  and their spears into pruning hooks;
nation shall not lift up sword against nation;
  neither shall they learn war anymore.

Isaiah 2:1-4

The prophet Isaiah has a vision from God of a time when people will not result to violence to solve their disagreements. He predicts that there will be a day when war will be eradicated from the face of the earth. Christopher R. Seitz, in *Isaiah 1-39*, described Isaiah's ministry to all the nations for peaceful coexistence and God's intervention.

> A scene of judgment will be enacted, and the God of Jacob will finally settle the divisions between the nations, bringing an end to warfare. . . . On the other side of this judgment, in the latter days, Israel will join the nations to learn again God's ways and to be taught his Torah once more. . . . Isaiah is the prophet with a specific task to nations beyond Israel's borders. . . . Israel and the nations alike stand under a similar rule of universal justice. And as with images of restoration directed at Israel, so too God has a plan and a purpose involving every nation on earth.[1]

This is the challenge for people of faith, to work for the elimination of violent conflict even as the world continues to engage in warfare.

To no one's surprise, Christian Nationalism feeds upon militarism. When one is armed with a religious faith partnered with love and loyalty to nation, it is easy to be an apologist for actions committed in the name of national interest. Support for military actions is quite easy to adopt with a critique of the morality or appropriateness of the actions. Military invasions are seen as justifiable as a battle between the righteous armies of God defeating the demonic forces of evil.

Christian Militarism

The United States had not always been as ready to engage in militarism. It took more than a century to move out of periods of isolationism after the founding and two world wars. Even during Manifest Destiny and colonialism the faith community was not possessed by a spirit of masculinity that defined what it meant to be a Christian and brought with it a strong militarism.

In the United States, there is a high acceptance of violence by the public with 40% of Christian nationalists affirming that patriots might have to resort to violence to save their country. Many of the former are in favor of proliferating the spread of Christianity through Crusade-like holy wars. Many are threatened by the advance of racial, gender, and identity justice and endorse the use of violence to halt its spread. According to Brookings, white supremacists are willing to use violence as a means to delay or prevent progress in American society that improves the lives of people of color. The PRRI/Brookings Christian Nationalism Survey found that 16% of Americans agree with the statement "Because things have gotten so far off track, true American patriots may have to resort to violence in order to save our country."[2]

Previously, the faith community was a voice of opposition to military conquest as a means of expressing patriotism. But by the 1950s, the country was feeling under attack from systemic evils eating away at its core, rendering it feeling impotent. The John Wayne effect replaced a gentle savior with one who was a warrior. Fundamentalists, conservatives, and evangelicals adopted a patriarchal system where the image of a soldier was the Christian prototype. The Japanese attack on Pearl Harbor did something similar to the 9/11 attack six decades later. It brought to the surface a vulnerability that made most Americans uncomfortable and resulted in widespread support for military aggression. The war was framed in a religious dogma as a battle between the forces of good and evil prevalent in premillennialist theology. From Billy Sunday, Billy Graham, and Jerry Falwell, to today's clergy, ministers transformed a gospel of grace to a ministry of war. Billy Graham supported a foreign policy that was militarist as he promoted U.S. aggression as a tool for Christian evangelism. He equated warfare as acceptable to spread the gospel around the world regardless of the cost in human life. His ideology was a merger between the political aspirations of leadership to stop the spread of communism and atheism. Christian militarism was Christian Nationalism.

Christian militarism registers high during times of war and immediately afterward. Abraham Lincoln initially questioned whether God was on the side of either the North or the South. He wrote an 1862 memo, later titled by his secretary, "*Meditation on the Divine Will.*" He acknowledged that opponents feel that their cause is righteous, and that God endorses their position. "In great contests, each party claims to act in accordance with the will of God. Both may be, and one must be wrong. God cannot be for and against the same thing at the same time." He later concluded that God took a position, but not on behalf of the battling armies. God's intervention was not for either the Union or the Confederacy, but on behalf of the enslaved. God brought the conflict into being and would not end it until slavery was destroyed. "I am almost ready to say this is probably true—that God wills this contest, and wills that it shall not end yet—By his mere quiet power, on the minds of the now contestants, He could have either saved or destroyed the Union without a human contest—Yet the contest began—And having begun He could give the final victory to either side any day—Yet the contest proceeds." Holding on to his Emancipation Proclamation until a Union victory at Antietam, he felt compelled to admit that God favored the enslaved: "God had decided this question in favor of the slaves. He was satisfied that it was right, was confirmed and strengthened this action by the vow and the results." Franklin D. Roosevelt wrapped World War II in religious terminology:

> Our enemies are guided by brutal cynicism, by unholy contempt for the human race. We are inspired by a faith that

> goes back through all the years to the first chapter of the Book of Genesis: 'God created man in his own image.' We on our side are striving to be true to that divine heritage. We are fighting, as our fathers have fought, to uphold the doctrine that all men are equal in the sight of God.[3]

Truman viewed the Cold War as essentially a moral conflict. He believed that communism was "a tyranny led by a small group who have abandoned their faith in God. These tyrants have forsaken ethical and moral beliefs."[4] George W. Bush acknowledged a God who chooses between good and evil as he waged war against the "axis of evil." He confirmed that the U.S. was on God's side. "Freedom and fear, justice and cruelty have always been at war. And we know that God is not neutral between them."[5]

After 911, a militant Christianity promoted an angry, wrathful response to the attack on the World Trade Centers. The bulk of the antagonism was directed toward the Muslim community. Franklin Graham labeled Islam as "a very evil and wicked religion." Pat Robertson regularly compared Muslims to the Nazis. James Dobson used his programming to warm Christians that their families were endangered by Islamic fundamentalism. Ted Haggard predicted that unless Christians resisted their children would be nurtured by an Islamic state. By 2002, 77 percent of evangelical leaders registered an unfavorable view of Islam. Seventy percent concurred that Islam was "dedicated to world domination."[6]

During the 2003 Gulf War with Iraq, *Sojourners Magazine* countered with a call for love and justice for all. There must be, they said,

> a shared commitment to confront injustice and stand up for the defenseless. . . . Meanwhile, those resolved to respond first as Christians will continually wonder how to live out Christian love of neighbor. . . . In the lead up to the

> November elections, one secular anti-war group coined the slogan, 'Regime change begins at home—vote!' Christians might better say something else: 'Regime change begins at home—worship!'"[7]

Christian Nationalism and Guns

Death by gun violence has reached epidemic levels throughout the United States. The disagreement revolves around Second Amendment rights verses the proliferation of guns on the streets of America. For Christian Nationalists, there is no question about the centrality of the American Constitution in American life. On issues involving religious freedom and gun rights, the Constitution is the judge and provides sanction and justification. The First and Second Amendments are quoted as legitimate sources supporting gun ownership and religious freedom to discriminate. There is no question that one can interpret the Constitution, albeit loosely, to say that American citizens have the "right to bear arms;" but it is an unresolved argument as to whether the intent was directed at all citizens or only the militia. While the Bible does not speak directly on gun violence, it does speak on violence. The right to bear arms is informed by the damage that guns do around the world, and one must consider the consequences upon the global community and other persons' lives. This country has an epidemic of gun violence for which it has no remedy where dozens of children are murdered in a single massacre.

The Bible states that people of faith are to be lovers of peace. Jesus said that those who live by the sword shall die by the sword. We are called to melt down our weapons of war into spoons and forks to feed others. Christians are called to be willing to make sacrifices in order that others might have life. Jesus said that the greatest love one can have is to sacrifice one's life for something. For Christians, there is no higher authority than the Bible. When it comes to the highest authority in the lives of Christian, Scripture must inform even our political opinions. And when there are conflicts with our political beliefs, the Word of God should have the last word. Scripture calls believers to consider not only their desires and opinions but to consider how their opinions impact others. The Constitution and the Bible each have their own unique purpose. The Constitution is a tool to establish democratic governance; the Bible is a book of revelation that opens the reader to the will of God. For Christians, both have value but require a different set of allegiance. To equate them places a Christian in a dangerous position of heretical alignment. The Bible constantly warns of the danger of placing anything above our loyalty to God or on an equal plane. The Ten Commandments open with a demand that one cannot give allegiance to any other gods, forbids the making of graven idols, and condemns taking the name of the Lord our God in vain (Exodus 20). To hold the Constitution as a document of equal worth to the word of God grants a level of equal worth to human life and meaning.

Amanda Tyler warned that Christian militarism is "not new" and that the country has endured a concerning increase in rhetoric endorsing violence. "Over the past several years, we seem to be stuck on high in Christian nationalism. We've seen it in violent, even deadly ways. Christian nationalist views can inspire violence—even against houses of worship."[8] Philip S. Gorski and Samuel L. Perry, in their book *The Flag + The Cross: White Christian Nationalism and the Threat to American Democracy*, write that Christian Nationalism can lead to violence. White Christian Nationalists are willing to fight to reclaim their rightful place in society, utilizing a radical justification of white supremacist ideology, claiming religious freedom and patriotism. Violence is defined as righteous when the actors are defending the rights of whites under the mantles of religion, government, and civil society. It is then done in the name of maintaining order against those whose intent is to disrupt the status quo. When done by people of color and their representative organizations, such as Black Lives Matter, it is illegal and a sign of moral degradation. White order produces order while Black aggression results in disorder. White Christian violence is an expression of freedom and suppresses the illegality and immorality of rebellion against freedom."[9] They wrote of America's self-perception of her violent actions overseas; rather than being imperialistic, they were honorable and benevolent. America was stated to have different motivations apart from other nations despite overwhelming evidence that she was imperialistic and aggressively violent to achieve her goals of wealth accumulation.

> America's imperial adventurism was a form of noble self-sacrifice. Like Christ—and the Protestant theologians of the era did not hesitate for a moment to draw that comparison—America was acting out of compassion, altruism, and benevolence, never vengefulness, self-interest, or greed. America's motives were always and ever innocent, perfectly so. Even when it employed the most savage violence, it was doing God's will. There was a secular justification, too. . . . When America employs violence, this argument goes, it does so to spread freedom to others. Now, military violence will be used to spread the blessings of freedom throughout the world. Once again, we see how white Christian nationalism is entangled with the holy trinity of racial order, Christian freedom, and male violence."[10]

Donald Trump lost his bid for reelection in 2020 and told his supporters to "fight like hell." Many of those who marched up to the Capitol on January 6 were from the ranks of Christian Nationalism and saw this as their moment. There was a natural appeal of his words as they already defined the present age as a period of conflict. They were determined to fight to take what had been stolen from them, an election. Many were hoping that January 6 would be the pivotal event instigating the new period. During the insurrection, followers had

Christian and American flags, along with statues of the Virgin Mary and Jesus. Stickers read, "Trump is my president; Jesus is my savior." Many had become radicalized to violence. Mauricio Garcia, a Latino man in Allen, Texas, was a supporter of white supremacy. He murdered eight people in a mass killing in Allen, Texas, at a local mall. Investigators did background checks on his internet history and discovered searches on racist and misogynistic webpages. He tattooed his body with Nazi symbols, including a hooked cross and SS lightning bolt. Enrique Tarrio, Afro-Cuban, led the Proud Boys, who shared many of the same characteristics, including racist rhetoric.[11]

Shannon N. Brown, in her paper, "Backwards Christian Soldiers," wrote that the religious right played a major role in the increase of militarization of U.S. foreign policy before and following the attack of 9/11. Following the protest movements of the 1960s, religious conservatives interpreted the movements as representing a decline in American morality. A further motivator was the decrease in support for the military following the protest against the Vietnam War. A weird configuration utilizing military in the service of foreign policy for the implementation of a moral society. This effort was motivated by a desire to fulfill God's purpose for the nation. To bring about world peace meant the implementation of American military might. Beginning in the 1970s, a dual partnership with the U.S. military whose catchwords of "duty, honor, and country" aligned with their Christian values. The Republican Party promoted "traditional values," patriotism, and military strength. This effort gained momentum after 9/11. Brown wrote,

> [T]he Religious Right [is] a particularly significant player in the militarization of U.S. foreign policy in the post-9/11 era. . . . [T]here appears to be at least four important themes trending on the issue: the first being that, with the conclusion of the Cold War era, the Religious Right found impetus for greater *political mobilization* through strategic

> political and military alliances, the rise of the movement's leadership, and its growth in organizational strength. Secondly, in the post-9/11 era, the movement's *proximity to power*—through the election of an evangelical president and a neoconservative alliance—helped to advance the Religious Right as a major player in U.S. foreign policy. Thirdly, after the terrorist attacks of September 11, 2001, the combination of a *religiously infused political ideology* with *nationalistic ideals* surrounding notions of American Exceptionalism helped to provide the moral justification for a broader, more militaristic foreign policy agenda. Fourth, and lastly, that the Christian *fundamentalism* of the movement, tied to militaristic, right-wing politics after 9/11 constitutes a dangerous brand of bad theology. . . . [W]ith their dogmatic messages of intolerance and hard-lined politics, the Religious Right has overlooked the loving and peaceful message of Jesus' gospel, by promoting a militaristic and nationalistic brand of American theocracy."[12]

Scholar Irfan Nooruddin of Ohio State's Mershon Center conducted a study that concluded that "religious nationalism (is) a significant predictor of certain attitudes toward U.S. military intervention abroad." These attitudes include support for using the military to defend the American oil supply and the idea that military service should be required of all males. "These attitudes are consistent with an understanding of America as a chosen nation whose resources must be protected from its enemies and which has an obligation to spread American values—but drawing the line at using the military to defend non-Americans."[13]

Jesus and Militarism

Jesus's position on violence for any reason is consistent in the Gospels; he offers no support or justification for any reason. His followers have never completely adopted his complete rejection of violence and have created various exceptions, the most prominent being the just war ideology. Two criteria are required. There must be a just cause to wage war, and certain limits must be conditional for warring parties. Considerations are that there are worse consequences than war, such as the installation of an authoritarian, cruel regime. Egyptians had a policy that the Pharaoh was the official representative of their god and could declare war on its behalf. Hindus made the first written references to rules for war in the *Mahabharata*. The Chinese demanded that war be fought only as a last resort and that only the country's ruler could rightfully declare it. The Japanese largely adopted those considerations alongside Chinese neighbors. The Greeks, following the guidance of Aristotle, dictated that war be fought only to maintain peace. The military should be maintained only for self-defense, never for conquering or enslaving others. The Romans refused to justify fighting between nations, with the only exceptions being to repel an invasion, retaliatory action, or treaty breach. War was a moral evil and had to have the sacramental blessing of a priest. They stressed that all nations abide by humane considerations and treatment for civilians and troops. The theologian St. Augustine first used the just war term based upon Romans 13:14. War was a necessary evil being justifiable and abstaining from war to stop preventable suffering is sin. Thomas Aquinas set up three mandatory factors necessary for war: it must be declared by a monarch, for a just cause, and for the promotion of goodness and righteousness. Not all agreed that there were any justifications for humans committing acts of violence, even under the war banner. They were labeled as pacifists, those who refused to fight for any reason, nor accepted any reasons for nations to send their young men into battle. Quakers are known as Friends and the Peace denomination.

The New Interpreter's Study Bible determined that the Great Commission reversed the mission of followers of deity.

Military campaigns were no longer to be viewed through the lens of fulfilling the aims of the empire, but those of Jesus for community and acceptance.

> Matthew's community is given a goal, not by Jupiter and the gods but by Jesus. And its means are very different. Instead of military power, it employs compassionate power, healing mercy, and inclusive community, and life-giving words to proclaim and enact God's empire (10:7-8).[14]

During his arrest Jesus denied his disciples the opportunity to prevent his arrest and stopped their resistance to the soldiers sent to apprehend him. When Peter cut off the ear of one of his arresters he instructed against violence for any reason, even in his defense (Luke 22:52b-53). As he was being questioned by the high priest, Annas, a soldier did not like the manner in which he answered and struck him. Jesus turned to him and questioned his use of violence (John 18:19-23).

For many Christians, divine authority and guidance is found in the pages of the Bible. When it comes to the highest authority in the lives of Christian, Scripture must inform even our political opinions. And when there are conflicts with our political beliefs, the Word of God should have the last word. Scripture calls believers to consider not only their desires and opinions but to consider how their opinions impact others. While the Bible does not speak directly on gun violence, it does speak on violence. The right to bear arms is informed by the damage that guns do around the world, and one must consider the consequences upon the global community and other persons' lives. This country has an epidemic of gun violence for which it has no remedy where dozens of children are murdered in a single massacre. The Bible states that people of faith are to be lovers of peace. Jesus said that those who live by the sword shall die by the sword. We are called to melt down our weapons of war into spoons and forks to feed others.

Christians are called to be willing to make sacrifices in order that others might have life. Jesus said that the greatest love one can have is to sacrifice one's life for something.

Martin Luther King, Jr., in his speech, "Remaining Awake Through a Great Revolution," maintained a high level of consistency in his admonitions rejecting violence on every level. It matters little whether it was the state or individuals, a commitment to nonviolence was the only way. Humanity must adopt nonviolence as a way of life or we will destroy one another. "We must all learn to live together as brothers—or we will all perish together as fools."[15]

24

Christian Nationalism and The Media

Then King Ahasuerus said to Queen Esther and to Mordecai the Jew, . . . "You may write as you please with regard to the Jews, in the name of the king, and seal it with the king's ring, for an edict written in the name of the king and sealed with the king's ring cannot be revoked."

The king's secretaries were summoned at that time, in the third month, which is the month of Sivan, on the twenty-third day, and an edict was written, according to all that Mordecai commanded, to the Jews and to the satraps and the governors and the officials of the provinces from India to Cush, one hundred twenty-seven provinces, to every province in its own script and to every people in its own language, and also to the Jews in their script and their language. He wrote letters in the name of King Ahasuerus, sealed them with the king's ring, and sent them by mounted couriers riding on fast steeds bred from the royal herd. . . . A copy of the writ was to be issued as a decree in every province and published to all peoples. . . . So the couriers, mounted on their royal steeds, hurried out, urged by the king's command. The decree was issued in the citadel of Susa.

Esther 8:7-14

The term *media* came into popular usage in the 1920s as means of communication became more varied. Over the centuries technology has developed from cave paintings, oral traditions, writing (papyrus), printing press (books, newspapers, magazines), radio, television, and the internet. In antiquity people communicated to the masses utilizing a variety of means: public verbal announcements, scrolls, and letters. Letters are among the oldest form of communication, and when issued by authority figures, can be considered a form of media.

Each civilization has developed means to communicate across distances. Writing is the long-recognized method, but different societies utilized ingenious methods. Native Americans used smoke signals to spread news, warn of danger, and coordinate with different tribes. Different patterns, a long stream, puffs, or even different colors, communicated different messages over long distances. Africans developed a sophisticated system of using drums to share news, warnings, and complex ideas. Different drums produced different sound qualities, pitches, and rhythms interpreted through secret codes. Some drummers were so skilled that they could mimic the human language and were understood by the receiver. Drummers were stationed in different locations and passed the messages along over great distances.

In the book of Esther, letters play a prominent role communicating the threat of genocide and then rescue. An evil plot was planned against the Jewish people that originated from a letter in the name of King Ahasuerus circulated throughout the Babylonian Empire. The proclamation is reversed as the Jewish people are empowered by another letter that they can defend themselves and keep any property of the defeated.

Christians have a long history of writing and preserving letters as a means of communicating and preserving the story of the faith. Many have been compiled into a book, the Bible, revered as revelations from God. They are read on a daily basis, studied, and interpreted for insight and wisdom into what it means to be obedient to God's will.

Christian Nationalists claim a high degree of belief in the sanctity of Scripture and justify many of their actions based on what they read and believe. A problem arises when any person of faith attempts to be too orthodox and apply literally every word, nuance, and commandment. It can lead to a blindness to what is really important in living a faithful existence by attempting to dictate modern existence by ancient moral codes. For example, women are confined to submissive roles in much of the Bible. This is an issue of patriarchal dominance in a world where women cannot vote, hold positions of authority over men, or exercise a place of equality made in the image and likeness of God.

Christian Nationalists have become rather sophisticated in their use of media as a means of communicating the gospel. Unfortunately, many of the books and videos produced are sexist, homophobic, and racist. Corporal punishment is condoned and there is a distaste for public education. Media empires are created that spoon-feed many looking for spiritual guidance yet are being led down roads of intolerance and judgment of others. Is this really the heart of the gospel message?

Shannon N. Brown challenged unhealthy means of being a Christian:

> [I]f Christians truly want to reflect the light of Jesus into the world, they need to cast off such mentalities as the Religious Right and embrace the pursuit of social and economic justice, political and religious diversity, and the primacy of human rights and multilateral cooperation in foreign policy.[1]

A Media Empire

After WWII evangelicals realized the power of mass media as a tool of evangelism, church growth, and entrepreneur success.

Their initial market was parachurch organizations and institutions founded by evangelists and megachurches with no denominational leanings. Billy Graham was one of the first to extend his outreach to the printed word, writing two dozen books and serving as a founding member of *Christianity Today*. His sermons went across the globe as 700 radio stations regularly broadcast his sermons and talks. His was the start of a media infrastructure with a variety of preachers, authors, and individuals dedicated to the cause of spreading the gospel, or getting rich. It was the establishment of the Christian Booksellers Association (CBA) in 1950 when the problem of distribution was solved. Previously, distribution was managed by religious publishing houses to a small market, primarily in urban areas, along denominational networks, walking salesmen, and by mail. The CBA made the Christian bookstore a viable investment. In its first year, there were only 270 such stores. The number grew to 725 in the 1960s and by the 1970s there were 3,000 in numerous locations in the United States. Part of its success was not only a network of stores, but it also broadened the market to include other forms of media. Its greatest accomplishment was the creation of a Christian culture that was modern and yet conservative enough not to offend. It became cool to be Christian and to proudly wear that identity. The recruitment of popular celebrities added enticement as singers, actors, and well-known evangelists promoted products.[2]

Christian Nationalists created an aggressive media culture, clothed in religious garb, with an expansive global impact. A network of mass communications utilizes television, radio, social media, and print media. Evangelicals created a vast, media empire that effectively spread the message of Christian Nationalism around the world. For over fifty years, a slew of products, Christian books, magazines, CCM, and contemporary Christian music have developed. Christian radio, television, and films have entered into the churches and homes, spreading the ideology known as Christian Nationalism. Readily accessible blogs and podcasts make it easy to communicate scripted messages. Conferences hawk T-shirts so that messages can be broadcast to the wider public and serve as reminders of the experience. There is even a home decor market. All for the digestion of a hungry population seeking help in maintaining a Christian identity. A sophisticated media machinery teaches everything from parenting, sexual purity, and faith. Teens have taken purity vows and worn silver rings as evidence. Kids have watched *VeggieTales* with delight as parents were moved by church viewings of *The Passion of the Christ* and *Soul Surfer*. Christian Nationalists have had impact beyond evangelical congregations as mainline churches have consumed and promoted such merchandise with little recognition of the subliminal messages from producers Pat Robinson, John Piper, Joyce Meyer, and the Gospel Coalition.[3]

Talk radio took it to another level as secular stations promoted what was referred to as Christian values. Or at least values assumed to be Christian. Unhampered by the repealed FCC fairness doctrine nothing was out of bounds concerning topics broadcast around the nation. Far-right hosts, not known for their Christian faith, were listened to by evangelicals daily. Rush Limbaugh and Bill O'Reilly were hired by Roger Ayers of Fox News, and they attacked anyone and anything considered progressive. Sexist, militarist, masculinity, racist, and homophobic ramblings bombastically spread anti-democratic populism with great aplomb. Rage was the sentiment of the day, and it was directed at anyone they deemed to be the enemy. Conservative white men were especially receptive. Fox News became the mouthpiece of conservation America and later the Republican Party.

Fox News' motto, "Fair and Balanced" has been criticized as anything but that. Since its founding, it has painted a nostalgic picture of white men in control upholding a militant masculinity defending the family against liberals and feminists. White evangelicals saw in it a network committed to their cause and watched it in isolation. It helped to center the positions of the Religious Right and political conservatives to the degree that network programming became socially conservative and catered to the Republican Party. Its poli-religious journalism overshadowed and became the news. Du Mez wrote, "Within two decades, the influence of Fox News or conservative evangelicalism would be so profound that journalists and scholars alike would find it difficult to separate the two."[4]

Conclusion

The Christian Response to Christian Nationalism

> As I urged you when I was going to Macedonia, remain at Ephesus so that you may charge certain persons not to teach any different doctrine, nor to devote themselves to myths and endless genealogies, which promote speculations rather than the stewardship from God that is by faith. The aim of our charge is love that issues from a pure heart and a good conscience and a sincere faith. Certain persons, by swerving from these, have wandered away into vain discussion, desiring to be teachers of the law, without understanding either what they are saying or the things about which they make confident assertions.
>
> 1 Timothy 1:3-7 ESV

From its earliest days, the Christian church has wrestled with the persistent challenge of false teaching. The Apostle Paul devoted significant attention to confronting doctrines that threatened to distort the gospel and mislead believers. In his letters—particularly to Timothy—he warned of teachers motivated not by truth, but by a desire for influence, status, and control. These individuals cloaked their ideas in spiritual language while leading communities away from the core message of Christ.

Several of his letters were written to churches warning them of misleading and heretical teachers who were a danger to the faith. Churches were infected by teachings propounded by those who desired power, influence, and status. He charged Timothy to refute ancient mythologies that distorted the gospel. His concern was not merely theological precision for its own sake. False teaching, in his view, was spiritually dangerous because it reshaped how believers understood God, themselves, and their responsibilities to others. He urged vigilance, discernment, and a commitment to truth grounded in the life and teachings of Jesus.

That same challenge persists today as Christians are called to be watchful for doctrines that mislead those eager for the latest trends and receptive of charismatic speakers. The forms have changed, but the underlying dynamic remains. Ideas that appear sincere on the surface can, upon closer examination, distort the gospel in ways that are both subtle and profound. Among the most significant of these in the contemporary American context is the ideology commonly referred to as Christian Nationalism.

Christian Nationalism is one of the longest existing ideologies in the history of human civilization. Long before Christianity existed, there was the entanglement of religion and political entities. Although Christian Nationalism is often discussed as a modern phenomenon, the fusion of religious identity with political power is far older than Christianity itself. Across civilizations, rulers have invoked divine authority to legitimize their authority, unify populations, and secure loyalty. Monarchs were frequently portrayed as chosen—or even appointed—by the divine, and this belief was passed down through generations as part of a hereditary right to rule. Religious nationalism was an instrument used by those in power to give divine credence to their authority, as well as a means of ensuring a long rule. It became hereditary as it was passed from monarch to children who were also given the legacy of divine mandate to govern. Civilization after civilization adopted the precepts of religious nationalism, and even civilizations that never encountered one another install it in one form or another. The lesson for society is that it fails to provide stability or ensure competence. Eventually the populace will lose confidence in it as a political model and seek other means of governance.

This pattern has appeared in many forms, across cultures that never encountered one another. Despite differences in expression, the underlying principle remained consistent: aligning political authority with religious legitimacy strengthens both—at least for a time.

History, however, also reveals the limitations of this model. Systems that merge religious devotion with political power often struggle to maintain justice, accountability, and adaptability. Over time, populations frequently grow disillusioned, particularly when claims of divine sanction are used to justify inequality, oppression, or exclusion.

This historical backdrop provides an important lens through which to view contemporary expressions of Christian Nationalism. It is not an isolated development, but part of a longstanding pattern in which faith is intertwined with the pursuit of power.

Christian Nationalism is best understood as a political ideology that seeks to merge Christian identity with national identity, often portraying a particular nation as uniquely favored or ordained by God. It uses Christian language, symbols, and narratives to advance political goals, encouraging believers to see loyalty to the nation as intertwined with faithfulness to God.

It is important to distinguish this from other forms of engagement between faith and public life. Christians have long contributed to moral discourse, social reform, and civic responsibility. Christian Nationalism, however, goes further. It elevates the nation to a place of spiritual significance that rivals—or even replaces—primary allegiance to God.

Christian Nationalism is a danger to both the country and the church. It poses a threat to democratic principles, racial unity, religious freedom, and cultural expression. CN teachings do not align with what has been historically taught by most denominations. It is rather a political ideology that hides under the cover of Christian language and uses its symbols and signs to deceive believers into thinking it is Christian theology. It parallels political purposes with religious commitment. It incorporates deception and hypocrisy underlain by false theological justification in defense of its actions. The nation has struggled to live out the commands of God to love justice, do kindness, and walk humbly with our God. Rather the country, like all others, proclaimed that, because she was a Christian nation, she was righteous and just. But it was a limited righteousness for a select few. America, even as she called for liberty and justice for all, murdered Native Americans, enslaved Africans, interred Asians, and established overseas colonies.

Beyond its theological implications, Christian Nationalism also carries significant social consequences. When religious identity is tied to national identity, it can create boundaries that exclude those who do not fit a particular cultural or religious mold. This dynamic can undermine commitments to religious freedom, pluralism, and equal dignity. In the American context, the tension is particularly evident. The nation has long articulated ideals of liberty and justice for all, yet its history includes profound contradictions—moments in which entire groups were denied those very promises. Appeals to divine favor have at times been used to justify actions that stand in tension with the ethical demands of the gospel.

This is not to single out one nation as uniquely flawed, but to recognize a broader human tendency: to assume righteousness for ourselves while overlooking injustice. Christian Nationalism can reinforce this tendency by framing national identity in moral or even sacred terms, making self-critique more difficult.

At its core, Christian Nationalism presents a theological problem. The Christian tradition has consistently emphasized that God alone is worthy of ultimate allegiance. When any nation is portrayed as uniquely righteous, divinely mandated, or central to God's redemptive plan, it risks crossing into a form of idolatry.

This concern is not new. Scripture repeatedly warns against placing trust in human structures or attributing divine status to them. The biblical narrative calls God's people to humility, justice, and faithfulness—not national exaltation.

Moreover, Christian Nationalism often relies on selective use of Scripture. Isolated passages may be invoked to support particular political positions, while the broader biblical themes of love, mercy, justice, and care for the marginalized are minimized or overlooked. The result is a theology that reflects cultural and political priorities more than the life and teachings of Jesus.

Jesus himself consistently resisted attempts to align his mission with political ideology. He challenged systems of injustice, but he did not seek to establish a nationalistic movement. His teachings emphasized sacrificial love, humility, and a kingdom "not of this world"—one that transcends political boundaries and ethnic divisions.

So, what are we to do? Each one of us has a responsibility to be as informed as humanly possible on the elements in society that on the surface appear to be harmless, matters of faith, but, once investigated, reveal ideologies and beliefs dangerous to the functioning of a healthy society. Certain actions can be undertaken by those committed to withstanding the lure of Christian Nationalism.

To combat Christian Nationalism, the church must regain its prophetic voice. Persons of conscience must make a concerted effort to identify Christian Nationalism when it appears in their midst. Christian Nationalism is sustained by the silence of Christian leaders, clergy, and laity refusing to voice opposition to religious idolatry. Attributing righteousness to any nation is a problematic form of veneration that should be assigned only to God. Samuel Wells, writing in *Christian Century*, stated: "The rhetoric . . . that only a strong America prevents the world from lapsing into chaos, invites citizens to buy into a divine (or at least salvific) mission that has to be named as idolatry." It is difficult to criticize members of any community who profess a Christian identity and who occupy pulpits and seats of governance. But an informed faith demands that we are constantly in a mode of learning and old demons take on new shapes, often adopting the language of faith for nefarious purposes. The church, along with other religious institutions, has a special contribution advocating for the rights of others who are marginalized and ostracized within a community. Christians are called to walk in the same footsteps of a Savior who challenges injustice regardless of whom it is targeting. He especially has a harsh word for those who assume the mantle of leadership in his church as religious leaders. Christians are a people called in his name to be prophets and servant-leaders for society—to help to restore the balance of power so that all are treated fairly.

Hold discussions on the meaning of Christian Nationalism in your local congregation. Often members have not thought about what constitutes the ideology and ways it has infiltrated the cultures of congregations. Examine the ways in which elements have been taught within the life of congregations and accepted without debate. The rejection of Christian Nationalism is vital to the integrity and purity of the Christian faith. Christians who reside in the United States of America must work to overcome centuries of indoctrination into Christian Nationalism. It will take gaining an understanding of the history of the country beyond the affirmation that America is God's gift to the world. Christians must adopt an orthodox mentality when it comes to what it means to be a Christian. God calls us to be guided by the teachings and example of the biblical Jesus for whom the greatest commandment was to love God, self, and one another. Read Amanda Tyler's book, *How to End Christian Nationalism*, as she speaks directly to congregations providing effective strategies.

Dissuade against describing one's congregation using political language. Congregations are not red, blue, or purple but must find their identity as believers gathered to worship and serve God in the world. The conflict is not between conservative and progressive Christians but with a world that is selfish, violent, and exploitative. Christians are to be a people called to a higher level of living that is free from judgmental behavior or a desire for status and political power. The purity of the church is maintained by not allowing societal norms to become incorporated into the church's life. They are called to be that faithful remnant who dare to follow a different path in the footprints of a Savior who died in order that the world might have life. It is not an easy journey and requires a willingness to sacrifice all that we have been taught to value, but it is a life worth living.

Reevaluate the meaning and appropriateness of identifying oneself as a Christian patriot. Labeling oneself as a Christian patriot is the first step toward Christian Nationalism. It is extremely difficult to withstand cultural pressure to compromise the true purpose of the faith and cause the adoption of idolatrous practices such as bringing flags into the church or holding one's nation up as more moral than others simply because everyone is doing it. A Christian's identity must be first and foremost one of a follower of Christ without other allegiances. There can be no equal loyalty to both church and state, God, and the nation. As Jesus said of the choice between the desire for wealth and the love of God, "You will either love the one or hate the other." In the end, this dual identity, especially as it is being touted by politicians and preachers, will lead to the implosion of both institutions.

Organize small groups for national advocacy. Change usually starts through the initiative of an individual or a small group of invested persons. Begin your process by meeting on a regular basis to explore the meaning and complexities of CN. Participate in local advocacy efforts that challenge the legitimacy of Christian Nationalism. Hold public forums to discuss the meaning of the separation of church and state and the ways in which it benefits both church and society. Ensure that public schools are not used as political footballs by those seeking to violate the First Amendment by installing materials promoting Christianity on school grounds. Write letters to your local newspaper on opinion pages to counter dangerous expressions of intolerance in your community. Voters need information on candidates who have expressed CN views in the past or are associated with CN leaders and congregations. While a person cannot be judged by their personal associations, candidates must answer to tighter scrutiny and be asked how their religious and personal associations will influence their actions once in office

Hold ecumenical conversations on Christian Nationalism and expressions of it in your local community. Seek out relationships with ecumenical and interfaith neighbors to enlarge the participation of others with a similar interest. Openly discuss ways in which persons of faith and their communities are harmed by CN rhetoric and practices. Ensure that their voices are heard and use this as a time of learning about unintentional harms inflicted to your neighbors. Invite others to be a part of leadership to plan the way forward.

Utilize the resources provided by your denomination. Quite a few have advocacy offices, often situated in Washington D.C. with a long history of producing toolkits, study guides, and theological explanations on responses to CN and other justice issues. Write overtures challenging Christian Nationalism for your denomination's annual meetings. Backlash to CN has arisen primarily from within the faith community. Clergy have written books and articles, preached sermons, given lectures, and done everything imaginable to denounce Christian Nationalism as not being legitimate Christianity.

Organize visits with local, state, and national representatives. State legislatures are often leading the way with CN legislation promoting the placement of religious paraphernalia on state grounds. Engage them with why this is not having the intended impact and can actually be counterproductive, as many citizens will reject such efforts as coercion. Share the religious diversity within their district and how their voters might feel that their representative does not support them or their issues. Meet with your members of Congress to discuss a rigid enforcement of the Johnson Amendment and to oppose efforts to weaken it.

Connect with denominational offices that focus on advocacy and receive training on being a prophetic church. American Christianity has always courted a close relationship between church and politics believing that both benefited. This is definitely the case as the church promotes morality for every area of life. But too close a relationship means compromise on the principles that give the faith its purpose and meaning, belief in a God who calls for fairness for all people without bias or partiality. God loves all people and the Bible challenges nations to be equally just and impartial, especially when actions relate to the poor and migrants. Principles that run counter to Christian Nationalism are to be the rule of one's faith journey.

At it's 227th General Assembly the Presbyterian Church (USA) passed a paper, "Standing Against White Christian Nationalism," with several recommendations. *Presbyterians Today* summarized the report's recommendations.

- A call to urge the PC(USA) to become informed on the meaning of the ideology known as White Christian Nationalism, including clergy, members, and national leaders. Special consideration of the fact that 2026 was the 250th anniversary of the founding of the nation and citizens should become even more aware of domestic dangers to the health of the United States.
- It's national agency, Presbyterian Life and Witness (PL&W), should mount a well-focused strategy to challenge the impact of White Christian Nationalism on the policies and laws passed in the U.S.

- PL&W should promote the standards defining the stipulations of the Johnson Amendment that prohibits nonprofits from partisan participation, endorsing candidates for political office, and donating to a campaign. Congregations should refrain from any efforts that violate the policy.
- PL&W should distribute this document to ruling and teaching elders, mid-council staffs, and agency leaders.
- Encourage member congregations to engage in conversations on the presence of symbols of the country that are located on church property, sanctuaries, and the ways in which the worship of God contains elements of patriotic passion and content.
- Authorize the Stated Clerk to promote the use of this document when issuing public statements that are related to the issue of White Christian Nationalism.
- Communicate with academic institutions, seminaries, and the Association of Presbyterian Colleges and Universities, to incorporate lessons on White Christian Nationalism into their curriculum.
- In agreement with a previous overture, efforts should be made to promote the addition of an amendment to the *Book of Order* to promote religious freedom for all faiths and their right to worship freely.[1]

Christian Nationalism portrays itself as true Christian teachings, but it is really about gaining power and influence. Believers must always be on their guard against teachings and teachers who are teaching false doctrines and misinterpretations of the gospel. The combining of faith in a triune God with patriotic ideology is false and contrary to the biblical message. The doctrines of the church must remain true to Scripture, inspiration of the Holy Spirit, and theological expositions on the true meaning of the Christian faith. A measuring stick is that teachings must be grounded in more than just the teacher's words. To be able to quote Scripture is not enough, for almost any particular emphasis can be supported by random passages of Scripture. The key is to find support throughout the whole of Scripture for the message of love, grace, and redemption, which is consistent. Disciples must become reacquainted with the Jesus of the Bible, as many have a Lord who has been spoon-fed by generations of followers of a particular perspective.

We must be guided by the Greatest Commandment to love God, neighbor, and self. Jesus does not discriminate and urges caution on the part of his followers when issuing judgmental opinions on who is acceptable to God, charging that those who judge others are going to be judged by the same manner. Life in the 21st century is confusing as there are so many voices seeking to entice us to believe as they do. Truth is found in trusting the Spirit of God to lead us in the path trod by the Savior. But it is up to us to not be swayed by those whose words promote division and partiality to only a select few as favorable to God. God is not partial to people, institutions, or nations, but is Lord of all.

Bibliography

Achtemeier, Paul J. *Romans: Interpretation: A Bible Commentary for Teaching and Preaching*, Atlanta: John Knox Press, 1985.

ACLU, *The Constitution of the United States*, New York: ACLU, 2016.

Alberta, Tim. *The Kingdom, the Power, and the Glory: American Evangelicals in an Age of Extremism*, New York: Harper, 2024.

Anderson, Bernhard W. *Understanding the Old Testament*, New Jersey: Englewood Cliffs, 1975.

Angell, Stephen Ward. *Bishop Henry McNeal Turner and African-American Religion in the South*, Knoxville: The University of Tennessee Press, 1992.

Armstrong, Karen *A History of God*, New York: Ballantine Books, 1993.

Bennett, Jr., Lerone *Confrontation: Black and White*, Baltimore: Penguin Books Inc., 1968.

Blackwell, Amy Hackney and Christopher W. *Mythology for Dummies*, New Jersey: John Wiley & Sons, Inc., 2023.

Blount, Brian K. General Editor. *True to Our Native Land: An African American New Testament Commentary*, Minneapolis: Fortress Press, 2007.

Boesak, Allan A. Ed. by Leonard Sweetman. *Black and Reformed: Apartheid, Liberation, and the Calvinist Tradition*, New York: Orbis Books, 1986.

Borg, Marcus J. *Conflict, Holiness and Politics in the Teachings of Jesus*, Lampeter: The Edwin Mellen Press, 1984.

Boring, E. Eugene. *Revelation: Interpretation: A Bible Commentary for Teaching and Preaching*, Louisville: Westminster John Knox Press, 1989.

Brown, Dee. *Bury My Heart at Wounded Knee,* New York: Bantam Books: 1970.

Bruce, F. F. *Hard Sayings of Jesus*, Illinois: Intervarsity Press, 1983.

Brueggemann, Walter. *Genesis: (Interpretation: A Bible Commentary for Teaching and Preaching)*, Atlanta: John Knox Press, 1982.

Brueggemann, Walter. *First and Second Samuel: Interpretation: A Bible Commentary for Teaching and Preaching*, Louisville: Westminster John Knox Press, 1990.

Bruggink, Donald J. and Carl H. Droppers. *Christ And Architecture: Building Presbyterian / Reformed Churches*, Grand Rapids Michigan: William B. Eerdmans Publishing Company,1965.

Cash, W. J. *The Mind of the South*, New York: Vintage Books, 1991.

Casson, Lionel. *Ancient Egypt*, New York: Time Life Books, 1965.

Charles, Mark and Soong-Chan Rah, *Unsettling Truths: The Ongoing, Dehumanizing Legacy of the Doctrine of Discovery*, Downers Grove, IL: Inter Varsity Press: 2019.

Clark, Malcolm. *Islam for Dummies*, New Jersey: Wiley Publishing, 2003.

Clarke, William Newton, D.D., *An Outline of Christian Theology*, New York: Charles Scribner's Sons, 1898.

Cone, James H. *God of the Oppressed*, Minneapolis: The Seabury Press, Inc, 1975.

Cotterell, Arthur, ed. *The Encyclopedia of World Mythology*, New York: Barnes & Noble Books, 2001.

Craddock, Fred B. *Luke: Interpretation: A Bible Commentary for Teaching and Preaching*, Louisville: Westminster John Knox Press, 1990.

Egerton, Douglas R. *Death or Liberty: African Americans and Revolutionary America*, New York: Oxford University Press, 2009.

Ferm, Vergilius ed. *Classics of Protestantism*, New York: Philosophical Library, 1959.

Fischer, David Hackett, *American Founders: How Enslaved People Expanded American Ideals*, New York: Simon & Schuster, 2022.

Foner, Eric. *The Story of American Freedom*, New York: W.W. Norton & Company, 1998

Gorski, Philip S. and Samuel L. Perry, *The Flag + The Cross: White Christian Nationalism and the Threat to American Democracy*, New York: Oxford University Press, 2022.

Guthrie, Shirley C., Jr., *Christian Doctrine*, Louisville, Westminster/ John Knox Press, 1994.

FitzGerald, Frances. *The Evangelicals: The Struggle to Shape America*, New York: Simon & Schuster, 2017.

Frady, Marshall. *Jesse: The Life and Pilgrimage of Jesse Jackson*, New York: Random House, 1996.

Fox, Stephen R. *The Guardian of Boston: William Monroe Trotter*, New York: Atheneum, 1970.

Genovese, Eugene D. *Roll, Jordan, Roll: The World the Slaves Made*, New York: Vintage Books, 1974.

Gomes, Peter J., *The Good Book: Reading the Bible with Mind and Heart*, New York: Avon Books, 1998.

Graham, Shirley. *The Story of Phillis Wheatley (Poetess of the American Revolution)*, New York: Washington Square Press (Archway Paperback): 1970.

Hakim, Joy. *A History of US: Liberty for All*, New York: Oxford University Press: 1994.

Hannah-Jones, Nikole, Caitin Roper, Ilena Silverman, and Jake Silverstein, ed., *The 1619 Project: A New Origin Story*, New York: One World: 2021.

Hare, Douglas R. A. *Matthew: Interpretation: A Bible Commentary for Teaching and Preaching*, Louisville: Westminster John Knox Press, 1993.

Hartman, Andrew. *A War for the Soul of America: A History of The Culture Wars*, Chicago: The University of Chicago Press, 2019.

Hartz, Paula R. *Zoroastrianism: World Religions*, New York: Facts on File: 1999.

Hawkins, Jimmie R. *Unbroken and Unbowed: A History of Black Protest in America*. Louisville: Westminster John Knox, 2022.

Hewitt, Hugh. *Searching for God in America*, Dallas: Word Publishing, 1996.

Hinson-Hasty, Elizabeth L., *The Problem of Wealth: A Christian Response to a Culture of Affluence*, New York: Orbis Books, 2017.

The New Interpreter's Study Bible: New Revised Standard Version with the Apocrypha (NIB), Nashville: Abingdon Press: 2003.

Janz, Denis R., ed. *A Reformation Reader*, Minneapolis: Fortress Press: 1999.

Jones, Robert P. *The End of White Christian America*, New York: Simon & Schuster, 2016.

Jones, Robert P. *The Hidden Roots of White Supremacy and the Path to a Shared American Future*, New York: Simon & Schuster, 2023.

Kenny, Kevin. *Peaceable Kingdom: The Paxton Boys and the Destruction of William Penn's Holy Experiment*, New York: Oxford University Press, 2009.

Kimball, Dan. *They Like Jesus but Not the Church: Insights from Emerging Generations*. Grand Rapids: Zondervan, 2007.

Kobes Du Mez, Kristin. *Jesus and John Wayne: How White Evangelicals Corrupted a Faith and Fractured a Nation*, New York: Liveright Publishing Corporation, 2020.

Kramer, Samuel Noah. *Cradle of Civilization (The Great Ages of Man: A History of the World's Great Cultures)*, New York: Time Incorporated, 1967

Kunhardt III, Philip B., Peter W. Kunhardt, and Peter W. Kunhardt, Jr. *Looking for Lincoln: The Making of an American Icon*, New York: Alfred A. Knopf, 2008.

Kruse, Kevin. *One Nation Under God: How Corporate America Invented Christian America*, New York: Basic Books, 2015.

Loewen, James W. *Lies Across America: What Our Historic Sites Get Wrong*, New York: Touchstone, 1999.

Lincoln, C. Eric, ed. *The Black Experience in Religion*, New York: Anchor Books, 1974.

Lincoln, C. Eric and Lawrence H. Mamiya, *The Black Church in the African American Experience*, Durham: Duke University Press, 1990.

MacLean, Nancy. *Democracy in Chains: The Deep History of the Radical Right's Stealth Plan for America*, New York: Viking 2017.

Matkin, Michael J. *The Complete Idiot's Guide to the Gnostic Gospels*, New York: Watermill Books, 2005

Marks, Paula Mitchell. *In A Barren Land: American Indian Dispossession and Survival*, New York: Quill William Morrow, 1998.

McConnell, D. R. *A Different Gospel: A Historical and Biblical Analysis of the Modern Faith Movement*, Massachusetts: Hendrickson Publishers, Inc., 1988.

McNeill, John T. ed. *Calvin: Institutes of the Christian Religion, Volume 2*, Philadelphia: The Westminster Press: 1960.

Miller, Paul D. *The Religion of American Greatness: What's Wrong with Christian Nationalism*, Downer's Grove, Illinois: InterVarsity Press, 2022.

Morgan, Edmund S., *American Slavery, American Freedom: The Ordeal of Colonial Virginia*, New York: W. W. Norton & Company, 1995.

Niebuhr, H. Richard. *Christ and Culture*, New York: Harper Torchbooks, 1951.

Oden, Thomas C. *First and Second Timothy and Titus: (Interpretation: A Bible Commentary for Teaching and Preaching)*, Louisville: Westminster John Knox Press, 1989.

Park, Benjamin E. *American Zion: A New History of Mormonism*, New York: Liveright Publishing Corporation, 2024.

PBS Documentary, Joseph Campbell and the Power of Myth, Ep. 1: "The Hero's Adventure," 1988.

Peters, Rebecca Todd, *Trust Women: A Progressive Christian Argument for Reproductive Justice,* Boston: Beacon Press, 2018.

Phillips, Kevin. *American Theocracy: The Peril and Politics of Radical Religion, Oil, and Borrowed Money in the 21st Century,* New York: Viking, 2006.

Powell, Colin with Joseph E. Persico, *My American Journey: An Autobiography,* New York: Random House, Inc., 1995.

Quarles, Benjamin. *The Negro in the Making of America,* New York: Collier Books, 1971.

Rae, Noel, ed. *Witnessing America: The Library of Congress Book of Firsthand Accounts of Life in America 1600-1900,* New York: Penguin Books, 1996.

Reich, Robert B., *The Work of Nations: Preparing Ourselves for 21st Century Capitalism,* New York: Knopf Doubleday Publishing Group, 1992.

Reichley, A. James. *Faith in Politics,* Washington, D.C.: The Brookings Institution, 2002.

Richard Rothstein, *The Color of Law: A Forgotten History of How Our Government Segregated America,* New York: Liveright Publishing Corporation, 2017.

Russell, Dick. *Black Genesis: And the American Experience,* New York: Carroll & Graf Publishers, Inc., 1998.

Ryrie, Alec. *Protestants: The Faith That Made the Modern World,* New York: Viking, 2017.

Schiess, Kaitlyn. *The Ballot and the Bible: How Scripture Has Been Used and Abused in American Politics and Where We Go from Here,* Grand Rapids: Brazos Press, 2023.

Seitz, Christopher R. *Isaiah 1-39: Interpretation: A Bible Commentary for Teaching and Preaching,* Louisville: Westminster John Knox Press, 1993.

Sernett, Milton C. ed. *Afro-American Religious History: A Documentary Witness,* 2nd Edition, Durham: Duke University Press, 1985.

Smylie, James H., *American Presbyterians: A Pictorial History*, Philadelphia: Presbyterian Historical Society, 1985.

Stewart, Katherine. *The Power Worshippers: Inside the Dangerous Rise of Religious Nationalism*, New York: Bloomsbury Publishing, 2019.

Sweet, William Warren. *The Story of Religion in America*, New York: Harper & Brothers, Second Revised Edition, 1950.

Takaki, Ronald. *A Different Mirror: A History of Multicultural America*, Boston: Little, Brown and Company, 1991.

Towner, W. Sibley. *Daniel: Interpretation: A Bible Commentary for Teaching and Preaching*, Atlanta: John Knox Press, 1984.

Troeltsch, Ernst. *Religion in History*, Minneapolis: Fortress Press, 1991.

Tyler, Amanda. *How to End Christian Nationalism*, Minneapolis: Broadleaf Books: 2024,

Wallis, Jim. *God's Politics: Why the Right Gets It Wrong and the Left Doesn't Get It*, New York: HarperCollins Publishers, 2005.

Washington, James M., ed. A Testament of Hope: *The Essential Writings and Speeches of Martin Luther King, Jr.*, New York: HarperCollins, 1986.

Webb, Jeffrey B. *The Complete Idiot's Guide to Christianity*, New York: Alpha Books, 2004.

West, Cornel. *Democracy Matters: Winning the Fight Against Imperialism*, New York: The Penguin Press, 2004.

White, Ronald C., Jr., and C. Howard Hopkins, Jr., *The Social Gospel: Religion and Reform in Changing America*, Philadelphia: Temple University Press, 1976.

Williamson, Lamar, Jr. *Mark: Interpretation: A Bible Commentary for Teaching and Preaching*, Atlanta: John Knox Press, 1983.

Willimon, William H. *Acts: (Interpretation: A Bible Commentary for Teaching and Preaching)*, Louisville: Westminster John Knox Press, 1988.

Willis, Roy, ed., *World Mythology*, London: Duncan Baird Publishers, 1996.

Wilmore, Gayraud S. *Last Things First*, Philadelphia: The Westminster Press, 1982.

Yoder, John Howard. *The Politics of Jesus*, Grand Rapids, MI: William B. Eerdmans Publishing Company, 1995.

Yoo, William, *What Kind of Christianity: A History of Slavery and Anti-Black Racism in the Presbyterian Church*, Louisville, KY: Westminster John Knox Press, 2022.

Zunz, Olivier, ed., *Alexis De Tocqueville: Democracy in America*, New York: The Library in America, 2004.

Notes

Introduction

1. Frances FitzGerald, *The Evangelicals: The Struggle to Shape America,* New York: Simon & Schuster, 2017. 361.

2. *Center for American Progress,* April 13, 2022, "Christian Nationalism Is 'Single Biggest Threat' to America's Religious Freedom," https://www.americanprogress.org/article/christian-nationalism-is-single-biggest-threat-to-americas-religious-freedom/.

3. Paul D. Miller, "What Is Christian Nationalism?" February 3, 2021, https://www.christianitytoday.com/ct/2021/february-web-only/what-is-christian-nationalism.html.

1. Christian Nationalism

1. Jack Jenkins, *Religious News Service,* Joint Baptist Coalition for Religious Freedom, "Christians Against Christian Nationalism," July 2019, https://www.christiansagainstchristiannationalism.org/statement.

2. Kim, November 14, 2023, National Organization for Women, "Why Christian Nationalism Is a Feminist Issue," https://now.org/blog/why-christian-nationalism-is-a-feminist-issue/.

3. Gregory A. Smith, Michael Rotolo, and Patricia Tevington, October 27, 2022, Pew Research Center, "45% of Americans Say U.S. Should Be a Christian Nation,'" https://www.pewresearch.org/religion/2022/10/27/45-of-americans-say-u-s-should-be-a-christian-nation/.

4. Francis Wilkinson, *Deccan Herald (DH),* February 4, 2025, "MAGA's driving force is Christian nationalism," https://www.deccanherald.com/world/magas-driving-force-is-christian-nationalism-3390181.

5. Dorothy S. Boulware, *Word in Black,* March 19, 2025, "Bishop Michael Curry's Gospel of Love," https://wordinblack.com/2025/03/bishop-michael-curry-and-the-gospel-of-love/?utm_source=ActiveCampaign&utm_medium=email&utm_content=As%20Services%20Shrink%2C%20the%20Black%20Church%20Steps%20Up&utm_campaign=Religion%20newsletter%203%2022.

6. Pew Research Center, October 27, 2022, "In their own words: How Americans describe Christian nationalism," https://www.pewresearch

.org/religion/2022/10/27/in-their-own-words-how-americans-describe-christian-nationalism/

7. Cathy Young, *The Montanan,* April 27, 2024, "Christian Nationalism: A Grave Threat to America," https://dailymontanan.com/2024/04/27/christian-nationalism-a-grave-threat-to-america/.

8. Lamar Williamson, Jr., *Mark: Interpretation: A Bible Commentary for Teaching and Preaching*, Atlanta: John Knox Press, 1983. 217-219.

9. Lamar Williamson, Jr., *Mark.* 221.

10. Mark Charles and Soong-Chan Rah, *Unsettling Truths: The Ongoing, Dehumanizing Legacy of the Doctrine of Discovery*, Downers Grove, IL: InterVarsity Press, 2019. 59.

11. John Howard Yoder, *The Politics of Jesus*, Grand Rapids: William B. Eerdmans Publishing Company, 1995. 208.

12. Kaitlyn Schiess, *The Ballot and the Bible: How Scripture Has Been Used and Abused in American Politics and Where We Go from Here*, Grand Rapids: Brazos Press, 2023. 152, 153.

13. Kaitlyn Schiess, *The Ballot and the Bible*. 151.

14. Michael Horton, *Ligonier*, September 1, 2008, "A Tale of Two Kingdoms," https://www.ligonier.org/learn/articles/tale-two-kingdoms.

15. Alec Ryrie, *Protestants: The Faith That Made the Modern World*, New York: Viking, 2017. 48.

16. Denis R. Janz, ed. *A Reformation Reader*, Minneapolis: Fortress Press: 1999. 96.

17. Denis R. Janz, ed. *A Reformation Reader*. 157.

18. John T. McNeill, ed. *Calvin: Institutes of the Christian Religion Volume 2*, Philadelphia: The Westminster Press: 1960. 1485-1491, 1513, 1520-1521.

19. Rebecca Bratten Weiss, *Christian Century*, "Faith at the Expense of Freedom," October 2024 Issue, https://www.christiancentury.org/features/faith-expense-freedom.

20. *Wikipedia*, "Theocracy," https://en.wikipedia.org/wiki/Theocracy.

21. *Dictionary.com*, "Patriotism vs. Nationalism: What's the Difference? https://www.dictionary.com/e/patriotism-vs-nationalism/.

22. Kristin Kobes Du Mez, *Jesus and John Wayne: How White Evangelicals Corrupted a Faith and Fractured a Nation,* New York: Liveright Publishing Corporation, 2020. 19.

23. Shirley C. Guthrie, Jr. *Christian Doctrine*, Louisville, Westminster/John Knox Press, 1994, 163.

24. Patrick Schreiner, *TGC*, April 27, 2023, "The Good, The Bad, and The Ugly of Christian Nationalism," https://www.thegospelcoalition.org/article/good-bad-ugly-christian-nationalism/.

25. Berndt Ostendorf, September 15, 2019, "A Nation with the Soul of a Church? The Strange Career of Religion in America: A View from Europe," https://www.aisna.net/wp-content/uploads/2019/09/1516ostendorf.pdf.

26. Daniel K. Williams, *CURRENT*, February 29, 2024, "Civil Religion Is Different from Christian Nationalism," https://currentpub.com/2024/02/29/civil-religion-is-different-from-christian /nationalism.

27. Lawrence J. McCaffrey, *The Irish Diaspora in America* (Washington, D. C., 1984), pp. 6, 62.

28. Amanda Tyler, *How to End Christian Nationalism*, Minneapolis: Broadleaf Books: 2024. 107.

29. Kristin Kobes Du Mez, *Jesus and John Wayne*. 71.

30. Ronald Takaki, *A Different Mirror: A History of Multicultural America*, Boston: Little, Brown and Company, 1991. 176, 177.

31. Kalefa Sanneh, March 27, 2003, *The New Yorker*, "How Christian Is Christian Nationalism?" https://www.newyorker.com/magazine/2023/04/03/how-christian-is-christian-nationalism.

32. Katherine Stewart, *The Power Worshippers: Inside the Dangerous Rise of Religious Nationalism*, New York: Bloomsbury Publishing, 2019. 104.

33. Kristin Kobes Du Mez, *Jesus and John Wayne*. 75-76.

34. Kevin Phillips, *American Theocracy: The Peril and Politics of Radical Religion, Oil, and Borrowed Money in the 21st Century*, New York: Viking, 2006. 244.

35. Katherine Stewart, *The Power Worshippers*. 25.

36. Rick Pidcock, *Baptist News Global*, May 25, 2023, "Yes, Tim Scott is a Black Man, but he's still Promoting Christian Nationalism," https://baptistnews.com/article/yes-tim-scott-is-a-black-man-but-hes-still-promoting-christian-nationalism/.

37. Laura Barron-López and Sam Lane, *PBS News Hour*, February 1, 2024, "What is Christian Nationalism and Why It Raises Concerns About Threats to Democracy," https://www.pbs.org/newshour/show/what-is-christian-nationalism-and-why-it-raises-concerns-about-threats-to-democracy.

38. Terry Gross, NPR, February 29, 2004, "Tracing the rise of Christian nationalism, from Trump to the Ala. Supreme Court," https://www.npr.org/2024/02/29/1234843874/tracing-the-rise-of-christian-nationalism-from-trump-to-the-ala-supreme-court."

39. Terry Gross, NPR, February 29, 2004, "Tracing the rise of Christian nationalism, from Trump to the Ala. Supreme Court."

40. Tom Mockaitis, *The Hill*, August 5, 2023, "Flynn is 'Reawakening' the dangerous Alliance of Christianity and Nationalism," https://thehill

.com/opinion/campaign/4151643-flynn-is-reawakening-the-darkest-sides-of-christianity-and-nationalism/.

41. Michelle R. Smith, *PBS,* OCTOBER 7, 2022, "Michael Flynn is Recruiting an 'Army of God' in Growing Christian Nationalist Movement," https://www.pbs.org/newshour/politics/michael-flynn-is-recruiting-an-army-of-god-in-growing-christian-nationalist-movement.

42. Kristin Kobes Du Mez, *Jesus and John Wayne*. 153-154.

43. Yonat Shimron, "A Campaign to Blitz the Country with 'In God We Trust' Laws Takes Root," *Religious News Service,* July 2, 2018, https://religionnews.com/2018/07/02/a-campaign-to-blitz-the-country-with-in-god-we-trust-laws-takes-root/.

44. Brian Duignan, *Britannica.com,* August 20, 2024, "Project 2025," https://www.britannica.com/topic/Project-2025.

45. *PBS,* August 29, 2023, "Conservatives aim to restructure U.S. government and replace it with Trump's vision," https://www.pbs.org/newshour/politics/conservatives-aim-to-restructure-u-s-government-and-replace-it-with-trumps-vision.

46. "Project 2025," by Brian Duignan. Britannica.com. April 21, 2026. https://www.britannica.com/topic/Project-2025

47. Pew Research Center, October 28, 2021, "In the U.S., Far More Support Than Oppose Separation of Church and State, https://www.pewresearch.org/religion/2021/10/28/in-u-s-far-more-support-than-oppose-separation-of-church-and-state/

48. Chicago Tribune Content Agency, August 16, 2019, *The Chicago Tribune,* "The Bible Stands as the Supreme Constitution for All Mankind," https://www.chicagotribune.com/sns-201907300011--tms--bgrahamctnym-a20190816-20190816-story.html.

49. Morgan Lee, "Christian Nationalism Is Worse Than You Think," January 13, 2021, https://www.christianitytoday.com/ct/podcasts/quick-to-listen/christian-nationalism-capitol-riots-trump-podcast.html.

50. Peter Smith, *AP,* May 15, 2024, "Jesus is their savior, Trump is their candidate. ex-president's backers say he shares faith, values," https://apnews.com/article/trump-christian-evangelicals-conservatives-2024-election-43f25118c133170c77786daf316821c3.

51. Kristin Kobes Du Mez, *Jesus and John Wayne*. 297, 298.

52. Americans United for Separation of Church and State, "White Christian Nationalism: Attacking Our Democracy," https://www.au.org/how-we-protect-religious-freedom/issues/religious-racial-equality/white-christian-nationalism/.

53. Adam Volle, *Britannica*, "Christian Nationalism," https://www.britannica.com/topic/Christian-nationalism.

54. Peter Smith, *AP*, May 15, 2024, "Jesus is their savior, Trump is their candidate. Ex-president's backers say he shares faith, values."

55. Katherine Stewart, *The Power Worshippers*. 211.

56. Adam Volle, *Britannica*, "Christian Nationalism."

57. *Center for American Progress*, April 13, 2022, "Christian Nationalism Is 'Single Biggest Threat' to America's Religious Freedom."

58. Josephine von Dohlen, *CRUX*, July 10, 2017, "Images of Faith Preserved at Capitol Attest to Role of Religion in U.S." https://cruxnow.com/church-in-the-usa/2017/07/images-faith-preserved-capitol-attest-role-religion-u-s.

59. Josephine von Dohlen, *CRUX*, July 10, 2017, "Images of Faith Preserved at Capitol Attest to Role of Religion in U.S."

60. Josephine von Dohlen, *CRUX*, July 10, 2017, "Images of Faith Preserved at Capitol Attest to Role of Religion in U.S."

61. Kirby Anderson, *Probe*, January 29, 2007, "God in Our Nation's Capital," https://probe.org/god-in-our-nations-capital/.

62. David Mikkelson, *Scopes*, November 5, 2003, "Religious Symbols in the U.S. Capitol," https://www.snopes.com/fact-check/national-capital/.

63. Kirby Anderson, *Probe*, January 29, 2007, "God in Our Nation's Capital."

64. Kirby Anderson, *Probe*, January 29, 2007, "God in Our Nation's Capital."

65. Gregory A. Smith, Michael Rotolo, and Patricia Tevington, October 27, 2022, Pew Research Center, "45% of Americans Say U.S. Should Be a Christian Nation."

66. Frances FitzGerald, *The Evangelicals: The Struggle to Shape America*. 358.

67. Pew Research Center, March 15, 2024, "Christianity's Place in Politics, and 'Christian Nationalism,' https://www.pewresearch.org/religion/2024/03/15/christianitys-place-in-politics-and-christian-nationalism/.

68. Daniel Silliman, *Christianity Today*, October 31, 2022, "Christianity Nationalism Debates Expose Clashing Views of Power," https://www.christianitytoday.com/news/2022/october/evangelical-christian-nationalism-nationalist-midterm-pew.html.

2. Global Origins of Christian Nationalism

1. William Newton Clarke, D.D., An Outline of Christian Theology, New York: Charles Scribner's Sons, 1898. 8.

2. Vergilius Ferm, ed. *Classics of Protestantism*, New York: Philosophical Library, 1959. 531, 532.

3. Vergilius Ferm, ed. *Classics of Protestantism*. 531.

4. Frances FitzGerald, *The Evangelicals: The Struggle to Shape America*. 200.

5. Bernhard W. Anderson, *Understanding the Old Testament*, New Jersey: Englewood Cliffs, 1975. 202.

6. Roy Willis, ed., *World Mythology*, London: Duncan Baird Publishers, 1996. 126.

7. Samuel Noah Kramer, *Cradle of Civilization*, New York: Time Incorporated, 1967. 108.

8. James H. Smylie, *American Presbyterians: A Pictorial History*, Philadelphia: Presbyterian Historical Society, 1985, 44.

9. Elizabeth Dias, *The New York Times*, February 10, 2021, "A Century Ago, White Protestant Extremism Marched on Washington," https://www.nytimes.com/2021/02/07/us/white-protestants-ku-klux-klan.html.

10. Paul D. Miller, *The Religion of American Greatness: What's Wrong with Christian Nationalism*, Downer's Grove, Illinois: InterVarsity Press, 2022. 3- 4.

11. S. B. F. Brandon and Friedrich Heer, eds. *Forty Centuries: From the Pharaohs to Alfred the Great*, Italy: The Britannica society, 1972. 28.

12. Arthur Cotterell, ed., *The Encyclopedia of World Mythology*, New York: Barnes & Noble Books, 2001, 8, 9.

13. Lionel Casson, *Ancient Egypt*, New York: Time Life Books. 1965. 267, 270, 290.

14. Arthur Cotterell, ed., *The Encyclopedia of World Mythology*. 7.

15. Francis Wilkinson, *Deccan Herald (DH)*, February 4, 2025, "MAGA's driving force is Christian nationalism."

16. Lionel Casson, *Ancient Egypt*. 267, 270, 290.

17. Lionel Casson, *Ancient Egypt*. 56.

18. Amy Hackney Blackwell and Christopher W. Blackwell, *Mythology for Dummies*, New Jersey: John Wiley & Sons, Inc: 2023. 77-86, 104-105.

19. Donald L. Wasson, July 28, 2016, *World History Encyclopedia*, "Alexander the Great as a God," https://www.worldhistory.org/article/925/alexander-the-great-as-a-god/.

20. Roy Willis, ed., *World Mythology*. 111, 34, 52, 56, 126, 160, 174.

21. Roy Willis, ed., *World Mythology*. 174, 234, 243, 248, 252, 256, 267, 267, 270, 290.

22. Matthew Wills, December 18, 2020, *JSTOR Daily*, "Making Sense of the Divine Right of Kings, https://daily.jstor.org/making-sense-of-the-divine-right-of-kings/.

23. CNE: Christian Network Europe, "The Coronation of King Charles is Full of Religious Symbolism," https://cne.news/article/3026-the-coronation-of-king-charles-is-full-of-religious-symbolism.

24. Jodi Eichler-Levine, Washington Post, March 20, 2020, "Why Christian nationalists think Trump is heaven-sent," https://www.washingtonpost.com/outlook/why-christian-nationalists-think-trump-is-heaven-sent/2020/03/20/a3c42734-5983-11ea-9b35-def5a027d470_story.html.

25. Arthur Cotterell, ed., *The Encyclopedia of World Mythology*. 30.

26. Paula R. Hartz, *Zoroastrianism: World Religions*, New York: Facts on File: 1999, 9-11.

27. Bernhard W. Anderson, *Understanding the Old Testament*. 50.

28. Bernhard W. Anderson, *Understanding the Old Testament*. 38.

29. *World Atlas*, 2024, "Zoroastrianism," https://www.worldatlas.com/articles/zoroastrianism.html.

30. Basil Davidson, *African Kingdoms,* New York: Time Life Books, 1966. 123-124.

31. Lionel Casson, *Ancient Egypt*. 80, 143.

32. Amy Hackney Blackwell and Christopher W. Blackwell, *Mythology for Dummies*. 32-38.

33. Samuel Noah Kramer, *Cradle of Civilization*. 99.

34. Amy Hackney Blackwell and Christopher W. Blackwell, *Mythology for Dummies*. 241.

35. Amy Hackney Blackwell and Christopher W. Blackwell, *Mythology for Dummies*. 32-38.

36. Samuel Noah Kramer, *Cradle of Civilization*. 100.

37. Bernhard W. Anderson, *Understanding the Old Testament*. 210.

38. Arthur Cotterell, ed., *The Encyclopedia of World Mythology*. 200.

39. Amy Hackney Blackwell and Christopher W. Blackwell, *Mythology for Dummies*. 130, 243.

40. Amy Hackney Blackwell and Christopher W. Blackwell, *Mythology for Dummies*. 176.

41. Noel Rae, *Witnessing America | : The Library of Congress Book of First-hand Accounts of Life in America 1600-1900*, New York: Penguin Books, 1996. 5.

42. Jared Krebsback, *The Collector*, December 30, 2024, "What Was the Religion of the Ancient Phoenicians and Carthaginians?" https://www.thecollector.com/phoenicians-carthaginians-religion/.

43. Jared Krebsback, *The Collector*, December 30, 2024, "What Was the Religion of the Ancient Phoenicians and Carthaginians?"

44. Amy Hackney Blackwell and Christopher W. Blackwell, *Mythology for Dummies*. 328.

45. Sierra Boucher, *Livescience*, "'An Offering to Energize the Fields': 76 Child Sacrifice Victims, All With Their Chests Cut Open, Unearthed at Burial Site in Peru," November 4, 2024, https://www.livescience.com/archaeology/an-offering-to-energize-the-fields-76-child-sacrifice-victims-all-with-their-chests-cut-open-unearthed-at-burial-site-in-peru.

46. Arthur Cotterell, ed., *The Encyclopedia of World Mythology*. 209.

47. Amy Hackney Blackwell and Christopher W. Blackwell, *Mythology for Dummies*. 262, 332, 341.

48. Jessica Suess, *The Collector*, October 21, 2024, "Valhalla & The Other Afterlives in Norse Mythology," https://www.thecollector.com/valhalla-other-afterlives-norse-mythology/.

49. Noel Rae, ed. *Witnessing America: The Library of Congress Book of Firsthand Accounts of Life in America 1600-1900*. 360-361.

50. Erin Blakemore, *National Geographic*, October 7, 2024, "Witch Hunts Were Common in the 17th Century. Here's What We Know," https://www.nationalgeographic.com/history/article/salem-witch-trials?rid=A873ED5F20435DB2C79F24AED330767F&cmpid=org%3Dngp%3A%3Amc%3Dcrm-email%3A%3Asrc%3Dngp%3A%3Acmp%3Deditorial%3A%3Aadd%3DWeeklyEscape_20241009&loggedin=true&rnd=1728497961126.

51. Lionel Casson, *Ancient Egypt*. 71-77.

52. Moses Hadas, *Imperial Rome*, New York: Time-Life Books, 1965. 72, 127.

53. Bernhard W. Anderson, *Understanding the Old Testament*. 143.

54. Jessica Suess, *The Collector*, October 21, 2024, "Valhalla & The Other Afterlives in Norse Mythology."

55. Malcolm Clark, *Islam for Dummies*, New Jersey: Wiley Publishing, 2003. 68-71.

56. Philip B. Kunhardt III, Peter W. Kunhardt, and Peter W. Kunhardt, Jr., *Looking for Lincoln: The Making of an American Icon*, New York: Alfred A. Knopf, 2008. 24.

57. Basil Davidson, *African Kingdoms*, New York: Time Life Books, 1966. 126.

58. Amy Hackney Blackwell and Christopher W. Blackwell, *Mythology for Dummies*.131-136.

59. Arthur Cotterell, ed., *The Encyclopedia of World Mythology*. 209.

60. Arthur Cotterell, ed., *The Encyclopedia of World Mythology*. 101.

61. Robert P. Jones, *Time Magazine*, August 31, 2023, "The Roots of Christian Nationalism Go Back Further Than You Think," https://time

.com/6309657/us-christian-nationalism-columbus-essay/. Also see Romanus Pontifex, https://www.papalencyclicals.net/nichol05/romanus-pontifex.htm.

62. Joey Schneider, *Fox2now*, July 10, 2024, "Missouri U.S. Sen. Josh Hawley Advocates for Christian Nationalism, https://fox2now.com/news/missouri/missouri-u-s-sen-josh-hawley-advocates-for-christian-nationalism/.

63. Bryan N. Massingale, *National Catholic Review*, July 10, 2023, "As the election cycle cranks up, Christians need to call out white Christian nationalism," https://www.ncronline.org/opinion/guest-voices/election-cycle-cranks-christians-need-call-out-white-christian-nationalism.

64. Stephen M. Walk, October 11, 2022, *Foreign Policy*, "The Myth of American Exceptionalism," https://foreignpolicy.com/2011/10/11/the-myth-of-american-exceptionalism/.

65. W. J. Cash, *The Mind of the South*, New York: Vintage Books, 1991. 337.

66. Cathy Young, *The Montanan*, April 2, 2024, "Christian Nationalism: A Grave Threat to America."

67. *WordWay*, September 9, 2020, "Worship is Protest," https://wordandway.org/2020/09/09/worship-is-protest/.

68. Allan Boesak. Leonard Sweetman, ed. *Black and Reformed: Apartheid, Liberation, and the Calvinist Tradition*, New York: Orbis Books, 1986. 106.

69. *European Academy of Religion and Society*, "The Dutch Reformed Church and its contribution to Apartheid'" December 7, 2021, https://europeanacademyofreligionandsociety.com/news/the-dutch-reformed-church-and-its-contribution-to-apartheid/.

70. *Wikipedia*, "Theocracy," https://en.wikipedia.org/wiki/Theocracy.

71. Adam Volle, *Britannica*, "Christian Nationalism."

72. Rainumdo Barreto and Joao B. Chaves, *The Christian Century*, December 1, 2021, "Christian nationalism is thriving in Bolsonaro's Brazil," https://www.christiancentury.org/article/critical-essay/christian-nationalism-thriving-bolsonaro-s-brazil.

73. Angelina E. Theodorou, November 25, 2014, Pew Research Center, "64 Countries Have Religious Symbols on Their National Flags," https://www.pewresearch.org/short-reads/2014/11/25/64-countries-have-religious-symbols-on-their-national-flags/.

74. Angelina E. Theodorou, November 25, 2014, Pew Research Center, "64 Countries Have Religious Symbols on Their National Flags."

75. Olivia Munson, *USA Today*, March 18, 2023, "The State Flag for all 50 States: See the State Flags (Plus D.C.) and the Meaning

Behind Each," https://www.usatoday.com/story/news/2023/03/18/complete-us-state-flags-list/11025139002/.

3. American Origins of Christian Nationalism

1. Moses Hadas, Imperial Rome. 128.

2. H. Richard Niebuhr, *The Social Sources of Denominationalism*, New York: The World Publishing Company: 1971. 106, 111.

3. H. Richard Niebuhr, *The Social Sources of Denominationalism*. 111-112.

4. H. Richard Niebuhr, *The Social Sources of Denominationalism*. 122-123, 127, 129, 133.

5. Berndt Ostendorf, September 15, 2019, "A Nation with the Soul of a Church? The Strange Career of Religion in America: A View from Europe," https://www.aisna.net/wp-content/uploads/2019/09/1516ostendorf.pdf.

6. Plimoth Patuxet, "Mayflower and Mayflower Compact," https://plimoth.org/for-students/homework-help/mayflower-and-mayflower-compact.

7. A. James Reichley, *Faith in Politics*, Washington, D.C.: The Brookings Institution, 2002. 56, 57.

8. William Warren Sweet, *The Story of Religion in America*, New York: Harper & Brothers, Second Revised Edition, 1950. 51, 53.

9. Philip S. Gorski and Samuel L. Perry, *The Flag + The Cross: White Christian Nationalism and the Threat to American Democracy*, New York: Oxford University Press, 2022.47.

10. Frances FitzGerald, *The Evangelicals: The Struggle to Shape America*. 19-25.

11. Frances FitzGerald, *The Evangelicals: The Struggle to Shape America*. 40, 44-45.

12. A. James Reichley, *Faith in Politics*. 73.

13. Nikole Hannah-Jones, Caitin Roper, Ilena Silverman, and Jake Silverstein, eds., *The 1619 Project*, New York: One World: 2021. 338.

14. Kevin Phillips, *American Theocracy: The Peril and Politics of Radical Religion, Oil, and Borrowed Money in the 21st Century*. 129, 121, 122.

15. A. James Reichley, *Faith in Politics*. 95.

16. Nikole Hannah-Jones, Caitin Roper, Ilena Silverman, and Jake Silverstein, eds., *The 1619 Project*. 338.

17. James H. Smylie, *American Presbyterians: A Pictorial History*. 44.

18. Kaitlyn Schiess, *The Ballot and the Bible*. 22-27.

19. *PBS American Experience*, "God in the White House," https://www.pbs.org/wgbh/americanexperience/features/godinamerica-white-house/.

20. *PBS American Experience,* "God in the White House."

21. A. James Reichley, *Faith in Politics*. 96-99.

22. A. James Reichley, *Faith in Politics*. 95.

23. American Civil Liberties Union (ACLU), *The Constitution of the United States,* New York: ACLU, 2016. 25.

24. Olivier Zunz, ed. *Alexis De Tocqueville: Democracy in America,* New York: The Library in America, 2004. 332, 344, 345, 347.

25. A. James Reichley, *Faith in Politics*. 111-112.

26. Kevin Phillips, *American Theocracy: The Peril and Politics of Radical Religion, Oil, and Borrowed Money in the 21st Century*. 141.

27. Kevin Phillips, *American Theocracy: The Peril and Politics of Radical Religion, Oil, and Borrowed Money in the 21st Century*. 150.

28. Glenn Hastedt, *One World, Many Voices: Global Perspectives on Political Issues,* New Jersey: Prentice-Hall, Inc., 1995. 17-31.

29. Eric Foner, *The Story of American Freedom,* New York: W. W. Norton & Company, 1998. 50.

30. Kalefa Sanneh, March 27, 2003, *The New Yorker,* "How Christian Is Christian Nationalism?"

31. William McKinley, First Inaugural Address, March 4, 1897. https://avalon.law.yale.edu/19th_century/mckin1.asp

32. General James Rusling, "Interview with President William McKinley," *The Christian Advocate* 22 January 1903, 17. Reprinted in Charles Sumner Olcott, *The Life of William McKinley,* Volume 2 (New York: Houghton Mifflin, 1916), 109-111.

33. Kevin Phillips, *American Theocracy: The Peril and Politics of Radical Religion, Oil, and Borrowed Money in the 21st Century*. 125, 130, 138, 143, 144, 145, 148, 152.

34. Ronald C. White, Jr. and Howard C. Hopkins, *The Social Gospel: Religion and Reform in Changing America,* Philadelphia: Temple University Press, 1976. 37-39.

35. Timothy B. Tyson, *News and Observer,* "The Ghosts of 1898: Wilmington's Race Riot and the Rise of White Supremacy," http://media2.newsobserver.com/content/media/2010/5/3/ghostsof1898.pdf.

36. Danny E. Olinger, "The Christianity of Woodrow Wilson," *New Horizons,* October 2018. https://opc.org/nh.html?article_id=962.

37. Rhys Long, *Americans United for Church and State,* August 29, 2023, "Origin Story: The history of Christian Nationalism is littered with hate and extremism, https://www.au.org/the-latest/church-and-state/articles/origin-story-the-history-of-christian-nationalism-is-littered-with-hate-and-extremism/.

38. A. James Reichley, *Faith in Politics*. 232-234.

39. Richard Rothstein, *The Color of Law: A Forgotten History of How Our Government Segregated America*, Liveright Publishing, 2017, xii.

40. Constantine Dzink, quoted in Robert P. Jones, *White Too Long: The Legacy of White Supremacy in American Christianity*, Simon & Schuster, 2020. 77-78.

41. Richard Rothstein, quoted in Robert P. Jones, *White Too Long*. 79.

42. Frances FitzGerald, *The Evangelicals: The Struggle to Shape America*. 169-207.

43. Frances FitzGerald, *The Evangelicals: The Struggle to Shape America*. 185-186.

44. Dianne Kirby, "The Cold War and American Religion," https://doi.org/10.1093/acrefore/9780199340378.013.398.

45. Frances FitzGerald, *The Evangelicals: The Struggle to Shape America*.236-238.

46. Ashley Lopez, NPR, February 14, 2023, "More than half of Republicans support Christian nationalism, according to a new survey," https://www.npr.org/2023/02/14/1156642544/more-than-half-of-republicans-support-christian-nationalism-according-to-a-new-s.

47. David Sessions, *Daily Beast*, August 18, 2011, "Tea Party: Is It the Christian Right in Disguise?" https://www.thedailybeast.com/tea-party-is-it-the-christian-right-in-disguise.

48. Scott Clement and John C. Green, Pew Research Center, February 23, 2011, "The Tea Party and Religion," https://www.pewresearch.org/religion/2011/02/23/tea-party-and-religion/.

49. Huma Khan, ABCNews, October 18, 2011, "Is the Tea Party a Religious Movement? 'Anthem' Invokes God, Judgment Day," https://abcnews.go.com/blogs/politics/2011/10/is-the-tea-party-a-religious-movement-anthem-invokes-god-judgment-day.

50. Daniel Cox and Robert P. Jones, PRRI, October 5, 2010, "Religion and the Tea Party in the 2010 Elections," https://www.prri.org/research/religion-tea-party-2010/.

51. Huma Khan, ABCNews, October 18, 2011, "Is the Tea Party a Religious Movement? 'Anthem' Invokes God, Judgment Day."

52. Barbara Bradley Hagerty, NPR, September 30, 2010, "The Tea Party's Tension: Religion's Role in Politics, https://www.npr.org/2010/09/30/130238835/the-tea-partys-tension-religions-role-in-politics.

53. "Confronting Christian Nationalism" podcast, first episode "What is Christian Nationalism," *Common Good Media*, Executive Director of Vote Common Good, Doug Pagitt.

4. White Christian Nationalism

1. Gabriel R. Sanchez, Keon L. Gilbert, and Carly Bennett, *Brookings*, "White nationalism remains major concern for voters of color, March 30, 2023, https://www.brookings.edu/articles/white-nationalism-remains-major-concern-for-voters-of-color-and-appears-to-be-connected-ideologically-to-the-growing-christian-nationalism-movement/

2. "2020 PRRI Census of American Religion: County-Level Data on Religious Identity and Diversity." Public Religion Research Institute. https://prri.org/research/2020-census-of-american-religion/

3. Ashley Lopez, *NPR*, February 14, 2023, "More Than Half of Republicans Support Christian Nationalism, According to a New Survey."

4. Adam Volle, *Britannica*, "Christian Nationalism."

5. Katherine Stewart, "The Power Worshippers," Free Inquiry, August/September 2021, Volume 41, No.5, https://secularhumanism.org/2021/08/the-power-worshippers/?gclid=Cj0KCQiA5OuNBhCRARIsACgaiqVPTCcLep-MnYZI02kgkXHqkh1Utggi9AHj_hhU3kRvXoZDeYE4EDAaAp8HEALw_wcB.

6. Jemar Tisby, *The Emancipator*, November 4, 2022, "Faith on the ballot; White Christian nationalism vs. Black Christian tradition," https://theemancipator.org/2022/11/04/elections/faith-ballot-white-christian-nationalism-vs-black-christian-tradition/.

7. Kristin Kobes Du Mez, *Jesus and John Wayne*. 4, 52.

8. Kristin Kobes Du Mez, *Jesus and John Wayne*. 4, 9, 13, 52.

9. Kristin Kobes Du Mez, *Jesus and John Wayne*. 173.

10. Kristin Kobes Du Mez, *Jesus and John Wayne*. 173-179.

11. Bryan N. Massingale, *National Catholic Review*, July 10, 2023, "As the election cycle cranks up, Christians need to call out white Christian nationalism."

12. Robert P. Jones, *The End of White Christian America*, New York: Simon & Schuster, 2016. 1, 234, 236.

5. Black Christian Nationalism

1. Gabriel R. Sanchez, Keon L. Gilbert, and Carly Bennett, *Brookings*, "White nationalism remains major concern for voters of color," March 30, 2023.

2. Anthea Butler, March 2, 2024, *MSNBC*, "The political views of these Christian nationalists might surprise you," https://www.msnbc.com/opinion/msnbc-opinion/trump-black-latino-christian-nationalists-rcna140794.

3. Besheer Mohamed and Kiana Cox, June 15, 2020, *Pew Research Center*, "Before protests, black Americans said religious sermons should address race relations," https://www.pewresearch.org/short-reads/2020/06/15/before-protests-black-americans-said-sermons-should-address-race-relations/.

4. Nikole Hannah-Jones, *The 1619 Project*. 8, 9, 36.

5. C. Eric Lincoln and Lawrence H. Mamiya, *The Black Church in the African American Experience*, Durham: Duke University Press, 1990. 200-214.

6. Janell Ross, *The Washington Post*, July 28, 2026, "The Rev. William Barber Dropped the Mic," https://www.washingtonpost.com/news/the-fix/wp/2016/07/28/the-rev-william-barber-dropped-the-mic/.

7. Wikipedia, "Albert Cleage," https://en.wikipedia.org/wiki/Albert_Cleage.

8. C. Eric Lincoln, ed. *The Black Experience in Religion*, New York: Anchor Books, 1974. 168.

9. Nikole Hannah-Jones, Caitin Roper, Ilena Silverman, and Jake Silverstein, eds., *The 1619 Project*. 348.

10. Ben Carson, Keynote Address at the National Character and Leadership Symposium, Air Force Academy, February 24, 2022. https://www.youtube.com/watch?v=DTHibqmPd7E

11. Rick Pidcock, *Baptist News Global*, May 25, 2023, "Yes, Tim Scott is a Black man, but he's still promoting Christian nationalism," https://baptistnews.com/article/yes-tim-scott-is-a-black-man-but-hes-still-promoting-christian-nationalism/.

12. Mark Robertson, Speech at the Conservative Political Action Conference in Orlando, 2022. https://www.youtube.com/watch?v=NkdLquU8xVU&t=40s

13. Lee H. Walker, *Rediscovering Black Conservatism*, Chicago: The Heartland Institute, 2009. 13.

14. Cornel West, *Democracy Matters: Winning the Fight Against Imperialism*, New York: The Penguin Press, 2004. 171-172.

6. Hispanic Christian Nationalism

1. Erica Ramirez, "The particularly Pentecostal flavor of Mayra Flores' Christian nationalism," Religion News Service, July 11, 2022. https://religionnews.com/2022/07/11/the-particularly-pentecostal-flavor-of-mayra-flores-christian-nationalism/

2. Lourdes Hurtado, *NBC News*, March 11, 2024, "Latino evangelical support for Christian nationalism rises as Trump courts religious votes," https://www.nbcnews.com/news/amp/rcna142735.

3. Russell Contreras, *Axios*, February 29, 2024, "Survey: 55% of Latino Protestants support Christian nationalism," https://www.axios.com/2024/02/29/christian-nationalism-latino-hispanic-protestant-evangelical.

4. Erica Ramirez, *Religion News Service*, July 11, 2022, "The particularly Pentecostal flavor of Marya Flores' Christian nationalism," https://religionnews.com/2022/07/11/the-particularly-pentecostal-flavor-of-mayra-flores-christian-nationalism/.

5. Russell Contreras, *Axios*, February 29, 2024, "Survey: 55% of Latino Protestants Support Christian Nationalism."

6. Katherine Stewart, *The Power Worshippers*. 94, 95.

7. Sarah McCammon, NPR *All Things Considered*, "Latino evangelicals praise Donald Trump as president-elect who respects Christians, November 14, 2024, https://www.npr.org/2024/11/13/nx-s1-5181821/trump-latinos-evangelicals-economy-transgender-abortion-education.

8. Lourdes Hurtado, March 11, 2024, *NBC News*, "Latino evangelical support for Christian nationalism rises as Trump courts religious vote."

9. Michael Gonzalez, *The Guardian*, November 4, 2024, "Texas House candidate campaigning in churches, in potential legal violation," https://www.theguardian.com/us-news/2024/nov/04/texas-congressional-campaign-churches.

7. Asian American Christian Nationalism

1. Neil G. Ruiz, Carolyne Im, and Ziyao Tian, Pew Research Center, November 30, 2023, "Asian Americans and the 'model minority' stereotype," https://www.pewresearch.org/2023/11/30/asian-americans-and-the-model-minority-stereotype/.

2. *Faithfully Magazine*, FM Editors, January 29, 2021, "Possessed by Legion: Anti-Asian Hate and Christian Nationalism," https://faithfullymagazine.com.

3. Faithfully Magazine, FM Editors, January 29, 2021, "Possessed by Legion: Anti-Asian Hate and Christian Nationalism."

4. Gabriel R. Sanchez, Keon L. Gilbert, and Carly Bennett, *Brookings*, "White nationalism remains major concern for voters of color," March 30, 2023.

5. *Faithfully Magazine*, FM Editors, January 29, 2021, "Possessed by Legion: Anti-Asian Hate and Christian Nationalism."

8. The Church and Christian Nationalism

1. William H. Willimon, *Acts: Interpretation: A Commentary for Teaching and Preaching* (Westeminster John Knox Press, 2010), 41.

2. Dan Kimball, *They Like Jesus but Not the Church: Insights from Emerging Generations* (Zondervan, 2007), 78.

3. Shirley C. Guthrie, Jr. *Christian Doctrine.* 300.

4. Dion Forster, 2019, Stellenbosch Theological Journal, "Worship as 'Protest'" Johan Cilliers as a Public Theologian?" http://www.scielo.org.za/scielo.php?script=sci_arttext&pid=S2413-94672019000200010.

9. Evangelicals and Christian Nationalism

1. Tim Alberta, *The Kingdom, the Power, and the Glory: American Evangelicals in an Age of Extremism*, New York: Harper, 2024. 21.

2. Kristin Kobes Du Mez, *Jesus and John Wayne.* 3.

3. Kristin Kobes Du Mez, *Jesus and John Wayne.* 2-4.

4. Summer Evans and Adam Ragusea, March 21, 2018, *NPR,* "Why African-Americans Are Leaving White Evangelical Churches," https://www.gpb.org/news/2018/03/21/why-african-americans-are-leaving-white-evangelical-churches. The Pew Research Center information is found at https://www.pewresearch.org/fact-tank/2018/02/07/5-facts-about-the-religious-lives-of-african-americans/.

5. Kristin Kobes Du Mez, *Jesus and John Wayne.* 6.

10. Progressive Christians and Christian Nationalism

1. Donald J. Bruggink and Carl H. Droppers. *Christ And Architecture: Building Presbyterian / Reformed Churches*, Grand Rapids Michigan: William B. Eerdmans Publishing Company, 1965. 451.

2. "Christian Nationalism Is Worse Than You Think," interview with Paul Miller, Lutheran Advocacy Ministry in Arizona, January 13, 2021. https://lamaz.org/news-blog/christian-nationalism-is-worse-than-you-think.

3. Harold M. Daniels, statement written by the Presbyterian Church (USA) Office of Theology for Worship Resources in 1988.

4. Donald J. Bruggink and Carl H. Droppers. *Christ And Architecture: Building Presbyterian / Reformed Churches.*

11. Catholics and Christian Nationalism

1. Douglas R. A. Hare, *Matthew: Interpretation: A Commentary for Teaching and Preaching* (Louisville: John Knox Press, 1993), 190.

2. Ruth Braunstein, *National Catholic Reporter*, July 24, 2024, "Catholic Christian nationalism is having a moment," https://www.ncronline.org/news/catholic-christian-nationalism-having-moment.

3. Ruth Braunstein, *National Catholic Reporter*, July 24, 2024, "Catholic Christian nationalism is having a moment."

4. Ruth Braunstein, *National Catholic Reporter*, July 24, 2024, "Catholic Christian nationalism is having a moment."

5. Rachel Zoll, *AP*, July 13, 2017, "Confidant of Pope Francis condemns US religious right," https://apnews.com/article/ff74d0ef06a74e518f194069e1657e7e.

6. Jonathan Liedl, *National Catholic Register*, March 18, 2024, "Is 'Christian Nationalism' Really a Problem?" https://www.ncregister.com/news/christian-nationalism-potent-influence-or-political-bogeyman.

7. Jack Holloway, *The Christian Century*, Decembere 2025 edition, "Music for the Apocalypse," https://www.christiancentury.org/features/music-apocalypse.

8. Ruth Braunstein, *National Catholic Reporter*, July 24, 2024, "Catholic Christian Nationalism is Having a Moment."

9. Rachel Zoll, *AP*, July 13, 2017, "Confidant of Pope Francis Condemns US Religious Right."

10. Kate Scanlon, National Catholic Reporter, April 18, 2024, "'Christian nationalism' is opposed to Catholic teaching," https://www.ncronline.org/news/christian-nationalism-opposed-catholic-teaching.

11. Jack Jenkins, *Religion News Service*, April 3, 2024 "The strange world of Catholic 'integralism'—and Christian nationalism" https://religionnews.com/2024/04/03/the-strange-world-of-catholic-christian-nationalism/.

12. John Stoehr, *The Editorial Board*, March 15, 2024, "The anti-Catholic hatred hidden inside 'Christian nationalism,'" https://www.editorialboard.com/the-anti-catholic-hatred-hidden-inside-christian-nationalism/.

13. Ben Howe, *The Immoral Majority: Why Evangelicals Chose Political Power Over Christian Values,* New York: HarperCollins Publishers Inc., 2019.

12. Clergy and Christian Nationalism

1. Thomas C. Oden, First and Second Timothy and Titus: Interpretation: A Bible Commentary for Teaching and Preaching, John Knox Press, 1989. 141.

2. Clarice J. Martin, "1–2 Timothy and Titus," in True to Our Native Land: An African American New Tesetament Commentary. Minneapolis: Fortress Press, 2007. 409-436.

3. Quoted in Noel Rae, "How Christian Slaveholders Used the Bible to Justify Slavery," Time Magazine, February 23, 2018. https://time.com/5171819/christianity-slavery-book-excerpt/

4. Rhys Long, *Americans United for Church and State*, August 29, 2023, "Origin story: The history of Christian Nationalism is littered with hate and extremism," https://www.au.org/the-latest/church-and-state/articles/origin-story-the-history-of-christian-nationalism-is-littered-with-hate-and-extremism/.

5. Frances FitzGerald, *The Evangelicals: The Struggle to Shape America*. 232-233,3 35.

6. Randall Balmer, *Politico*, May 27, 2014, "The Real Origins of the Religious Right: They'll tell you it was abortion. Sorry, the historical record's clear: It was segregation." https://www.politico.com/magazine/story/2014/05/religious-right-real-origins-107133/.

7. Frances FitzGerald, *The Evangelicals: The Struggle to Shape America*. 290 292.

8. Randall Balmer, *Politico*, May 27, 2014, "The Real Origins of the Religious Right: They'll tell you it was abortion. Sorry, the historical record's clear: It was segregation."

9. Cornel West, *Democracy Matters: Winning the Fight Against Imperialism*. 146, 148.

10. Adam Volle, *Britannica*, "Christian Nationalism."

11. Kristin Kobes Du Mez, *Jesus and John Wayne*. 136.

12. Frances FitzGerald, *The Evangelicals: The Struggle to Shape America*. 412.

13. Francis Wilkinson, *Deccan Herald (DH)*, February 4, 2025, "MAGA's driving force is Christian nationalism."

14. Frances FitzGerald, *The Evangelicals: The Struggle to Shape America*. 446, 447.

15. Katherine Stewart, "The Power Worshippers," August/September 2021, Volume 41, No.5.

16. Randall Balmer, *Politico*, May 27, 2014, "The Real Origins of the Religious Right: They'll tell you it was abortion. Sorry, the historical record's clear: It was segregation."

17. Randall Balmer, *Politico*, May 27, 2014, "The Real Origins of the Religious Right: They'll tell you it was abortion. Sorry, the historical record's clear: It was segregation."

18. Kenneth F. Mott, EBSCO, 2022, "Prayer in schools," https://www.ebsco.com/research-starters/religion-and-philosophy/prayer-schools.

19. Deirdre Jonese Austin, October 23, 2020, "How One Worship Leader Made Racial Justice Protests About Christian Persecution," https://sojo.net/articles/how-one-worship-leader-made-racial-justice-protests-about-christian-persecution.

20. Jack Jenkins, *The Presbyterian Outlook*, "Christian leaders condemn Christian nationalism in new letter," August 2, 2019, https://pres-outlook.org/2019/08/christian-leaders-condemn-christian-nationalism-in-new-letter/.

21. Letter sent by Rev. Paula White to the author on July 17, 2024, from pastorpaula@nationalfaithadvisoryboard.org.

22. Carol Kruvilla, *Huffington Post*, January 22, 2018, "Franklin Graham Praises Trump As Staunch Defender Of Christianity," https://www.huffpost.com/entry/franklin-graham-claims-trump-has-defended-christianity-more-than-any-recent-president_n_5a663c12e4b0dc592a0b86bb.

23. *AP*, May 4, 2018, "Billy Graham's Son: God Put Trump into Office," https://www.usatoday.com/videos/news/nation/2018/05/04/billy-grahams-son-god-put-trump-office/34543485/.

13. Politicians and Christian Nationalism

1. Douglas R. A. Hare, *Matthew*, 44-45.

2. Kalefa Sanneh, March 27, 2003, *The New Yorker*, "How Christian Is Christian Nationalism?"

3. Abram Van Engen, *National Endowment for the Humanities*, Winter 2020, "How America Became 'A City Upon a Hill,'" https://www.neh.gov/article/how-america-became-city-upon-hill#:~:text=Hardly%20anyone%20knew%20this%20sermon,Carter%2C%20Ronald%20Reagan%2C%20George%20H.%20W..

4. Ronald Reagan, "Farewell Address to the Nation," January 11, 1989. https://www.reaganlibrary.gov/archives/speech/farewell-address-nation.

5. Gregory A. Smith, Michael Rotolo, and Patricia Tevington, October 27, 2022, Pew Research Center, "45% of Americans Say U.S. Should Be a Christian Nation."

6. Gabriel R. Sanchez, Keon L. Gilbert, and Carly Bennett, *Brookings*, "White nationalism remains major concern for voters of color," March 30, 2023.

7. Gregory A. Smith, Michael Rotolo, and Patricia Tevington, October 27, 2022, Pew Research Center, "45% of Americans Say U.S. Should Be a Christian Nation."

8. Gabe Whisnant, *Newsweek*, "Full List of 'Black Americans for Trump' Coalition Partners," June 15, 2024, https://www.newsweek.com/full-list-black-americans-trump-coalition-partners-1913346.

9. Yonat Shimron, "A Campaign to Blitz the Country with 'In God We Trust' Laws Takes Root," *Religion News Service*, July 2, 2018, https://religionnews.com/2018/07/02/a-campaign-to-blitz-the-country-with-in-god-we-trust-laws-takes-root/.

10. Mark Walsh, *EducationWeek,* May 28, 2024, "Federal Judge Overturns New Hampshire Law on Teaching 'Divisive Concepts,'" https://www.edweek.org/policy-politics/federal-judge-overturns-new-hampshire-law-on-teaching-divisive-concepts/2024/05.

11. Marvin Olasky, *Religion Unplugged*, July 1, 2024, "Olasky's Books For July: Christian Nationalism And Critical Race Theory," https://religionunplugged.com/news/olaskys-books-for-july-christian-nationalism-and-critical-race-theory.

12. Eric Bates, *Mother Jones*, May/June 1995, "What You Need to Know about Jesse Helms," https://www.motherjones.com/politics/1995/05/what-you-need-know-about-jesse-helms/.

13. Bill Peterson, *The Washington Post,* November 3, 1984, "Helms' Religion Stand Rallies Christian Group," https://www.washingtonpost.com/archive/politics/1984/11/03/helms-religion-stand-rallies-christian-group/75666066-9132-4292-8b6d-6840571fe500/.

14. Laura Barron-López and Sam Lane, *PBS News Hour,* February 1, 2024, "What is Christian nationalism and why it raises concerns about threats to democracy."

15. Joey Schneider, *Fox2now*, July 10, 2024, "Missouri U.S. Sen. Josh Hawley advocates for Christian nationalism," https://fox2now.com/news/missouri/missouri-u-s-sen-josh-hawley-advocates-for-christian-nationalism/.

16. "More than half of Republicans support Christian Nationalism, according to a new survey," NPR, February 13, 2023. https://www.npr.org/transcripts/1156642544.

17. Terry Gross, *NPR*, February 29, 2004, "Tracing the rise of Christian nationalism, from Trump to the Ala. Supreme Court."

18. Jack Jenkins and Emily MacFarlan Miller, August 27, 2020, "Pence altered a biblical reference, changing 'Jesus' to the American flag in his convention speech," https://www.washingtonpost.com/religion/2020/08/27/pence-bible-rnc-jesus-flag/.

19. John Blake, *CNN*, January 12, 2025, "White Christian nationalists are poised to remake America in their image During Trump's second term, author says," https://www.cnn.com/2025/01/12/us/white-christian-nationalism-du-mez-cec/index.html.

20. *Freedom from Religion Foundation*, November 27, 2024, "FFRF exposes Christian nationalist bent of Trump's proposed cabinet," https://

ffrf.org/news/releases/ffrf-exposes-christian-nationalist-bent-of-trumps-proposed-cabinet/.

21. Alexander Ward and Heidi Przybyla, *Politico*, February 2, 2024, "Trump Allies Prepare to Infuse 'Christian Nationalism' in Second Administration," https://www.politico.com/news/2024/02/20/donald-trump-allies-christian-nationalism-00142086.

22. *Freedom from Religion Foundation*, November 27, 2024, "FFRF exposes Christian nationalist bent of Trump's proposed cabinet."

23. Francis Wilkinson, *Deccan Herald (DH)*, February 4, 2025, "MAGA's driving force is Christian nationalism."

24. *Freedom from Religion Foundation*, November 19, 2024, "Christian crusader Pete Hegseth unfit to lead the Pentagon," https://ffrf.org/news/releases/christian-crusader-pete-hegseth-unfit-to-lead-the-pentagon/.

25. Heath Druzin, *Alabama Reflector*, November 26, 2024, "Trump's Defense secretary nominee has close ties to Idaho Christian nationalists," https://alabamareflector.com/2024/11/26/trumps-defense-secretary-nominee-has-close-ties-to-idaho-christian-nationalists/.

26. *Freedom from Religion Foundation*, November 27, 2024, "FFRF exposes Christian nationalist bent of Trump's proposed cabinet."

27. Charles M. Blow, *New York Times*, July 12, 2023, "Tommy Tuberville Is Whitewashing White Nationalism," https://www.nytimes.com/2023/07/12/opinion/tommy-tuberville-white-nationalism.html.

28. *Freedom from Religion Foundation*, November 27, 2024, "FFRF exposes Christian nationalist bent of Trump's proposed cabinet."

29. *PBS American Experience*, "God in the White House."

30. Kevin M. Kruse, *One Nation Under God: How Corporate America Invented Christian America*, New York: Basic Books, 2015. 39.

31. *PBS American Experience*, "God in the White House."

32. Stephen M. Walt, October 11, 2022, *Foreign Policy*, "The Myth of American Exceptionalism," https://foreignpolicy.com/2011/10/11/the-myth-of-american-exceptionalism/.

33. Kevin M. Kruse, *One Nation Under God: How Corporate America Invented Christian America*, New York: Basic Books, 2015. ix.

34. Kevin M. Kruse, *One Nation Under God: How Corporate America Invented Christian America*. x.

35. Kevin M. Kruse, *One Nation Under God: How Corporate America Invented Christian America*. xii.

36. *PBS American Experience*, "God in the White House."

37. Kalefa Sanneh, March 27, 2003, *The New Yorker*, "How Christian Is Christian Nationalism?"

38. Kevin M. Kruse, *One Nation Under God: How Corporate America Invented Christian America*. 11-26, 46, 48, 72, 87.

39. Bill Scher, *Politico*, July 17, 2015, "When Reagan Dared to Say 'God Bless America,'" https://www.politico.com/magazine/story/2015/07/reagan-god-bless-america-120286/.

40. *PBS American Experience*, "God in the White House."

41. *PBS American Experience*, "God in the White House."

42. Frances FitzGerald, *The Evangelicals: The Struggle to Shape America*. 458-461, 466, 467, 498, 500.

43. Kristin Kobes Du Mez, *Jesus and John Wayne*. 172.

44. Frances FitzGerald, *The Evangelicals: The Struggle to Shape America*. 472-473.

45. Jim Wallis, *God's Politics: Why the Right Gets It Wrong and the Left Doesn't Get It*, New York: HarperCollins Publishers, 2005. 141.

46. *Mt Vernon Webpage*, "George Washington and Religion," https://www.mountvernon.org/library/digitalhistory/digital-encyclopedia/article/george-washington-and-religion/.

14. Christian Nationalism and Abortion

1. Walter Brueggemann, Genesis: Interpretation: A Commentary for Teaching and Preaching (Louisville: Westminster John Knox, 1986), 32.

2. Rebecca Todd Peters, *Trust Women: A Progressive Christian Argument for Reproductive Justice*, Boston: Beacon Press, 2018. 52.

3. Rebecca Todd Peters, *Trust Women: A Progressive Christian Argument for Reproductive Justice*. 9.

4. Sarah Posner, *The Nation*, May 9, 2022, "Overturning *Roe* Is the Crowning Achievement of Christian Nationalism," https://www.thenation.com/article/society/dobbs-christian-right/tnamp/.

5. Carter Sherman, *The Guardian*, March 2, 2024, "What Alabama's IVF ruling reveals about the ascendant Christian nationalism Movement," https://www.theguardian.com/world/2024/mar/02/christian-nationalism-alabama-ivf-ruling-politics.

6. Carter Sherman, *The Guardian*, March 2, 2024, "What Alabama's IVF ruling reveals about the ascendant Christian nationalism movement."

7. Carter Sherman, *The Guardian*, March 2, 2024, "What Alabama's IVF ruling reveals about the ascendant Christian nationalism movement.

8. Phoebe Petrovic, *ProPublica*, July 10, 2024, "The Gospel of Matthew Trewhella: How a Militant Anti-Abortion Activist Is Influencing Repub-

lican Politics," https://www.propublica.org/article/matthew-trewhella-pastor-activist-republican-politics.

9. Rebecca Todd Peters, *Trust Women: A Progressive Christian Argument for Reproductive Justice*. 6.

10. Rebecca Todd Peters, *Trust Women: A Progressive Christian Argument for Reproductive Justice*. 174-175.

11. *PBS American Experience*, "God in the White House."

15. Christian Nationalism and LGBTQIA

1. Walter Brueggemann, *First and Second Samuel: Interpretation A Bible Commentary for Teaching and Preaching*, Louisville: Westminster John Knox Press, 1990. 136, 149.

2. Erin Blakemore, *History*, June 5, 2018, "How LGBT Civil Servants Became Public Enemy No. 1 in the 1950s," https://www.history.com/news/state-department-gay-employees-outed-fired-lavender-scare.

3. Kevin M. Kruse, *One Nation Under God: How Corporate America Invented Christian America*. 130.

4. *Capitol History*, "A Summary History of LGBTQ+ Legislation and Representation within Congress," https://capitolhistory.org/capitol-history-blog/a-summary-history-of-lgbtq-legislation-and-representation-within-congress/.

5. Michael Heard, *HistoryHub.info*, "The Enemy Within: Patriotism, Un-Americanism & Coercion in Postwar America, 1945-1960. Introduction: Defining un-Americanism," https://historyhub.info/the-enemy-within-patriotism-un-americanism-coercion-in-postwar-america-1945-1960-introduction-defining-un-americanism/.

6. *PBS American Experience*, "Milestones in the American Gay Rights Movement," https://www.pbs.org/wgbh/americanexperience/features/stonewall-milestones-american-gay-rights-movement/.

7. Jack Jenkins and Emily MacFarlan Miller, August 27, 2020, "Pence Altered a Biblical Reference, Changing 'Jesus' to the American Flag in His Convention Speech."

8. Anthea Butler, *Dissent*, "The Black Church: From Prophecy to Prosperity," Winter 2014, https://www.dissentmagazine.org/article/the-black-church-from-prophecy-to-prosperity/#:~:text=After%20the%20heyday%20of%20the%20freedom%20movement,individual%20morality%20and%20a%20gospel%20of%20prosperity.&text=Jakes%20used%20the%20message%20of%20respectability%20and,are%20the%20majority%20in%20most%20black%20churches.

9. Kim, *National Organization for Women*, November 14, 2023, "Why Christian Nationalism Is a Feminist Issue."

10. *The Associated Press*, May 2024, "A milestone reached in mainline Protestant churches' decades-old disputes over LGBTQ inclusion," https://fox59.com/news/national-world/ap-us-news/ap-a-milestone-reached-in-mainline-protestant-churches-decades-old-disputes-over-lgbtq-inclusion/amp/.

11. *PBS American Experience*, "Milestones in the American Gay Rights Movement," https://www.pbs.org/wgbh/americanexperience/features/stonewall-milestones-american-gay-rights-movement/.

12. Anthea Butler, *Dissent*, "The Black Church: From Prophecy to Prosperity," Winter 2014.

13. David Crary, *AP*, January 7, 2024, "How to Deal with Same-Sex Unions? It's a question fracturing major Christian denominations," https://apnews.com/article/lgbtq-samesex-unions-christianity-catholic-anglican-methodist-00e3a4adaf4266dabbf730390eebd2d9.

16. Christian Nationalism and Gender Justice

1. Brian K. Blount, General Editor, *True to Our Native Land: An African American New Testament Commentary*, Minneapolis: Fortress Press, 2007. 274.

2. Kristin Kobes Du Mez, *Jesus and John Wayne*. 277-278.

3. Kim, November 14, 2023, National Organization for Women, "Why Christian Nationalism Is a Feminist Issue."

17. Christian Nationalism and White Supremacy

1. Philip S. Gorski and Samuel L. Perry, *The Flag + The Cross: White Christian Nationalism and the Threat to American Democracy*. 54, 61.

2. Benjamin Quarles, *The Negro in the Making of America, Third Edition*. Touchstone, 1996. 81.

3. William Warren Sweet, *The Story of Religion in America*. 306, 307.

4. Geoffrey C. Ward, Ric Burns, and Ken Burns, *The Civil War: An Illustrated History*, New York: Alfred A. Knopf, 1991. 85.

5. Benjamin Quarles, *The Negro in the Making of America*. 72.

6. William Warren Sweet, *The Story of Religion in America*. 294.

7. William Warren Sweet, *The Story of Religion in America*. 285.

8. Eugene D. Genovese, *Roll, Jordan, Roll: The World the Slaves Made*, New York: Vintage Books, 1974. 185, 202-209.

9. William Warren Sweet, *The Story of Religion in America*. 308.

10. Kaitlyn Schiess, *The Ballot and the Bible*. 43-49.

11. Eugene D. Genovese, *Roll, Jordan, Roll: The World the Slaves Made*. 162-166.

12. 373 Ibid.

13. Milton C. Sernett, ed. *Afro-American Religious History: A Documentary Witness*, Durham: Duke University Press, 1985. 103, 104.

14. Lerone Bennett, Jr., *Confrontation: Black and White*, Baltimore: Penguin Books Inc., 1968. 51.

15. Philip S. Gorski and Samuel L. Perry, *The Flag + The Cross: White Christian Nationalism and the Threat to American Democracy*. 55, 56.

16. Paula Mitchell Marks, *In a Barren Land: American Indian Dispossession and Survival*, New York: Quill William Morrow, 1998. xxiii.

17. Paula Mitchell Marks, *In a Barren Land: American Indian Dispossession and Survival*. 41.

18. Kevin Kenny, *Peaceable Kingdom Lost: The Paxton Boys and the Destruction of William Penn's Holy Experiment*, New York: Oxford University Press, 2009. 184, 231.

19. Kevin Kenny, *Peaceable Kingdom Lost: The Paxton Boys and the Destruction of William Penn's Holy Experiment*. 183.

20. Paula Mitchell Marks, *In a Barren Land: American Indian Dispossession and Survival*. 14, 15.

21. Benjamin E. Park, *American Zion: A New History of Mormonism*, New York: Liveright Publishing Corporation, 2024. 118.

22. Stephanie Sy, *PBS*, September 6, 2023, "Research uncovers role of churches and religious groups in Indigenous boarding schools," https://www.pbs.org/newshour/show/research-uncovers-role-of-churches-and-religious-groups-in-indigenous-boarding-schools.

23. Mark M. Lambert, *The University of Chicago Divinity School*, July 6, 2022, "Reckoning with Re-education: Christianity's Role in Native American Boarding Schools," https://divinity.uchicago.edu/sightings/articles/reckoning-re-education-christianitys-role-native-american-boarding-schools.

24. Mark M. Lambert, *The University of Chicago Divinity School*, July 6, 2022, "Reckoning with Re-education: Christianity's Role in Native American Boarding Schools."

25. Paula Mitchell Marks, *In a Barren Land: American Indian Dispossession and Survival*. 247, 376, 377, 380.

26. Kevin Phillips, *American Theocracy: The Peril and Politics of Radical Religion, Oil, and Borrowed Money in the 21st Century*. 138-145.

27. Joel A.Brown, *University of Chicago: Religion&Culture Forum*, June 26, 2017, "The Klan, White Christianity, and the Past and Present / a response to Kelly J. Baker by Randall J. Stephens," https://voices.uchicago.edu/religionculture/2017/06/26/the-klan-white-christianity-and-the-past-and-present-a-response-to-kelly-j-baker-by-randall-j-stephens/.

28. Robert Moats Miller, *The Journal of Southern History, Vol.22, No.3*, August 1956, "A Note on the Relationship between the Protestant Churches and the Revived Ku Klux Klan," https://www.jstor.org/stable/2954550.

29. Ruth Braunstein, *National Catholic Reporter*, July 24, 2024, "Catholic Christian nationalism is having a moment."

30. Elizabeth Dias, *The New York Times*, February 10, 2021, "A Century Ago, White Protestant Extremism Marched on Washington," https://www.nytimes.com/2021/02/07/us/white-protestants-ku-klux-klan.html.

18. Christian Nationalism and Religious Freedom

1. James W. Loewen, *Lies Across America: What Our Historic Sites Get Wrong*, New York: Touchstone: 1999. 359.

2. Allen D. Hertzke, editor, Charles C. Haynes, contributor, *Religious Freedom in America*, Americans United Research Foundation, 1986. 11-12.

3. Rev. Paul Brandeis and Rev. Dr. Sharon Harris-Ewing, *News-Press*, "Combating Christian nationalism to protect democracy," https://www.news-press.com/story/opinion/2023/02/12/combating-christian-nationalism-to-protect-democracy/69885057007/)

4. Philip S. Gorski and Samuel L. Perry, *The Flag + The Cross: White Christian Nationalism and the Threat to American Democracy*. 101-102.

5. *Center for American Progress,* April 13, 2022, "Christian Nationalism Is 'Single Biggest Threat' to America's Religious Freedom."

6. Adam Liptak, The New York Times, September 16, 2017, "Cake Is His 'Art,' So Can He Can Deny One to a Gay Couple?" https://www.nytimes.com/2017/09/16/us/supreme-court-baker-same-sex-marriage.html?action=click&module=RelatedCoverage&pgtype=Article®ion=Footer.

7. *Center for American Progress,* April 13, 2022, "Christian Nationalism Is 'Single Biggest Threat' to America's Religious Freedom."

8. Noah Feldman, September 14, 2022, *Bloomberg,* "A Texas Judge Just Took Religious 'Freedom' Too Far," https://www.bloomberg.com/opinion/articles/2022-09-14/texas-prep-drug-ruling-in-braidwood-case-should-be-overturned?utm_medium=email&utm_source=newsletter&utm_term=220917&utm_campaign=sharetheview&leadSource=uverify%20wall.

9. *Center for American Progress,* April 13, 2022, "Christian Nationalism Is 'Single Biggest Threat' to America's Religious Freedom."

10. Guthrie Graves-Fitzsimmons, *Center for American Progress,* April 13, 2022, "Christian Nationalism Is 'Single Biggest Threat' to America's Religious Freedom."

11. Amanda Tyler, *How to End Christian Nationalism.* 109.

12. Robert P. Jones, *The End of White Christian America.* 144-145.

13. Advisory Committee on Social Witness Policy, "Religious Freedom Without Discrimination," https://pcusa.org/sites/default/files/2024-12/religious-freedom.pdf

14. Testimony of the Rev. Jimmie Hawkins Before the U.S. House committee on Education and Labor Hearing on *Do No Harm: Examining the Misapplication of the Religious Freedom Restoration Act,* June 25, 2019, https://democrats-edworkforce.house.gov/imo/media/doc/HawkinsTestimony062519.pdf.

15. Sarah Ventre, Oregon Public Broadcasting (OPB), November 16, 2024, "This county is the most religiously diverse in the U.S.," https://www.opb.org/article/2024/11/16/the-most-religiously-diverse-county-in-the-u-s/.

19. Christian Nationalism and the War on Christians

1. Willimon, *Acts,* 166.

2. Philip S. Gorski and Samuel L. Perry, *The Flag + The Cross: White Christian Nationalism and the Threat to American Democracy.* 4-5, 8.

3. Sarah Posner, *The Nation,* May 9, 2022, "Overturning *Roe* Is the Crowning Achievement of Christian Nationalism."

4. Alexander Ward and Heidi Przybyla, *Politico,* February 20, 2024, "Trump Allies Prepare to Infuse 'Christian Nationalism, in Second Administration," https://www.politico.com/news/2024/02/20/donald-trump-allies-christian-nationalism-00142086.

5. Frances FitzGerald, *The Evangelicals: The Struggle to Shape America.* 417.

6. Frances FitzGerald, *The Evangelicals: The Struggle to Shape America.* 417.

7. Rachel Zoll, *AP,* July 13, 2017, "Confidant of Pope Francis Condemns US Religious Right."

8. Tim Aberta, *The Kingdom, the Power, and the Glory: American Evangelicals in an Age of Extremism,* New York: Harper, 2024. 21.

9. Peter Smith, *AP,* February 13, 2025, "Given Christianity's dominance in US, Trump raises eyebrows with anti-Christian bias initiative.," https://apnews.com/article/eradicating-anti-christian-bias-trump-religious-freedom-c4a01b2d75b471e7329f84a6e662c934.

10. Carol Kruvilla, *Huffington Post*, January 22, 2018, "Franklin Graham Praises Trump As Staunch Defender Of Christianity."

11. Jason Whitlock, *Blazemedia*, April 27, 2023, "Whitlock: Corporate Media, please quit calling me a 'conservative,'" https://www.theblaze.com/fearless/whitlock-corporate-media-please-quit-calling-me-a-conservative.

12. CP Staff, *Christian Post*, March 13, 2024, "Candace Owens warns 'Christian nationalism' label meant to 'divide and brainwash Christians,'" https://www.christianpost.com/news/candace-owens-says-christian-nationalism-being-used-to-divide.html

13. *Pew Research Center*, December 12, 2017, "Americans Say Religious Aspects of Christmas Are Declining in Public Life," https://www.pewresearch.org/religion/2017/12/12/americans-say-religious-aspects-of-christmas-are-declining-in-public-life/.

14. Paul D. Miller, *Christianity Today*, February 3, 2021, "What Is Christian Nationalism?"

15. Phoebe Petrovic, *ProPublica*, July 10, 2024, "The Gospel of Matthew Trewhella: How a Militant Anti-Abortion Activist Is Influencing Republican Politics."

16. Peter Smith, *AP*, February 13, 2025, "Given Christianity's dominance in US, Trump raises eyebrows with anti-Christian bias initiative."

20. Christian Nationalism and Islamophobia

1. Lamar Williamson, Jr., *Mark: Interpretation, a Bible Commentary for Teaching and Preaching*. 171.

2. *Aljazeera*, September 11, 2022, "Decades after 9/11, Muslims battle islamophobia in US," https://www.aljazeera.com/news/2022/9/11/decades-after-9-11-muslims-battle-islamophobia-in.

3. Eric Love, *Islamophobia and Racism in America*, New York: New York University Press, 2017. 20, 117.

4. Rose Marie Berger and Kate Bowman, *Sojourners Magazine*, January-February 2003, "Evangelical, Not Zionist." 10.

5. *Gallup*, "Islamophobia: Understanding Anti-Muslim Sentiment in the West," https://news.gallup.com/poll/157082/islamophobia-understanding-anti-muslim-sentiment-west.aspx.

6. Contributed to by White House Bureau Chief Patsy Widakuswara, *VOA News*, May 10, 2022, "US Muslims See Rise in Islamophobia," https://www.voanews.com/a/us-muslims-see-rise-in-islamophobia-/6565523.html.

7. Richa Karmarkar, August 29, 2022, *the Washington Post,* "Anti-Hindu attacks grow, from N.Y. to a California Taco Bell," https://www.washingtonpost.com/religion/2022/08/29/hindu-gandhi-taco-bell-punjab/?utm_campaign=wp_evening_edition&utm_medium=email&utm_source=newsletter&wpisrc=nl_evening&carta-url=https%3A%2F%2Fs2.washingtonpost.com%2Fcar-ln-tr%2F37c7917%2F630d28e81930ae1d206d59d2%2F5972b45eae7e8a1cf4adae58%2F40%2F51%2F630d28e81930ae1d206d59d2&wp_cu=d8f949609fb8c948f29c069f05c07f1c%7C48AD084A9ABE4F11E0530100007F93E8.

8. Seshadri Kumar, January 7, 2022, FB Independent, "Hindus Raise The Red Flag Over Islamophobic Bill At The Capitol," https://fbindependent.com/hindus-raise-the-red-flag-over-islamophobic-bill-at-the-capitol-p15219-1.htm.

9. Francois Gautier, November 25, 2016, *The Times of India,* "Islamophobia and Hinduphobia," https://timesofindia.indiatimes.com/blogs/francois-gautiers-blog-for-toi/islamophobia-and-hinduphobia/. The author reposed it October 8, 2019, on his blog at https://www.francoisgautier.com/2019/10/08/islamophobia-hinduphobia/.

10. Dennis Johnson and Valerie Merians, eds. *What We Do Now: Standing Up for Your Values in Trump's America,* New York: Melville House, 2017, 54.

21. Christian Nationalism and Christian Zionism

1. Brian K. Blount, General Editor, *True to Our Native Land: An African American New Testament Commentary*. 552.

2. E. Eugene Boring, *Revelation: Interpretation, a Bible Commentary for Teaching and Preaching,* Louisville: Westminster John Knox Press, 1989. 202.

3. PRRI Staff, February 28, 2024, "Support for Christian Nationalism in all 50 States: Findings from PRRI's 2023 American Values Atlas," https://www.prri.org/research/support-for-christian-nationalism-in-all-50-states/.

4. Nancy Gibbs, *TIME,* July 1, 2002, "Apocalypse Now," https://time.com/archive/6666729/apocalypse-now/.

5. *History Skills,* "How the modern state of Israel was created in 1948," https://www.historyskills.com/classroom/modern-history/formation-of-modern-israel-reading/.

6. Frances FitzGerald, *The Evangelicals: The Struggle to Shape America*. 477.

7. Nancy Gibbs, *TIME,* July 1, 2002, "Apocalypse Now."

8. Sarah Posner, *MSNBC,* December 14, 2022, "The major role of Christian nationalism on Jan 6," https://www.msnbc.com/opinion/msnbc-opinion/major-role-christian-nationalism-jan-6-rcna61531.

9. *Freedom from Religion Foundation*, November 14, 2024, "Mike Huckabee as Israeli ambassador would be a disaster of biblical proportions," https://ffrf.org/news/releases/mike-huckabee-as-israeli-ambassador-would-be-a-disaster-of-biblical-proportions/.

10. Jeffrey B. Webb, *The Complete Idiot's Guide to Christianity*, New York: Alpha Books, 2004. 228.

11. Jeffrey B. Webb, *The Complete Idiot's Guide to Christianity*. 232.

12. Gayraud S. Wilmore, *Last Things First*, Philadelphia: The Westminster Press, 1982. 48-49.

13. Jeffrey B. Webb, *The Complete Idiot's Guide to Christianity*. 226.

14. Gayraud S. Wilmore, *Last Things First*. 46.

15. Frances FitzGerald, *The Evangelicals: The Struggle to Shape America*. 477.

16. Gayraud S. Wilmore, *Last Things First*. 41-44, 48-49, 50.

17. Joseph Menn, December 2, 2022, *The Washington Post*, "Surging Twitter antisemitism unites fringe, encourages violence, officials say," https://www.washingtonpost.com/technology/2022/12/03/twitter-antisemitism-violence-jan-6/?utm_campaign=wp_todays_headlines&utm_medium=email&utm_source=newsletter&wpisrc=nl_headlines&carta-url=https%3A%2F%2Fs2.washingtonpost.com%2Fcar-ln-tr%2F387c3d7%2F638c7de99d88976ba34a2ee9%2F5972b45eae7e8a1cf4adae58%2F14%2F59%2F638c7de99d88976ba34a2ee9&wp_cu=d8f949609fb8c948f29c069f05c07f1c%7C48AD084A9ABE4F11E0530100007F93E8.

18. Jonathan Sarda, *Brandeis University*, "The Jewish Experience: The Long, Ugly, Antisemitic History of 'Jews Will Not Replace Us'," https://www.brandeis.edu/jewish-experience/jewish-america/2021/november/replacement-antisemitism-sarna.html.

19. Chile Eboe-Osuji, May 31, 2022, *Just Security*, "Beyond a 'Hate Crime': 'Replacement' Rhetoric and the Genocide Worry," https://www.justsecurity.org/"81687/beyond-a-hate-crime-replacement-rhetoric-and-the-genocide-worry/.

20. Maegan Vazquez and Betsy Klein, *CNN*, Dec 7, 2022, "Second gentleman warns of 'rapid rise' in antisemitism during White House roundtable," https://www.cnn.com/2022/12/07/politics/doug-emhoff-antisemitism-roundtable/index.html.

21. Will Carless, April 26, 2022, *USAToday*, "2021 saw highest-ever number of incidents targeting Jewish Americans: Report," https://www.usatoday.com/story/news/nation/2022/04/26/antisemitic-incidents-hit-record-number-2021/7441062001/.

22. U.S. Department of State, "Defining Antisemitism," https://www.state.gov/defining-antisemitism/.

23. Josh Healey, *Sojourners Magazine*, January-February 2003, "Not in My Name." 16.

24. Abraham Gutman, May 27, 2021, *Think: Opinion, Analysis Essays*, "Supporting Palestinian rights is antisemitic because Israel wants it to be," https://www.nbcnews.com/think/opinion/how-jews-can-support-palestinian-rights-condemn-antisemitism-ncna1268680.

22. Christian Nationalism and Capitalism

1. F. F. Bruce, *The Hard Sayings of Jesus* (Downers Grove, Ill.: InterVarsity Press, 1983), 184-186.

2. David T. Adamo, 2021, "The African background of the Prosperity Gospel, *Theologia Viatorum* 45(1), a71. https://doi.org/10.4102/tv.v45i1.71. 8.

3. Elizabeth Bruenig, April 20, 2015, *The New Republic*, "Gods and Profits: How capitalism and Christianity aligned in modern America," https://newrepublic.com/article/121564/gods-and-profits-how-capitalism-and-christianity-aligned-america.

4. Kevin M. Kruse, *One Nation Under God: How Corporate America Invented Christian America*. 8.

5. Katherine Stewart, *The Power Worshippers*. 116, 117.

6. David T. Adamo, 2021, "The African background of the prosperity gospel."

7. Kevin M. Kruse, *One Nation Under God: How Corporate America Invented Christian America*. 53.

8. Timothy L. O'Brien, *Bloomberg*, July 17, 2024, "Trump's 'Divine Intervention' May Be Just a Talking Point," https://www.bloomberg.com/opinion/articles/2024-07-17/trump-s-divine-intervention-may-be-just-a-talking-point?utm_medium=email&utm_source=newsletter&utm_term=240717&utm_campaign=sharetheview.

9. Kevin M. Kruse, *One Nation Under God: How Corporate America Invented Christian America*. 130, 132, 134, 137.

10. Kevin M. Kruse, *One Nation Under God: How Corporate America Invented Christian America*. 130, 132, 134, 137.

11. Anthea Butler, *Dissent*, "The Black Church: From Prophecy to Prosperity," Winter 2014.

12. John Blake, *CNN: Black in America2*, April 6, 2008, "Modern black church shuns King's message," https://www.cnn.com/2008/US/04/06/mlk.role.church/index.html.

13. John Blake, April 6, 2008, *CNN: Black in America2*, April 6, 2008, "Modern black church shuns King's message."

14. Joe Carter, September 1, 2015, *The Gospel Coalition*, "Why are Black and Hispanic Evangelicals More Favorable Toward the Prosperity Gospel?" https://www.thegospelcoalition.org/article/why-are-black-and-hispanic-evangelicals-more-favorable-toward-the-prosperit/.

15. Anthea Butler, *Dissent*, "The Black Church: From Prophecy to Prosperity," Winter 2014.

16. TIME.**GRAPHICS**, May 17, 2023, "Latino faith leaders to gather for summit on Christian nationalism," https://time.graphics/pt/event/8730578.

17. Elizabeth L. Hinson-Hasty, *The Problem of Wealth: A Christian Response to a Culture of Affluence*, New York: Orbis Books, 2017. 14, 15, 34, 38.

18. Jolene Almendarez, December 9, 2022, *Yahoo!*, "The Ark Encounter site in Kentucky is bigger than Disneyland and still growing," https://news.yahoo.com/ark-encounter-kentucky-bigger-disneyland-100505742.html.

19. Shirley C. Guthrie, Jr., *Christian Doctrine*. 163, 164.

20. Najuma Smith-Pollard, quoted in "Jesus vs. Santa Claus: Who really rules the season?" by Cynthia Gibson, *Our Weekly, Los Angeles*, December 17, 2015.

21. D. R. McConnell, *A Different Gospel: A Historical and Biblical Analysis of the Modern Faith Movement*, Massachusetts: Hendrickson Publishers, Inc., 1988. 158, 144, 151, 166.

22. Cynthia Gibson, *Our Weekly*, December 17, 2015, "Jesus vs. Santa Claus: Who really rules the season?" https://ourweekly.com/news/2015/12/17/jesus-vs-santa-claus-who-really-rules-season/.

23. Christian Nationalism and Militarism

1. Christopher R. Seitz, *Isaiah 1-39: Interpretation: A Bible Commentary for Teaching and Preaching*, Louisville: Westminster .John Knox Press, 1993. 38, 39, 40.

2. Gabriel R. Sanchez, Keon L. Gilbert, and Carly Bennett, *Brookings*, March 30, 2023, "White nationalism remains major concern for voters of color."

3. *PBS American Experience*, "God in the White House."

4. *PBS American Experience*, "God in the White House."

5. *PBS American Experience*, "God in the White House."

6. Kristin Kobes Du Mez, *Jesus and John Wayne*. 219-220.

7. Gerald W. Schlabach, *Sojourners Magazine*, January-February 2003, "Evangelical, Not Zionist." 15, 16.

8. Paul D. Miller, *Christianity Today*, February 2, 2021, "What Is Christian Nationalism?", https://www.christianitytoday.com/ct/2021/february-web-only/what-is-christian-nationalism.html.

9. Philip S. Gorski and Samuel L. Perry, *The Flag + The Cross: White Christian Nationalism and the Threat to American Democracy*. 102.

10. Philip S. Gorski and Samuel L. Perry, *The Flag + The Cross: White Christian Nationalism and the Threat to American Democracy*. 66-67.

11. Russell Contreras, *Axios*, February 29, 2024, "Survey: 55% of Latino Protestants support Christian nationalism," https://www.axios.com/2024/02/29/christian-nationalism-latino-hispanic-protestant-evangelical.

12. Shannon N. Brown, "Backwards Christian Soldiers: The Role of the Religious Right on the Militarization of U.S. Foreign Policy in the Post-9/11 Era," https://digitalcommons.tacoma.uw.edu/cgi/viewcontent.cgi?article=1004&context=ppe_prize.

13. The Ohio State University College of Arts and Sciences Mershon Center, "Religious Nationalism and American Militarism," https://mershoncenter.osu.edu/research-projects/religious-nationalism-and-american-militarism.

14. *The New Interpreter's Study Bible: New Revised Standard Version with the Apocrypha (NIB)*, Nashville: Abingdon Press: 2003. 1800.

15. James M. Washington, ed. *The Essential Writings and Speeches of Martin Luther King*, Jr., New York: HarperCollins, 1986,276, 269.

24. Christian Nationalism and the Media

1. Shannon N. Brown, "Backwards Christian Soldiers: The Role of the Religious Right on the Militarization of U.S. Foreign Policy in the Post-9/11 Era."

2. Kristin Kobes Du Mez, *Jesus and John Wayne*. 29-30.

3. Kristin Kobes Du Mez, *Jesus and John Wayne*. 7.

4. Kristin Kobes Du Mez, *Jesus and John Wayne*. 147-149.

Conclusion: The Christian Response to Christian Nationalism

1. John A. Bolt, *The Presbyterian Outlook*, April 28, 2026, "PC(USA) to consider policy rejecting White Christian nationalism," https://pres-outlook.org/2026/04/debate-over-white-christian-nationalism-comes-to-ga227/.